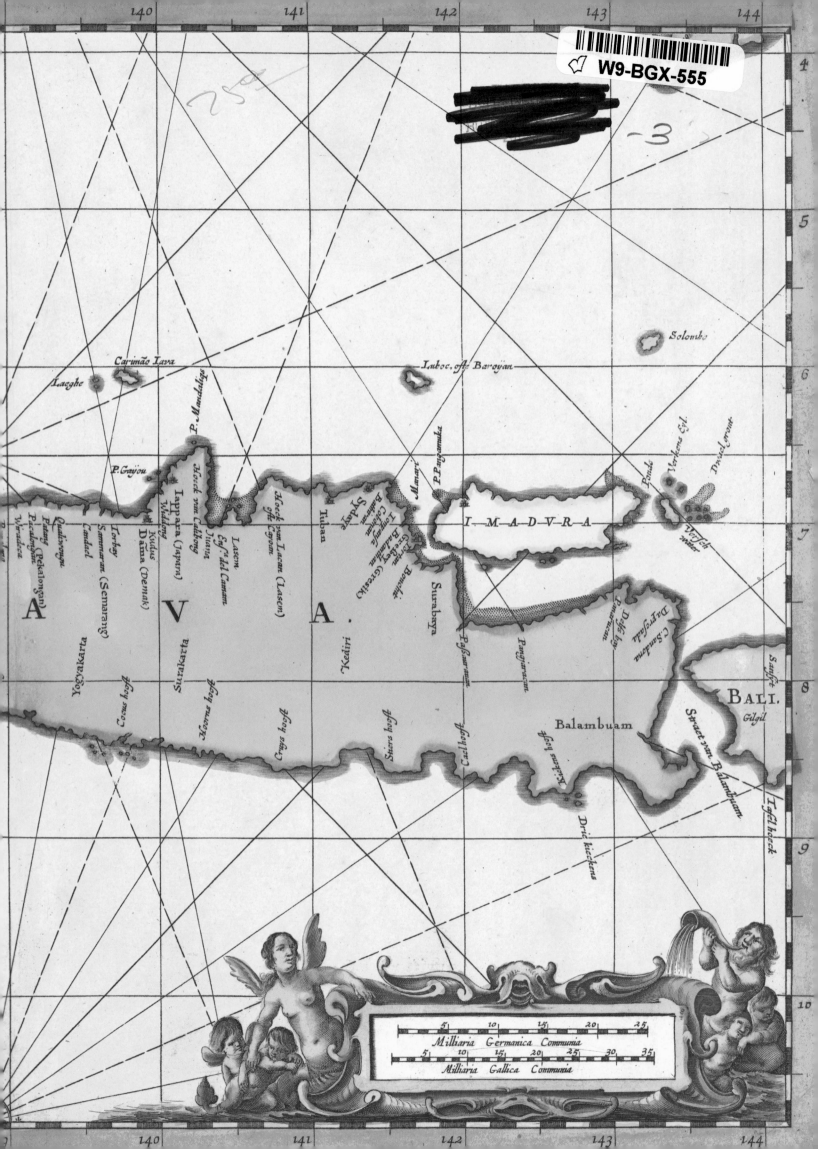

BATIK

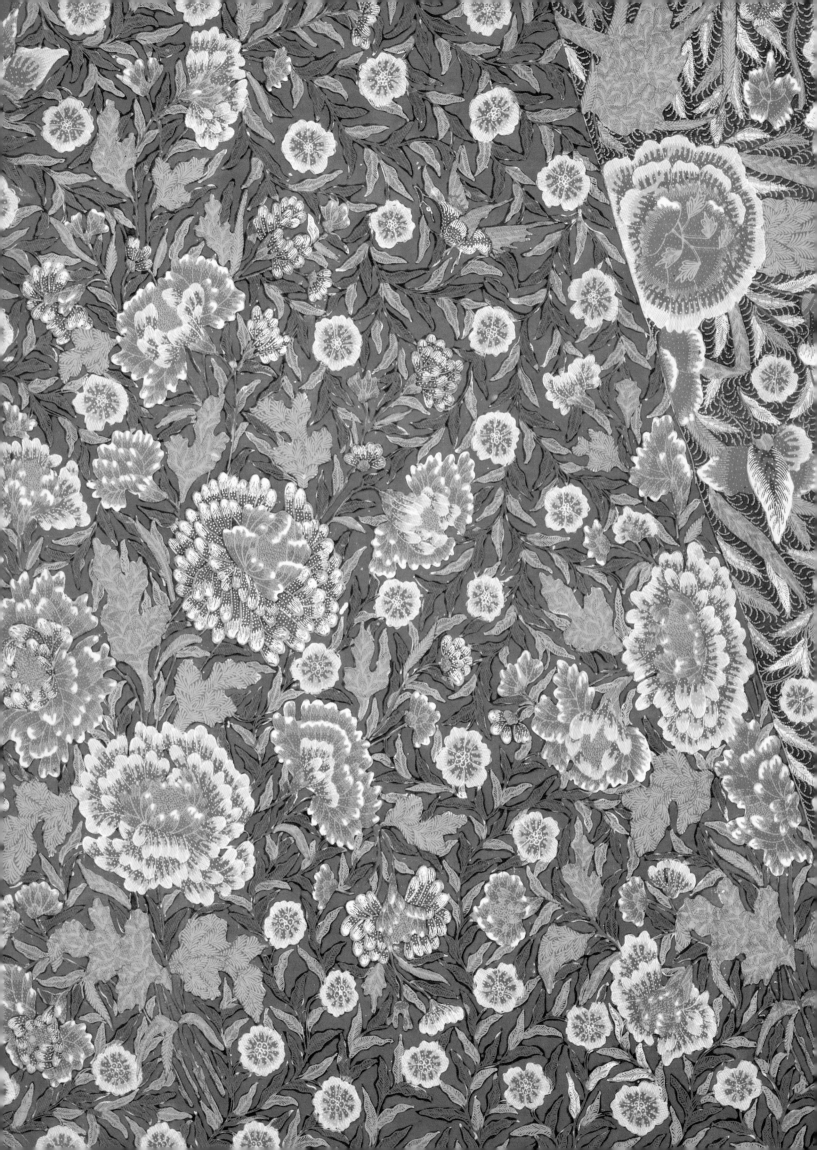

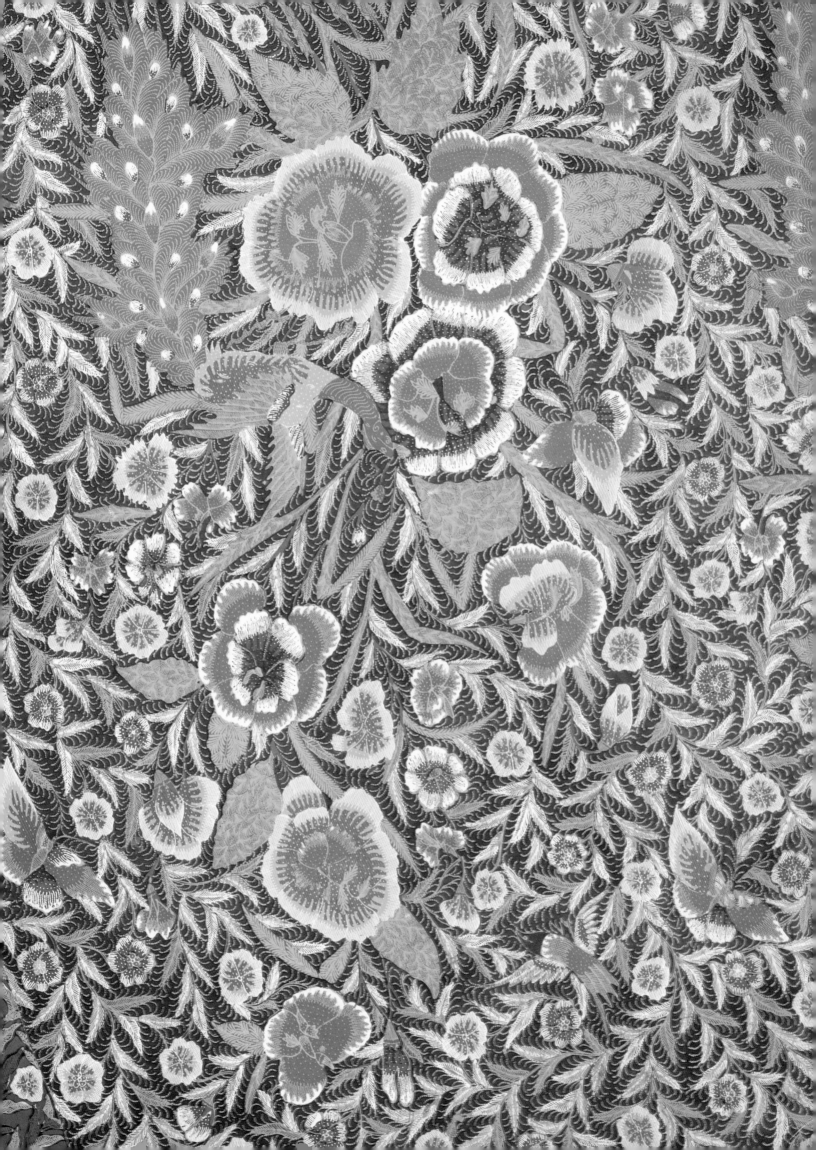

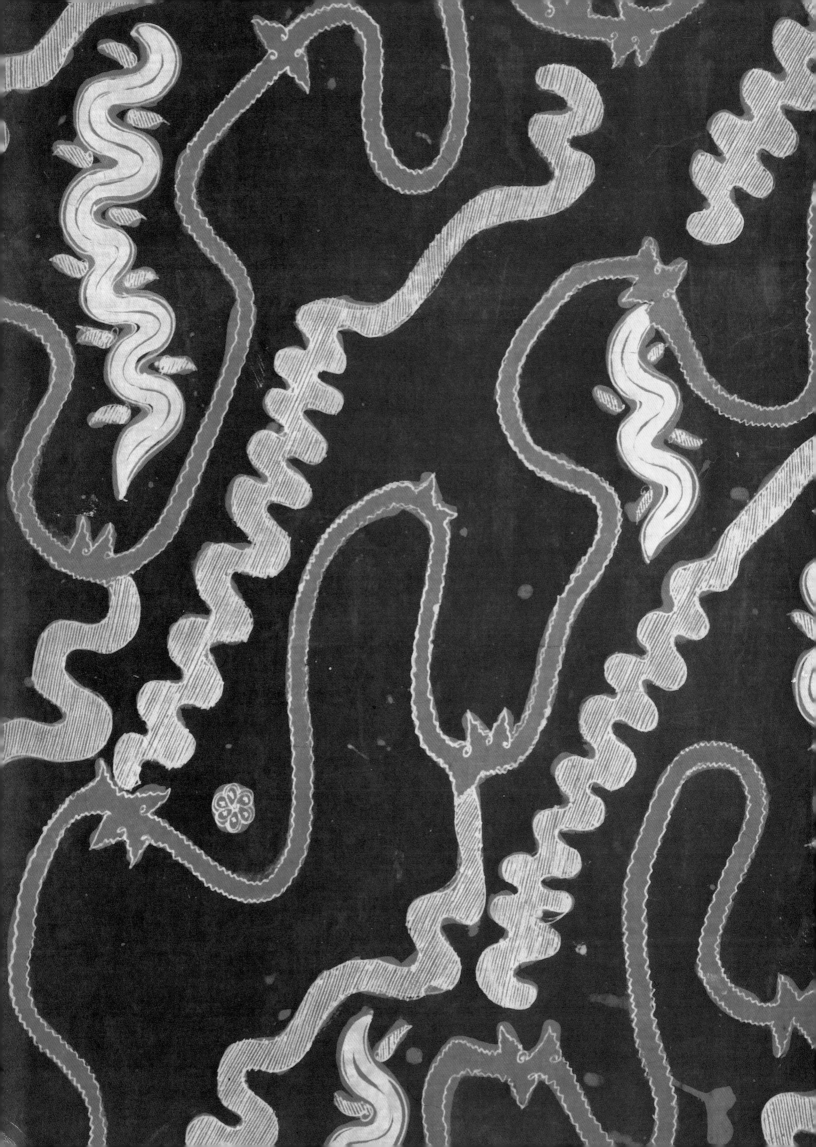

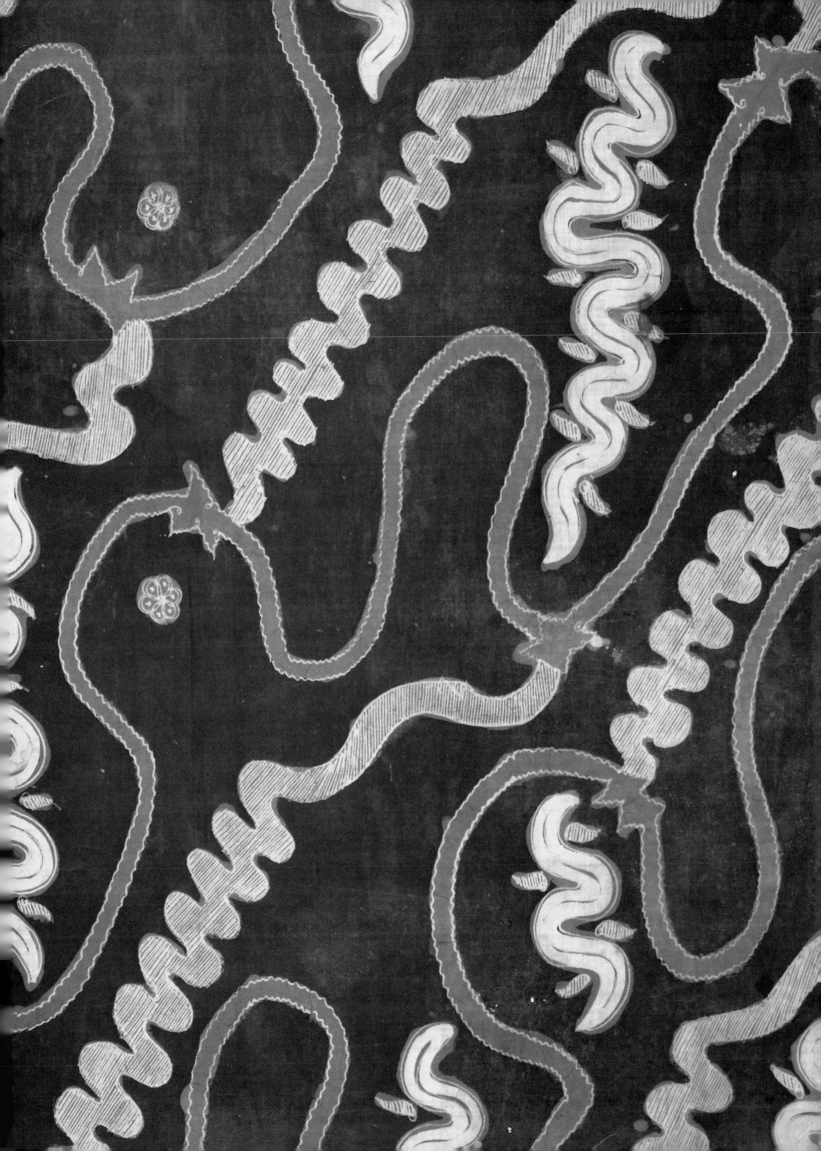

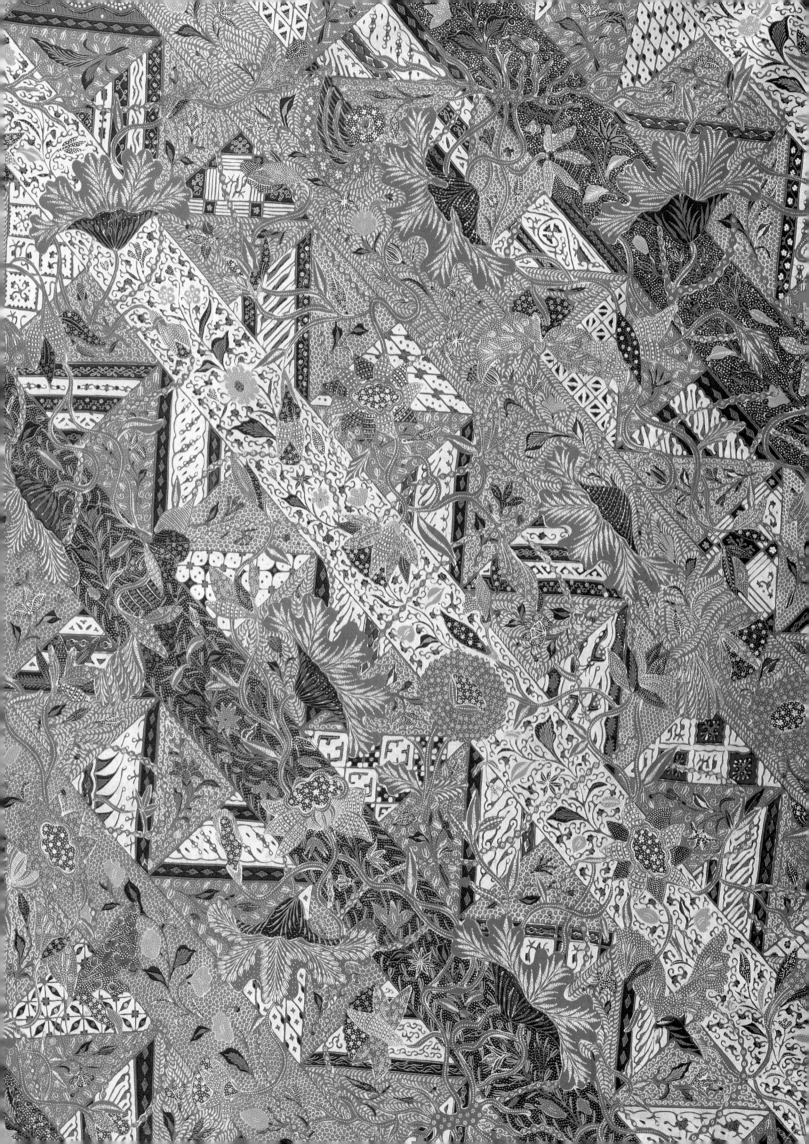

BATIK
FABLED CLOTH OF JAVA

Inger McCabe Elliott

PHOTOGRAPHS
Brian Brake

CONTRIBUTIONS
Paramita Abdurachman
Susan Blum
Iwan Tirta

DESIGN
Kiyoshi Kanai

Clarkson N. Potter, Inc./Publishers
DISTRIBUTED BY CROWN PUBLISHERS, INC., NEW YORK

Editor's note: The number at the end of each caption refers to the concordance, p. 205.

Published by Clarkson N. Potter, Inc., One Park Avenue, New York, New York 10016 and simultaneously in Canada by General Publishing Company Limited.

The author gratefully acknowledges permission for the use of photographs from the following: Paramita Abdurachman; Jane Hendromartono; Photographic Archives of the Royal Tropical Institute; Rare Books and Manuscript Division, the New York Public Library, Astor, Lenox and Tilden Foundations; Rob Nieuwenhuys; Time Inc.; and to the Trustees of the British Museum for allowing me to reproduce the batik of Raffles.

The generous support of Mobil Corporation is also deeply appreciated.

Manufactured in Japan

Library of Congress Cataloging in Publication Data
Elliott, Inger McCabe.
    Batik, fabled cloth of Java.
    Bibliography: p.
    Includes index.
    1. Batik—Indonesia—Java. I. Title.
TP930.E63 1984   746.6'62'095982   84-2127
ISBN 0-517-55155-1
10 9 8 7 6 5 4 3 2 1
First Edition

Endpaper: Map of Java, drawn nearly three hundred years ago. To make the north-coast batik journey more easily understood, towns such as Yogyakarta and Lasem were added.
Pp. 2–3: A typical Hokokai batik made between 1942 and 1945. (Detail) 2
Pp. 4–5: Detail of a western Javanese kain panjang, primitively and boldly rendered. 3
Pp. 6–7: A late nineteenth-century batik with the dragon or naga motif. (Detail) 4
Pp. 8–9: "Three countries" or tiga negeri sarong with a patchwork body. (Detail) 5
Pp. 10–11: A 1916 kain panjang common to the northern towns of Kudus and Juana. (Detail) 6

For Oz

When you are old and gray and full of sleep,
And nodding by the fire, take down this book.

—W. B. Yeats, *When You Are Old*

Batik from the Collections of:

Asmara Arifin, Jakarta
Joop Avé, Jakarta
China Seas Inc., New York
Brian Brake and Lau Wai Man, Auckland
Wieneke de Groot, Jakarta
Winnifred de Groot, Leiden
Deutsches Textilmuseum, Krefeld-Linn
H. Sa'adiah Djody, Jakarta
Inger McCabe Elliott, New York
Sergio Feldbauer, Milan
Jacques Gadbois
Henry Ginsburg and Lisbet Holmes, London
K.R.T. Hardjonagoro, Surakarta
Jane Hendromartono, Pekalongan
Robert J. Holmgren and Anita Spertus, New York
Jonathan Hope, London
Mary Kahlenberg and Dr. Anne Summerfield, Los Angeles
Koninklijk Instituut voor de Tropen, Amsterdam
Museum of Mankind, London
Museum Nasional, Jakarta
Oey Soe Tjoen, Kedungwuni
Ardiyanto Pranata, Yogyakarta
Soelaeman Pringgodigdo, Jakarta
Rijksmuseum voor Volkenkunde, Leiden
Hans W. Siegel, Ronco
Smend Gallery, Cologne
State Museum of Yogyakarta Sonobudoyo, Yogyakarta
Iwan Tirta, Jakarta

CONTENTS

PROLOGUE

For much of my professional life I worked as a photojournalist, shooting in black and white. Those were my colors. Soldiers bleeding and dying in Phnom Penh—black and white; Galina Ulanova in performance with the Bolshoi ballet—black and white; Puerto Rican schoolchildren in the barrio of New York—black and white; Marlon Brando cavorting on location in Bangkok—black and white.

Then one day in 1963, in a modest shop in Hong Kong, my black and white world turned into glorious color. That was the moment when the splendors of Java's north-coast batik burst upon me.

All great art pleases, teases, even disturbs the viewer—and so it was for me that day. What I saw in the little Hong Kong shop was a tiny sample of what you will see in these pages—glorious textiles where lions roar ferociously, ducks paddle serenely, mythical animals leap, and grains of rice dapple the cloth.

The batik artists of Java's north coast splash their colors with controlled abandon. They break all the rules. Somehow they are able to use green with red and end up with something that does *not* look like a Christmas card; somehow they can combine pink, yellow, brown, and aqua without bringing to mind Mae West's boudoir.

Entranced by what I had seen first in Hong Kong, and later in other markets around Southeast Asia, I set out about fifteen years ago to unravel the mystery of batik. What was its history? Where did these fabrics come from? Who made batik and how? I made my way to Indonesia, and before long I was working with Javanese artists, helping them design new patterns and rearranging old ones— moving butterflies, flowers, and peacocks around the "canvas"—and mixing colors the artists had never used before. "Impossible to get the washed-out peach," they would say. "It's never been done." But we did it.

In numerous visits since, I have worked with these artists on the intricate batik process as well—all the steps of patterning, waxing, the repeated dyeing and scraping of the cloth. Traditionally, manufacturers would batik only two yards of cloth at a time. By building long tables for drawing and waxing, I showed them that they could batik as many as sixteen or even thirty-two yards

Spectacular prada *sarong with red and blue* (bang-biru) *colors may have originated in Lasem. The head, or* kepala, *shown here has curvilinear geometrics and the body (not shown) is covered with the phoenix, a symbol of longevity.* 7

in one continuous process. These greater lengths, at reasonable prices, enabled my company, China Seas, to help open new markets for batik in Europe and the United States.

I was always on the lookout for the unusual. As best I could, I would discover where and when a piece was made, and by whom. It soon became evident that geography, history, and religion all played crucial roles in the evolution of batik.

Indonesia's official motto is "Unity in Diversity" and it could well have been written to describe the wonders of batik and how they came to be. Indonesia's geography is Malaysian, its predominant religion Islamic, its architecture a mixture of Dutch colonial and petrodollar glass, its middle class Chinese, its *lingua franca* Bahasa Indonesia. Its great monuments were built to both Buddhist and Hindu gods. Each and every one of these cultural, geographic, and religious influences can be found in the many-splendored batik of Java's north coast.

For hundreds of years the Javanese coast has lain at a crossroads of trade, near the course sailed by Marco Polo, Magellan, Sir Francis Drake, and St. Francis Xavier. It is even probable, although as yet unproved, that the Javanese themselves sailed to other parts of Asia as early as the pre-Christian era. Trade brought with it a succession of religions—Hinduism, Buddhism, Islam—and successive waves of colonization. Each of these influences left its imprint on the culture of Java and on its finest art form, batik.

Since this book focuses on the north coast, I have devoted little space to the batik of central Java—a subject which has been well covered elsewhere. But the cultural heritage and the court influence of central Java are important, and both are linked to the courts of Cirebon in the north.

It is not by chance that Java's major port cities, Jakarta, Semarang, and Surabaya, have received so little notice. With few exceptions, they were not major areas of batik making; rather, they provided the customers. Early on I discovered that the entire north coast, whether in western, central, or eastern Java, should be treated as one entity.

I waffled a bit about where to discuss *Hokokai* batik. These spectacular cloths can be seen in the context of north-coast Chinese batik; historically they are surely the last of the colonial batik. I chose, however, to place them with more recent batik because of their influence on several modern artists.

Organizing and cataloguing the materials for a book on batik is no easy task. Textiles are notoriously difficult to preserve in a tropical climate; I have found no existing batik which is dated before 1800. Furthermore, in 1942, when the Japanese invaded Indonesia, then called the Dutch East Indies, some important collections (notably those of Moens and Reesink) were spirited off to hiding places, sometimes sequestered in museums but often vanishing entirely. And finally, the history of batik is sketchy.

Sir Thomas Stamford Raffles, the energetic man who founded Singapore—which was to be a vital link with the China trade—was the first to write about the ancient art of batik. That was in 1817, after a five-year sojourn that established Raffles as an expert on the Indies. More than fifty years later, E. van Rijckovorsel, a Dutchman, spent four years in Java and collected batik that he donated to the Rotterdam Museum. In 1883 batik was shown in a colonial exhibit in Amsterdam, and fifteen years later another exhibit in The Hague spurred further interest. This show bore the curious title, "Colonial Women's Labor" (*Koloniale Frauenarbeit*). A monograph by G. P. Rouffaer and Dr. H. H. Juynboll appeared in 1900, and six years after that the Dutch colonial government assigned S. M. Pleyte and J. E. Jasper to a further study of folk art, including batik. These four men provided the cornerstone for all subsequent Javanese batik scholarship, by such notable experts as J. A. Loeber, Alfred Steinmann, Alfred Bühler, and more recently K.R.T. Hardjonagoro and Garrett and Bronwen Solyom.

Most scholarship in batik has concentrated on central Java; and while there have been several excellent works dealing with specific coastal areas by Paramita Abdurachman, M. J. de Raadt-Apell, and Harmen Veldhuisen, the study of north-coast batik has been spotty. Batik making has a long tradition in certain families there, but the artists have kept few records. Thus, I relied on oral history for some of the material in this book.

I also used my eyes. Being a photographer by training, my initial organization was visual. Did a certain batik resemble another in color, design, and technique? Chances were that they both came from the same region, the same town, the same period, even the same maker. As the great jigsaw began to come together, I drew on my earlier training as an aspiring historian. Doing my homework in the history books, I was gradually able to put most of the pieces into what seemed to be the proper cultural, geographic, and historic context. No two batik experts agree on very much—there is little "unity in diversity" in this field. And so I freely admit to breaking new ground and fully expect to hear numerous dissenting opinions on various of my conclusions.

This book, conceived seven years ago, represents a very considerable personal investment of time and energy—not only in terms of research and writing, but also in the continuing evolution of batik itself. I have been on four continents, crawled through cobwebbed attics, slogged through mud, batted away flying cockroaches, been apprehended by the police. I have pestered scholars and friends alike with the hope of showing what has never been shown before. From thirty collections around the world I have made my selections. I hope you will share my joy in these astonishing works of art.

Inger McCabe Elliott
New York
April 1978

I. TALES OF A TRADE ROUTE ISLAND

An early stone Hindu-Javanese deity in Surakarta.

The roots of batik are ancient, everywhere, and difficult to trace. No one knows exactly where and when people first began to apply wax, vegetable paste, paraffin, or even mud to cloth that would then resist a dye. But it was on the islands of Java and nearby Madura that batik emerged as one of the great art forms of Asia. Batik is known to have existed in China, Japan, India, Thailand, East Turkestan, Europe, and Africa, and it may have developed simultaneously in several of these areas. Some scholars believe that the process originated in India and was later brought to Egypt. Whatever the case, in A.D. 70, in his *Natural History,* Pliny the Elder told of Egyptians applying designs to cloth in a manner similar to the batik process. The method was known seven hundred years later in China. Scholars have ascertained that batik found in Japan was Chinese batik, made during the Tang Dynasty.

Thus batik was already an ancient tradition by the time the earliest evidence of such Javanese work appeared in the sixteenth century. Records from the coast of Malabar in 1516 suggest that painted cloth for export may have been batiked. The first known mention of *Javanese* batik occurred two years later, in 1518, when the word *tulis,* meaning "writing," appeared; the term survives today to specify the finest hand-drawn batik. One hundred years later the word *baték* actually appeared in an inventory of goods sent to Sumatra.

The word *batik* does not belong to the old Javanese language; in fact its origin is not at all clear. Most likely *batik* is related to the word *titik,* which in modern Indonesia and Mayalsia refers to a point, dot, or drop. Even that accomplished linguist, Sir Thomas Raffles, although he knew the word, neglected to translate *batik.* However, in compiling a list of occupations he did include *Tukang batik,* a "cotton printer."

Whatever its origins, the designs and uses of Javanese batik have reflected the vicissitudes of Java's ever-changing society. Three major religions have left their marks, as have a number of ethnic groups with their distinctive languages and customs. And over the years any number of invaders, explorers, and colonists have also brought change to Java and to its highest form of art.

◆

Java is a five-hundred-mile-long connecting link in an archipelago of nearly fourteen thousand islands that constitutes Indonesia—the world's fifth largest nation, with the world's largest Muslim population. About the size of Alabama, Java has an east-west mountain range flanked by limestone ridges and lowlands, with rivers that are navigable only in the wet season. Thirty-five of its one hundred twelve volcanoes are active. With nearly fifteen hundred people per square mile, it is the world's most densely populated island. The great majority of Java's 91 million people live in rural villages, their lives governed by the rhythmic cycles of their crops—rice, corn, sweet potatoes, tobacco. Because of the fierce overpopulation, most exist at a subsistence level.

By tradition and history Java is divided into three sections: west, central, and east. To the west lie the Sunda Strait and the cities of Jakarta (formerly Batavia), Bandung, Garut, and Tasikmalaya. This area was once the empire of the Sunda, and people there still call themselves Sundanese. Central Java, with its rich farmlands, is dominated by the cities of Yogyakarta and Surakarta—and features the great temples of Borobudur and Prambanan. To the east is the great port of Surabaya and the island of Madura. Stretching the length of Java lies the island's north coast with its mixed and vibrant heritage.

For two thousand years, Java's north coast was a lucrative trade area, luring sailors and merchants from all parts of the world. Situated in the calm and tranquil Java Sea, beyond the belt of typhoons and angry oceans, the island was on a spur of the trade route between Cairo and Nagasaki, Lisbon and Macao, London and the Moluccas, Amsterdam and Macassar. In Java, cloves and nutmeg from the Spice Islands to the east were traded for tea, silks, porcelains, and opium from China; for brightly patterned cloth from southern

THE LURE OF JAVA

India; for cinnamon from Ceylon; camphor from Siam; and a cornucopia of goods from Europe, Africa, and Japan. It was via the north coast of Java that Greeks, Malays, Indians, Chinese, Arabs, Portuguese, Dutch, British—as well as numerous pirates—sailed from the Indian Ocean to the South China Sea and thence to farther ports.

As long ago as the first century A.D., Syrian and Macedonian navigators discovered that seasonal monsoon winds enabled them to sail across the Indian Ocean without hugging the coastline. In about A.D. 150, Ptolemy wrote about Java in his *Geography,* and in the fourth century the Chinese Buddhist monk Fa-

Hsien wrote that he had reached Java ". . . where heresies and Brahmanism were flourishing, while the faith of Buddha was in a very unsatisfactory condition." Within another two hundred years, the silk routes—both overland and by sea—were well established, and the Strait of Malacca, between the Bay of Bengal and the South China Sea, became increasingly busy.

West and north of Java, on the island of Sumatra, the city of Palembang was a center of commerce for Southeast Asia in the fifth and sixth centuries. It was from here that the powerful Malay kingdom, Srivijaya-Palembang, came to dominate coastal Sumatra as well as the Strait of Malacca.

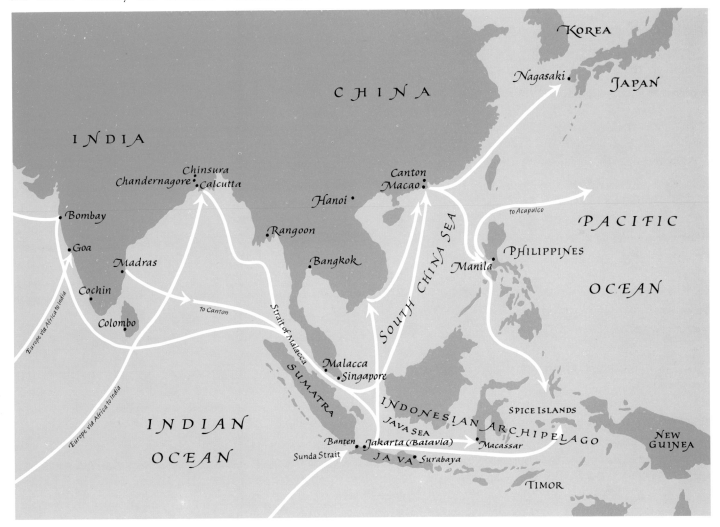

The main sea route from India via the Strait of Malacca and north toward China and Japan. To reach the Spice Islands ships skirted northern Java.

Three Religions

First Buddhism, then Hinduism, then Islam came to Java, and each profoundly affected its sacred and secular life as well as the development of its batik. Both Buddhism and Hinduism emphasized the "liberation of the soul from mortal ties as the ultimate purpose of life." But typically, the Javanese would adopt particular aspects of each religion that they found appealing and would mingle them with the others. Buddha and the Hindu god Śiva (Shiva), for example, were both looked upon as manifestations of the same being, and powerful rulers built monuments to each. The Sailendra family, of the princely courts in central Java, erected Borobudur in the ninth century. Its galleries and terraces and images of Buddha celebrated the spirit of Buddhism and the kinship between the secular leader and his god. Fifty miles away and about one hundred years later at Prambanan, another sacred monument called Lara Jonggrang was built; there the kings were united after death with the Hindu god Śiva. Design elements used in batik are found in both Buddhist and Hindu temples —the lotus, for example, in the reliefs of Borobudur; and the interlocking and intersecting circular designs —known in batik work as kawung—in the later Hindu temples of east Java.

With the spread of Hindu influence, a caste system was introduced: "No one dares stand in the presence of a superior . . . from the common laborer upward." The Javanese language developed different vocabularies and forms of salutation, depending on the age and position of the person being addressed. In the economic realm, the Hindus introduced such powerful innovations as wet-rice cultivation, wheeled vehicles, and draft animals, each in its own way contributing to the trading strength of the Indies. But for every grain of rice grown, tribute was extracted in a feudal system that was to endure for more than twelve hundred years.

By the thirteenth century, the Hindu-oriented kingdom of Majapahit claimed most of Java. It was a golden age, with Majapahit rulers spreading the idea of the divine right of kings, secure in the knowledge that royal divinity would flood the world and thereby cleanse it. On the political front, Majapahit rulers succeeded in defeating Kublai Khan's invading envoy on the northern coast of Java. But internal feuding and lack of access to overseas trade eventually eroded Majapahit power, and within two hundred fifty years the mighty kingdom had been reduced to the royal courts of Yogyakarta and Surakarta.

In the meantime, Java's north coast was becoming commercially active. Small harbor states, usually founded by rulers of obscure ethnic origin, began to appear. These states—Cirebon, Gresik, Japara, Demak, and Tuban among them—prospered because of their strategic location on the coast. They were on the sea route to the spice-producing Banda and Molucca islands farther east.

For thousands of years spices were valued by faraway people as medicines, aphrodisiacs, preservatives, and flavorings. Roman, Chinese, Indian, Arab, and European traders fought for centuries for the highly lucrative spice monopoly. Spices were light and compact and far easier to transport than bulky goods such as timber, porcelain, or even cloth. Great quantities of spices could be packed into the hold of a single small ship.

◆

Malacca, about two hundred miles north of Singapore on the southwestern coast of Malaysia, is a sleepy town today, and it is hard to realize that it was once the greatest commercial center in Southeast Asia. Geographic position accounted for Malacca's importance: at a time when deep-water ports were not necessary, it dominated the Strait of Malacca through which nearly all shipping passed, east and west. Malacca was also a trading post for religious ideas, and it was in this realm of the mind and the spirit, as much as in the marketplace, that Malacca's influence on Javanese batik would make itself felt.

Although Muslim communities had existed in Java as early as the twelfth century, it was from Malacca and Sumatra that the major drive for Javanese conversion came. The port became the meeting place for Chinese merchants from the east and for Muslims—Arabs and Indians—from the west. Traders from Java carried rice from Demak and Japara, nutmeg and cloves from Gresik and Tuban. If Javanese merchants were to win Arab support, they would have to open their doors to Islam.

The commercial and political advantages that attended religious conversion gave merchants real incentives to adopt Islam. Commercially, the Muslims were the world's leading traders, with connections throughout Asia, Europe, and Africa: association with them meant new routes and more riches. Politically, a community benefited when a former Hindu kingdom became Muslim because to some degree the caste system was eroded. A Muslim was judged by his fervor, not his rank. All believers were equal. By the end of the fifteenth century, there were twenty Muslim kingdoms on the north coast of Java, and Javanese traders from the north became the most influential people in Malacca. By 1523 Gresik's Muslim population totaled more than thirty thousand.

Like Hinduism and Buddhism, Islam also worked its way into the designs and uses of batik. The textile was "encouraged by the Muslim rulers as a major element of social expression in garments and hangings." Not only did Muslim traders expand the batik market but because of the Muslim prohibition against depicting human forms, design motifs also changed. New shapes—flat arabesques and calligraphy—were introduced and became integral in the evolution of batik.

Near Borobudur, the temple complex of Prambanan (also known as Lara Jonggrang) rises majestically. This sacred monu- *ment was built in the tenth century to honor the Hindu trinity of Śiva, Viṣṇu, and Brahma.*

A seventeenth-century Malay
and his wife selling their goods in
Batavia.

It is difficult to imagine that
today's sleepy Strait of Malacca
was once the main commercial
thoroughfare of Southeast Asia.

The Urban Chinese

The influence of the Chinese on Javanese batik was as profound as that of the Muslims, the Buddhists, and the Hindus. Trading such prestigious commodities as silk and porcelain for Java's textiles—not to mention its birds' nests—the Chinese had long been doing business in the area. From the ninth to the twelfth centuries, the princes of Java sent colored cotton cloth as tribute to Chinese leaders; indeed, they even sent silk to China. Now the Chinese brought mythical lions and lyrical flowers to batik designs along with a bright new palette of colors.

The city of Tuban, near the eastern end of Java's north coast, was known to the Chinese as early as the eleventh century, and by the fifteenth century it had become Java's greatest trading center, with many immigrants from southern China:

> In this city dwell very many noblemen who do great trade in the buying and selling of silk . . . cotton cloth, and also pieces of cloth which they wear on their bodies, some of which are made there. They have ships that they call junks, which . . . are laden with pepper and taken to Bali, and they exchange it for pieces of simple cotton cloth, for they are made there in quantity, and when they have exchanged their pepper there for that cloth, they carry the same . . . to other surrounding islands . . . and exchange the cloth in turn for mace, nutmeg, and cloves, and being laden . . . they sail home once more.

Whether the king of Tuban, pictured in the sixteenth-century book illustration (opposite), was Chinese we do not know. We do know from the vivid description that there was considerable pomp and ceremony as he sat on an elephant and received his Dutch visitors.

This king, in addition to treating the Dutch men in a humane manner, had his *keris* presented to Prince Mauritius. . . . The king's dress was a black silk tunic with wide sleeves. The elephant . . . was as high as two men one on top of the other. . . . History says that this king was able to gather several thousand armed men ready for war within 24 hours. . . . After the Dutch men had rendered to him the proper honor . . . [he] showed them his magnificence and majesty.

Nearby Gresik rivaled Tuban, and in the fourteenth century it boasted a Chinese-born ruler. *Fair Winds for Escort*, a navigation guide, gave instructions for sailing to Lasem, Tuban, Jaratan, Demak, and Banten. Farther west along Java's north coast, Cirebon had been visited by Chinese traders hundreds of years earlier.

Direct trade between China and Java virtually ceased after the beginning of the sixteenth century. The long-reigning Qing Dynasty (1644–1894) in fact forbade Chinese trade and overseas settlement. Yet, by 1700, Java had about ten thousand Chinese residents; within another hundred years there were one hundred thousand Chinese, many of them married to Javanese.

And even in those early times, the people now referred to as "overseas Chinese" exerted an influence beyond their numbers. The Chinese were mostly urban dwellers, settling in such large centers as Batavia (now Jakarta), Semarang, Surabaya, and Cirebon. A seventeenth-century observer wrote: "The Chinese drive here a considerable traffick being more industrious . . . mainly they are in merchandising and are great artists of thriftiness." They became entrepreneurs and middlemen, and their orders were big enough to cause batik making to become something of an industry, with factories spotted along the Java coast.

How the King of Tuban received the Dutch men.

Mesquita

LVBAN

Explorers from the West

Javanese history from about 1400 to 1600 was tumultuous and is still not well understood. By the sixteenth century, power in Europe had shifted from countries with armies to those with navies, and a struggle began among the European nations for control of Asia's riches. Portugal came to dominate a vast trade route, extending from Goa on the west coast of India to Malacca, thence to the Spice Islands, to Macao, and northward to Japan. The critical port of Malacca was in Portuguese hands. As Portuguese traders increasingly pushed the Javanese out of the spice trade, the reaction was predictable: local Javanese rulers bitterly contested the spreading Portuguese power. The ruler of Demak, for example, built up Banten in an effort to create a new trade route through the Sunda Strait to the south of Sumatra. Several coastal cities joined together to launch repeated and massive attacks against the Portuguese, resulting in the exhaustion of the cities' manpower and resources.

And from the kingdom of Mataram in central Java came more bad news for the north coast. With the northern cities already decimated, Mataram's ruler, Sultan Agung, decided that the time was ripe to strike. Japara, Gresik, Cirebon, Tuban, Madura, and Surabaya all fell. The devastation was frightful.

> The environs of Surabaya were completely laid waste, so that famine and loss of life forced the city to capitulate. Forty thousand Madurese were carried off prisoner to Java. . . . Countless inhabitants of the coastal centers took refuge on other shores.

The coast of northern Java was never to recover from such wanton destruction.

◆

By the end of the sixteenth century, the Dutch had sailed around the Cape of Good Hope to Java. They proved to be good organizers. Rather than relying on dozens of individual free lances to capture the spice trade, in 1602 the Dutch put together the Dutch East India Trading Company, known by its initials, VOC (*Vereenigde Oost-Indische Compagnie*). The VOC included a military force; more important, it was a monopoly operating in a single large geographic area. The VOC was the foundation of the Dutch commercial empire that was to last for nearly two hundred fifty years.

The VOC established a commercial settlement in Java. The Dutch settlers called it Batavia and built steep-roofed houses and dug canals that reminded them of home. Batavia flourished. Within fifty years it had become a center for trans-shipment of goods from the entire world. Wrote Adam Smith, the *laissez-faire* economist:

What the Cape of Good Hope is between Europe and every part of the East-Indies, Batavia is between the principal countries in the East-Indies. It lies upon the most frequented road from Hindustan to China and Japan. . . . Batavia is able to surmount the additional disadvantage, of perhaps the most unwholesome climate in the world.

Holland was now firmly established in Asia. Not only was Batavia thriving, the Dutch had also destroyed Banten in western Java, seized Malacca from the Portuguese, and were aggressively expanding their power. In return for Dutch protection, the sultans of the courts of Yogyakarta and Surakarta were forced to give the Dutch a strip of land on the north coast. They also granted the VOC permission to sell cotton cloth there, competing with Java's own home-grown cotton.

By 1755 VOC control was established throughout Java, except in the courts of Yogyakarta and Surakarta. And just as surely as Dutch influence would change all aspects of Javanese life, so would the establishment of the VOC affect north-coast batik.

At the end of the eighteenth century, several events were to seal the fate of the VOC and very nearly doom the prospects for later Dutch rule. The spice trade became less lucrative. Money was now to be made in produce shipped directly from Java: coffee, tea, and palm oil among other items. What virtually bankrupted the VOC, however, were savage doses of dysentery and malaria—along with piracy and corruption. Finally, the Napoleonic wars changed the fate of Java as well as Europe. Coincidentally, they also led to the first authoritative chronicling of baṭik.

The children's hospital of Batavia was actually an orphanage, built of brick with lodgings for servants and maintained by voluntary contributions.

Johan Nieuhoff was one of numerous brave, and sometimes foolhardy, seventeenth-century explorers.

BATIK AS COSTUME

Until well into the twentieth century, batik was used almost exclusively for clothing and for ceremonial occasions. In a rank-conscious society, class distinctions were made by the type of cloth worn and its pattern. In a tropical, humid climate such as Java, batik was ideal. As a costume, it was ingenious because batik demanded no zippers, buttons, or pins.

A **sarong,** usually sewn together at the ends, is only two yards long (180 cm.). A sarong has a "body," or *badan,* and a "head," or *kepala.* The *badan* is about three-quarters the length of the sarong. The *kepala* is a wide perpendicular band, usually in the middle or at the end of the sarong. Sometimes the *kepala* has two rows of equilateral triangles running down each side with the points of the triangles facing each other, much like a backgammon board; this design is called a *tumpal.*

The **dodot,** made by sewing two lengths of batik together, is a prerogative of royalty; *dodots* are usually worn only by the sultan, a bride or groom, or dancers at the courts, and are usually of unsurpassed quality. The *dodot* is worn draped and folded as an overskirt, sometimes with a train of fabric hanging at one side. Silk trousers are often worn underneath, with the pattern of the trousers showing in front.

Dodot

Sarong is a Malay word, but the idea of draping a cloth as a skirt probably originated in India. A young nineteenth-century girl from western Java wears a typical sarong with tumpal at its head. (Right)

Sarong

A **kain panjang** or "long cloth"—often simply called *kain*—is an ankle-length batik about forty inches wide (107 cm.) and about two and a half to three yards long (about 250 cm.). The entire surface is decorated, often with borders at the shorter ends. Worn by both men and women, a *kain* is usually considered more formal than a sarong. When worn by women, it is usually wrapped left over right, sometimes with narrow pleats in the front; men usually wear a *kain* with broader front pleats, wrapping it loosely right over left.

A **pagi-sore** or "morning-evening" batik is the Javanese version of reversible clothing. A little longer than a *kain,* the *pagi-sore* is divided diagonally, each half with a distinctive design and color. It is a simple matter to arrange the same cloth for two strikingly different effects.

The **selendang** (or *slendang*) is a long narrow cloth used exclusively by women as a carryall or a shawl. Draped over the shoulder, it can hold a baby, the day's marketing, or anything else that needs carrying. *Selendangs* often have striped borders at each end suggesting an imitation fringe; they are sometimes finished by a true fringe, which is attached, knotted, and twisted.

The **iket kepala,** worn only by men, is a square headcloth, tied elegantly to form a turban. The pattern of the *iket* may be distributed evenly over the surface of the cloth, but in the middle there is usually an undecorated area called *tengahan.* Often the perimeter has finely drawn stripes, imitating a real fringe.

A **kemben** is a "breast cloth," which is a narrow batik wrapped around the upper part of the body used to secure a *kain* or sarong. It is worn instead of a *kebaya* (a long-sleeved blouse usually decorated with lace and embroidery) or sometimes under the *kebaya.*

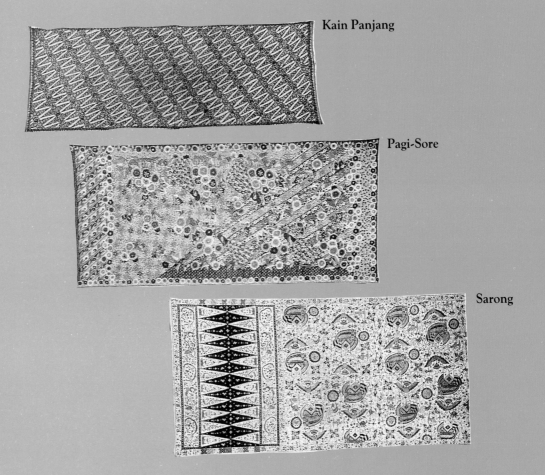

Kain Panjang

Pagi-Sore

Sarong

34

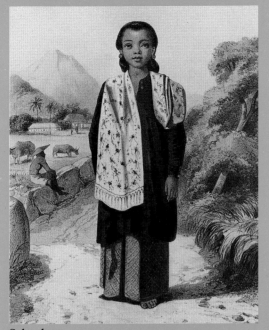

Selendang

Iket Kepala

Iket Kepala

Kemben

Dodot

Kain Panjang

Cotton for Sale—and to Wear

Cotton had been grown and spun in India for five thousand years, and by the middle of the fourteenth century it was probably the most important medium of exchange among Muslim, Hindu, and Arab traders. Within another three hundred years most merchants, except the Chinese—who traded mostly in porcelain—were carrying cotton throughout the East Indian archipelago. A single length of three or four yards was worth about forty pounds of nutmeg, and one ship might carry thirty or more different kinds of cloth, most likely including batik.

The export of batik from southeastern India to Java, Sumatra, Persia, and Siam reached its peak in the seventeenth and eighteenth centuries. Early batik designs imitated woven textiles and were called *djelemprang;* they were popular because the simulated woven design took far less time to produce than actual woven cloth. The double *ikat* weave (*patola*) was often copied as a batik design, and this and other geometrically patterned *djelemprangs* were to find their way into the batik of both central Java and the north coast.

The Indian textiles suggested the possibility of multicolored patterns, as well as new designs. They probably also inspired a new organization of the textile surface—as a framed rectangle. That seemingly simple change brought about a profound revolution in perspective: now the cloth could be viewed as a picture-plane to be filled with something other than stripes or plaids. All these innovations may well have suggested to local craftsmen the idea of filling major design elements in batik with a network of finer designs. This would later lead to the development of *isén*—the fine "filling" or pattern within a motif.

In a 1662 book by the Dutch explorer Johan Nieuhoff, numerous Javanese are shown dressed in what appear to be batiked garments. Shortly thereafter, a Dutch official visiting the central Javanese kingdom of Mataram reported four thousand women who were "painting" cloth. The numbers may have been inflated, but batik by then had become important enough to rival Dutch imported cloth. In fact, the ruler of Mataram encouraged his people to grow cotton in a vain attempt to free his people from the yoke of Holland.

By the end of the eighteenth century, the common people of Java were wearing plaid cloth (called *lurik*); others, more exalted, "preferred baték, or painted cloth," which came in a hundred different patterns. Not all these patterns were available to everyone, however. Certain designs, especially those used in the courts of central Java, were "forbidden" to commoners. But the freewheeling people of the north coast generally ignored such strictures.

Cotton, both locally grown and imported, was a key ingredient in the development of batik. Two types of cotton were grown in seventeenth-century Java. *Jerondo* was "used instead of feathers to stuff cushions, bolsters, and quilts . . . but not long enough for combing or weaving." A second type called *Kapas* was spun by the Javanese: "As soon as the flowers are gone, there buds out a knot, containing the cotton wool, this cotton fit for weaving." The labor required to produce handspun cloth limited the production of locally woven goods. Seven hours of continuous labor were required to produce one meter of cloth on a traditional Javanese loom, and this work, as well as the spinning of yarn, was done by women.

> The women of the family should provide the men with the cloths necessary for their apparel and from the first consort to the sovereign to the wife of the lowest peasant, the same rule is observed. In every cottage there is a spinning wheel and a loom, and in all ranks a man is accustomed to pride himself on [the] beauty of cloth woven by either his wife, mistress, or daughter.

For the women, only the planting and harvesting of crops took precedence over these homespun duties.

For the last four hundred years, however, cotton has not been a major commodity in Java's agricultural economy. As early as 1598, Jan H. Linschoten was persuaded that "if cloth of Holland were [in Java] to be found, it would be more esteemed than cotton linen out of India." Even under Dutch colonial rule, when a plantation system prevailed, coffee, rice, tobacco, and copra far outstripped cotton in importance. Batik makers have always relied on imported cotton, first from India and then from Holland and England. These imports were undoubtedly expanded in the third quarter of the eighteenth century, as Java's population tripled. The increased labor force, in turn, increased the production of batik.

An Arab of Java, *from a mid-nineteenth-century lithograph.*

Raffles the Remarkable

The leading witness to the development of batik was that extraordinary man, Thomas Stamford Raffles, who arrived in Java in 1811 as the English began a brief but important interregnum there. Some twelve thousand Englishmen landed in Java, capturing it from the Dutch. Raffles was appointed lieutenant governor of the island and forthwith set out to learn everything he could about his new surroundings. He abolished forced and "contingent" deliveries, upon which both the Dutch and Javanese had based their economy. Shocked that a country like Holland, which valued political liberty, would tolerate thirty thousand slaves in Java, Raffles set about eradicating slavery.

Not content with such far-reaching economic and social changes, Raffles steeped himself in the local culture. He studied the Javanese language; he uncovered the ancient monument at Borobudur, which by then was buried deep in the jungle; he encouraged restoration of other ancient temples. Raffles also wrote a monumental *History of Java,* which to this day stands as the most authoritative and exhaustive chronicle of the island and its folkways. He amassed one of the greatest collections of flora, fauna, textiles, and artifacts ever collected in the archipelago and packed it all up for shipment home. The boat and its contents burned fifty miles offshore. Undaunted, Raffles began a second collection, which he brought back safely to England.

Raffles may well have collected batik by the gross—he wrote that there were a hundred identifiable patterns—and his *History of Java* includes the first systematic study of the art. Only two of Raffles's Javanese pieces survive, and they seem to be the earliest in any collection. Illustrations in the Raffles *History* show numerous ways of wearing batik, along with many different patterns. He also wrote in detail about how batik is made.

During Raffles's time England began exporting its own printed cottons to Java, and local batik makers acquired a new perspective on their own work when they found the English prints were not colorfast. The English also exported a high-quality, tightly woven white cloth. This, along with European-made *mori,* as cambrics were called, began to replace Javanese hand-woven textiles. The smoother, mill-made textiles from Europe became the groundcloth of most nineteenth-century batik: it was possible for wax to be drawn in more detailed designs on these finer fabrics, and the motifs themselves began to change accordingly.

The subsequent hundred years witnessed a great flowering of batik, particularly on the north coast with its cosmopolitan exposure. Whereas Raffles had recognized a mere hundred designs, a century later the batik scholar G. P. Rouffaer described more than a thousand.

Sir Thomas Stamford Raffles, the remarkable man whose monumental History of Java *is still important to our knowledge of batik.*
One of the earliest (ca. 1810–1820) surviving examples of Javanese batik, this piece (right) remained in the Raffles' family until it was donated to London's Museum of Mankind in 1939. Its border was made separately and stitched to the fabric. 8

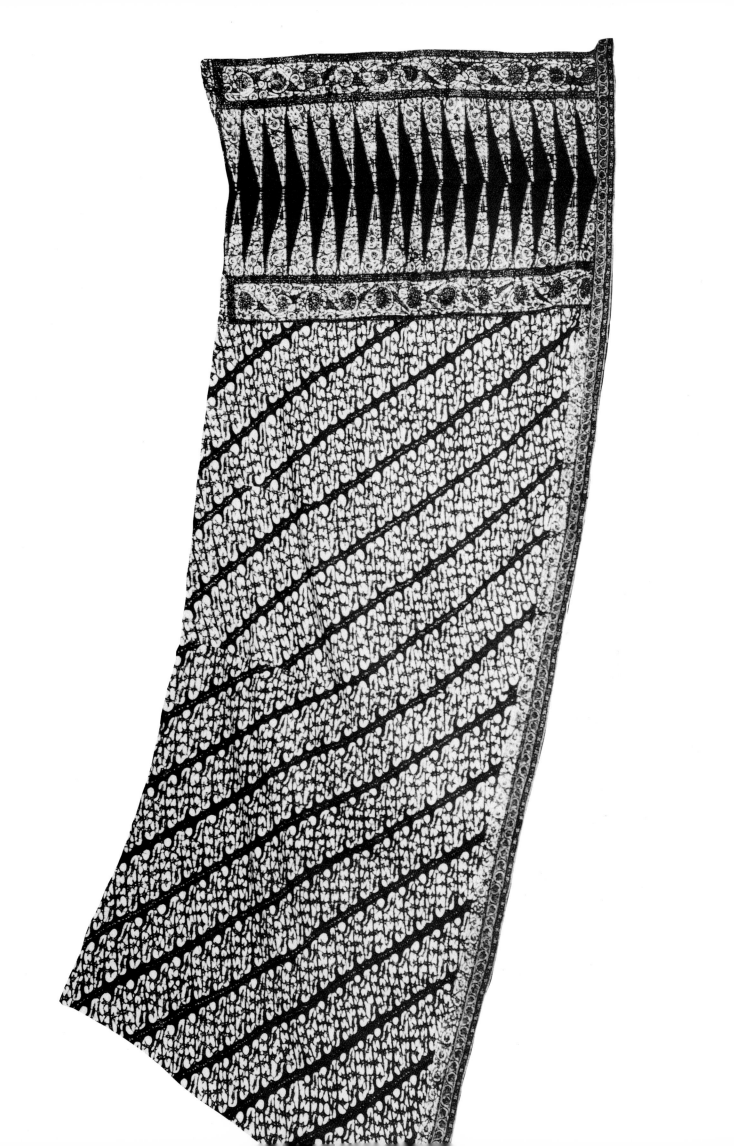

Birth of an Industry

In 1815, only four years after Sir Thomas Raffles and the British arrived in Java, the victorious nations at the Congress of Vienna decided that, in order to achieve world harmony, a balance of power would have to be imposed. Thus, the East Indies came to be restored to the Dutch who promptly revoked the reforms of Raffles.

The Dutch remained in the East Indies for almost another century and a half, turning much of the area—especially land-rich Java—into a vast state-owned plantation, cultivated by forced labor with product quotas. Java became a keystone of Holland's commercial empire in the Indies. Its pluralistic society, strengthened by Chinese immigration in the seven-

teenth century, now became stratified: Dutch on top, Chinese (and sometimes Arabs) in the middle, and the indigenous population at the bottom.

For most Javanese—excepting some Eurasians, a few nobles, some merchants and their families and friends —life was hard indeed. "No Dogs or Inlanders" was not an uncommon sign in public places. Dutch schools were closed to non-Dutch; land could be bought only by the Dutch. Although slavery was finally abolished in 1860, and a civil service was established along with some educational reforms, life for the people of Java continued grimly.

Nevertheless, profound changes were taking place beneath the surface. Between 1815 and 1860, the pop-

An 1855 lithograph entitled A Native School in the Kampung. *Javanese village life is still much the same, more than a century later. (Left)*
Chinese musician plays a popular instrument called the Kong-a-Hian. (Above)

ulation of Java doubled, then doubled again by 1900. The plantation system, which had cultivated cotton, tea, and coffee, now began to grow rubber and nut palm as well. The discovery of petroleum brought vast new wealth to the Netherlands, and a flood of Dutch civil servants came to oversee the empire—thousands of administrators and clerks, many of whom would come to view Java as "home."

All this was significant for the history of batik. The population explosion, both Javanese and Dutch, increased the availability of labor. New roads and railroads brought raw cotton and finished batik to growing markets. As the economy grew, there were more batik producers and more people who could afford to buy batik. From 1850 to 1939 the Javanese produced some of their finest work.

There were interruptions along the way, most notably the worldwide depression that began in 1929. Already threatened by cheap Japanese imports, Java's textile markets shriveled, and many men and women trudged from town to town in desperate search of employment. The economic dislocation was long and severe, resulting in the permanent loss of many local batik styles and specialties.

Then came the awful disruption of World War II as well as the culmination of the anticolonial struggle, which closed most batik factories and killed or exiled many of Java's batik entrepreneurs, their talents lost forever. In light of these travails, it was appropriate that when Indonesia achieved independence after the war, batik became the symbol of a unified nation.

This imposing house belonged to the mayor of the Chinese community in Batavia in the last half of the nineteenth century. (Left)
A wealthy nineteenth-century Chinese is borne by two Javanese in a hammock with a bamboo roof. (Below left)
A session of the colonial court in either Kudus or Japara after an uprising of the poor protesting famine. The Dutch resident acted as judicial chief, aided by representatives of the Chinese and Islamic communities as well as the local chief. (Below)

LIFE IN 19TH CENTURY JAVA

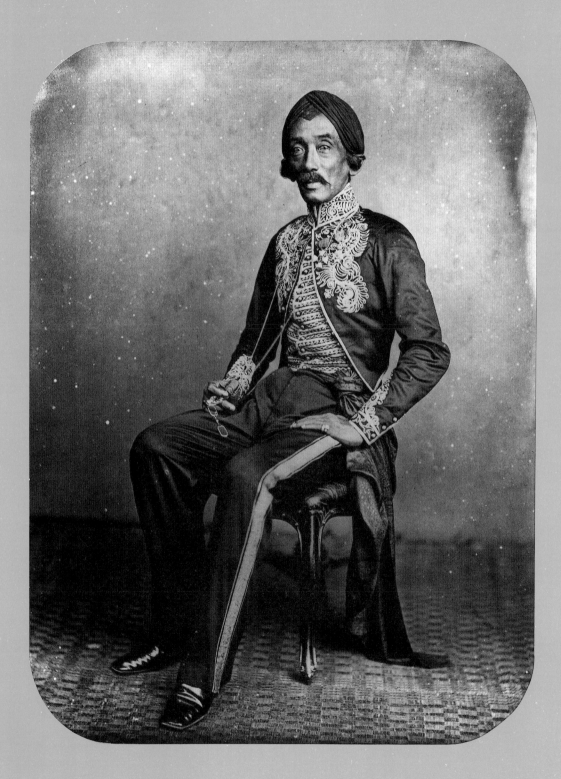

Raden Saleh, photographed in a costume he designed, was a nineteenth-century Javanese painter who had visited the courts of Europe. (Left)

Raden Aju, wife of the regent of Kudus, with retainers. (Above)

A dancer, probably from the regent's court.

Three girls, one reclining on a balek-balek, or bamboo bench.

Concubines, perhaps of the regent, or of some lesser official.

Wife of a Raden or regent, the highest non-Dutch official.

The regent of Cianjur astride a splendid beast.

This regent of Kudus was also a writer and poet.

Lower court officials.

Lounging in a palanquin or tandu.

Opium smokers with tools of their habit.

Javanese textile vendors.

Two Javanese women, one delousing the other.

The Batik Process

To appreciate batik fully, one must understand the extreme intricacy of the process and the great patience, care, and skill that it demands.

In Java, the long and laborious batik process begins at home or in factories that evoke William Blake's "dark Satanic mills" of nineteenth-century England. Since electricity is precious, workshops tend to be dim and dark. Often batikers must work by the natural light that somehow sneaks through the cracks and crevices of a workshop's roof.

With the unrelenting Javanese humidity and the unremittent vapors of molten wax, air hangs heavy in these factories, whose dirt floors are often muddied by rain. Women sit barefoot on mats or low stools, huddling in small circles around pans of heated wax, sharing the contents. Six days a week, they work from dawn to midafternoon for the equivalent of eighty cents to one dollar and fifty cents a day, about what it costs to feed a family. They range in age from ten to seventy, and they are considered no more than common laborers. From such sweatshop conditions come some of the most splendid textiles in the world.

In every true batik, wax is painstakingly applied to the cloth to *resist* successive dyes so that wherever the cloth is waxed, dyes cannot penetrate. For example, if the desired design is a red flower on a blue background, wax is first applied to the area that will become the flower. The white cloth is then immersed in blue dye and dried. After drying, the wax which covered the flower pattern is scraped from the cloth. Because the wax resisted the blue dye, there is now a white flower on a blue background. To make the flower red, the blue background is then covered with wax and the entire cloth is immersed in red dye. When the wax is scraped from the cloth for a second time, a red flower emerges on a blue background.

This process is repeated over and over again as more colors are used. The finest batik is reversible. Motifs are drawn, waxed, and dyed, first on one, then the other side of the fabric. Since the greatest Javanese batik is multicolored, it is not surprising that designers, waxers, dyers, and finishers take twelve months or more to complete a single piece of a yard or two.

Both silk and cotton are used for batik, and in certain areas, such as Juana on Java's north coast, silk is particularly popular. Unlike cotton, silk requires little preparation; its fibers are quite receptive to wax and dye without the elaborate series of treatments needed by cottons. Nevertheless, among Javanese batik makers the overwhelming preference is for cotton.

Children drawing batik designs on paper. (Left)
A typical tulis batik workshop. Several women share a pan of heated wax while each works on her own piece. (Right)

Centuries ago, cotton resembling coarse homespun was grown, spun, and woven in Java. That was serviceable for simple batik work. But to achieve the crisp, sharp, and intricate details of certain motifs, a finer cotton was necessary—and the Dutch were happy to oblige. About 1824, they introduced a fine, white, machine-woven cotton, and for more than a hundred years Java was dependent on this for its better batik. Sen was the name of one Dutch manufacturing company that exported a cloth that came to be known as *Tjap (Cap) Sen*, synonymous with finest quality. Javanese factories now produce machine-loomed cotton, but it is not as fine as the earlier Dutch material.

Before cotton is batiked, it must be prepared to receive wax and dyes. The cloth is first measured, torn into appropriate lengths, and hemmed at the ends to prevent fraying. Sometimes it is boiled to remove sizing or stiffness in the fibers. After boiling, the cloth is treated with oil and lye to give it a base color and to prepare the fibers to receive the dyes. The cotton is rinsed in yet another bath and while still wet, it is folded in approximately twelve-inch widths along its warp. Placed on a wooden baseboard, the cloth is then beaten with a mallet, to soften the fibers and enable the material to absorb wax.

After the baths and the beating, a design is applied by pencil to the prepared fabric. Some workers are so familiar with patterns—from a lifetime of repetition—that they can draw from memory. But for others, the designs are drawn on paper first, then fastened by pins (or even a few grains of cooked rice) to the fabric and finally traced in pencil on the cotton. The cloth is then ready to receive its first waxing, known as *ngrengreng*.

Mixing the Wax. Beeswax, often imported from the islands of Sumba and Timor, is the wax most commonly used in the batik process. The wax is mixed with resins: *gandarokan* (resin of the eucalyptus tree), *matakucing* (the Javanese word for "cat's eye," another resin), and *kendal* (the fat from cows). Because the composition of the wax mixture affects the appearance of the finished product, the recipe varies according to the type of design, and the proportions are always a well-guarded secret. Mrs. Oey Soe Tjoen of Kedungwuni, for example, believes the beauty of her exquisitely detailed designs is due to her wax recipe: the ingredients are known to many, the proportions only to her.

A Simple Tool. Hand-drawn batik is called *tulis*, after the Javanese word for "writing." Combining the finest designs with the best cottons, *tulis* is the most time-consuming, expensive, and highly prized batik. Except in the Cirebon area where, more than half a century ago, hand-drawing was a male prerogative, *tulis* batik is usually made by women. The basic tool is the *canting* (also spelled *tjanting*) with which liquid wax is drawn on cloth. This simplest of tools is not found in any other batik region in the world.

The *canting* works much like a fountain pen. It has a bamboo or reed handle, about six inches long, with a small, thin copper cup from which a tiny pipe protrudes. (Copper is used for both cup and pipe because it conducts heat and keeps the wax warm and fluid.) A woman holds the *canting* by its bamboo handle, scooping up the heated wax and blowing through the tip of the pipe to keep the wax fluid. Then, using the *canting*'s pipe as a pen, she draws the design on the fabric, outlining with wax instead of ink.

The first waxing, or ngrengreng, *is nearly completed. A worker would sit on a low stool with the wax and* canting *near at hand.*

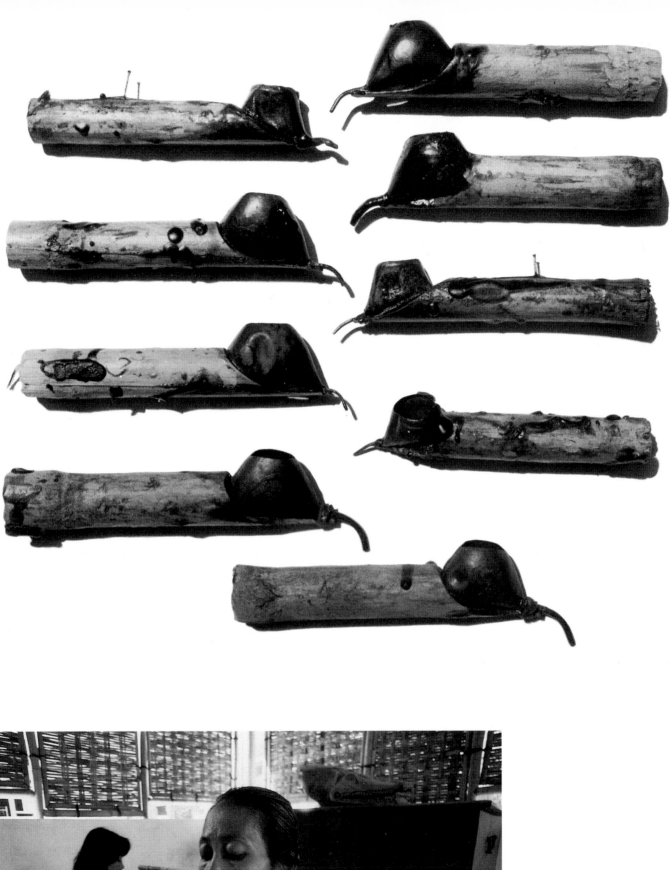

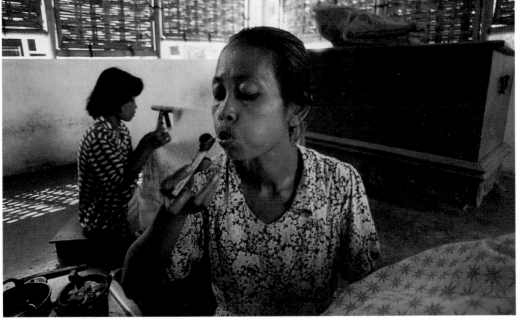

The essential tool of hand-drawn batik is the canting, which may have one or several spouts depending upon the design. (Top) A worker blows through the canting's tip to keep the wax flowing smoothly.

The size and diameter of the *canting*'s copper bowl and pipe are determined by the job at hand—whether the tool is to be used for coarse outlining or for fine details. Some *cantings* have two pipes, others as many as seven, with openings varying in size and shape—some are square instead of round. When there is a large area to be waxed, a wad of cotton is attached to the mouth of the pipe, to spread the wax more freely.

Before wax is applied, the cloth is draped over a bamboo frame called *gawungan* and weighted on one side to keep it from blowing in the wind while the waxing takes place. The batiker sits between the cloth and the pan of wax and begins her work with the *canting*. Her free hand supports the underside of the fabric, and she covers her lap with a napkin or *taplak* to protect herself from dripping hot wax.

Skilled workers are usually chosen to apply the first wax outline, the *ngrengreng*, to the cloth, because this will largely determine the quality of the batik. Less skilled workers perform the next step, retracing the outline in wax. Depending on the number of colors, the waxing process may be repeated again and again, each time by a different worker.

Enter, the Cap. Around 1840 the invention of the *cap* (or *tjap*)—a copper block that applies an entire design onto the cloth with a single imprint—revolutionized the batik industry. With *cap*, a worker can wax twenty pieces a day rather than spending up to forty-five days to hand-wax a single piece of cloth. Traditionally, men had dyed and women waxed, but with the introduction of the *cap*, a heavy block more easily handled by men than women, men became more important to the batik industry.

The *cap*, made by soldering copper shapes into the desired pattern, resembles a flat iron and is held by a metal handle attached to the back. In the *cap* process, the cloth is spread on a padded table, and the design is applied by dipping the copper block in wax and stamping it on the fabric. Small metal pins attached to the corners of the *cap* are used to align one *cap* impression with the next.

As with *tulis* batik, in fine *cap* work wax is applied to both sides of the cloth. Often two or three different *caps* are used for one batik, one for each successive color or design. Quite commonly, both *tulis* and *cap* techniques are combined to produce a piece of batik.

Another tool, used in both *tulis* and *cap* batiks, is the *cemplogen* (also *tjemplogen*). Especially common to the Indramayu region on Java's north coast, the *cemplogen* is a block of short gold, silver, or steel needles attached to a wooden handle—rather like a wire brush. Young school children spend their afternoons using this tool to puncture wax on solid background areas, and the dye then penetrates the small holes, producing hundreds of tiny dots.

With the efficient *cap*, the Javanese could begin to build a batik textile industry. The growing business also attracted Chinese and Arab middlemen who had the capital to acquire *caps*, cotton, wax, and dyes and to pay the workers. Eventually, the trade in *cap* batik extended beyond the East Indian archipelago to Singapore, Africa, and Europe.

Interestingly, the invention of the *cap* did not mean the end of fine, hand-drawn *tulis*; instead there evolved an almost symbiotic relationship between *tulis* and *cap* batik, with different classes of people adopting the two

The cemplogen, often used in tulis batik, punctures wax that has been poured onto a solid background. Dye penetrates these holes, producing hundreds of tiny dots on the finished batik. Cemplogens are especially common to the Indramayu area.

Unlike tulis, which is made by women, batik made by a printing block, or cap, is the work of men. Each man stands at a padded table with his own wax and caps, imprinting the white cotton.

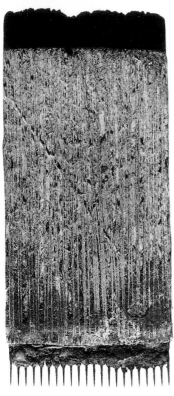

—or combinations of them. Competition from *cap*, of course, encouraged the *tulis* makers to find ways to get their goods to market faster.

Of several new production systems two were important. In the first, the work was organized by villages. Cloth and patterns would be consigned to women in a particular village by entrepreneurs or their agents, and the entire *tulis* process would be completed in that village. Either that, or people in one village might be assigned only to wax the cloth; middlemen would then take the waxed cloth to another village for dyeing and finishing.

The second system of production was an attempt to industrialize. Entrepreneurs established a series of batik factories, mostly on the north coast, so that they could control the quality of the cloth, designs, wax, and dyes. They introduced new motifs and techniques. With the introduction of aniline dyes at the end of the nineteenth century and synthetic dyes twenty years later, they were able to change the spectrum of colors. The factories proved that batik, even if hand drawn, need

Dye recipes are passed from generation to generation. Stones are often used to weigh down the batik while it is immersed in the secret dye. (Above)

Caps were first developed in the 1850s to "industrialize" the batik process. Made of copper, the finer ones today are collectors' items. (Right)

no longer be made at home. Batik, both *cap* and *tulis*—and sometimes a combination of the two—was now more readily available to a growing market.

Dyeing and Finishing. A well-executed dye is judged by its rich penetrating tone, the degree to which it is colorfast, and how well it resists abrasion. Small wonder that, in batik making, dye recipes are as secret as the wax mixtures, often passed by word of mouth from one generation to the next. Originally, the colors found in batik reflected the place of origin, as well as the cultural attitudes of the people who produced them. That is usually not the case today.

Though synthetic dyes have now largely replaced natural dyes, it was from nature that batik received its original colors. Certain roots and leaves of plants are known to produce color when boiled and mixed with special ingredients. Local water and local plant species greatly affect shades of color and thus each region of Java was to have its own characteristic tints.

Among the many colors found in Javanese batik, four are by far the most popular. The most common one, also believed to be the oldest, is indigo, derived from the plant of the same name and called *tom* by the Javanese. Forty of indigo's many species produce this particular shade of blue. Batik using this blue is called *biron* (from *biru*, the Javanese word for "blue").

A second common dye is *mengkudu*, a deep red from the bark and roots of the *Morinda citrifolia* plant; batik using this color is called *bangbangan* from *abang*, meaning red. *Tegerang*, from the *Cudriana javanesis* plant, is yellow. And *soga* is a rich, uniquely Javanese brown characteristic of batik from the central Javanese towns of Yogyakarta and Surakarta; it comes from the bark of the *Pelthophorum ferrugineum* tree. The Mangkunegara family in Surakarta was famous for its method of dying cloth with *soga* and the process is still used today by a family member, Ibu Praptini.

After each waxing cycle in the batik process, the cloth is ready to be dyed. In batches of twelve *kodi*—one *kodi* equals twenty pieces of batik—the cloths are placed in appropriate dye baths three times a day for ten days. They are then put into a bath of lime and water, which sets the dye. Traditionally on the fourth Sunday of each month the batik is dried on bamboo racks, ready for sale.

Under ordinary circumstances, cloth is usually dyed in boiling solutions. Not so with batik. Because wax has such a low melting point, batik must be dyed in a cold or lukewarm bath. This solution contains a pharmacopoeia of secret ingredients to facilitate penetration of

the dye into the fiber and to enhance the luster of the finished batik. These mysterious potions include oils from fruit seeds, brown palm sugar, fermented casava, bananas, even shredded chicken.

The cloth is immersed as often as necessary in a coloring vat to achieve the desired shade. It is then soaked in another solution of lye and water, to fix the dye. After each color has been set the wax is scraped off and reapplied; sometimes additional designs are drawn on the cloth between dyeings. Overdyeing is used to produce certain colors. Green, for example, starts off as a light blue (from indigo), which is then overdyed in a yellow bath; black is produced similarly, by overdyeing indigo with red or brown.

At the turn of the century, advances in science and technology produced synthetic dyes that gradually replaced the natural dyes of the Indies. Aniline dyes were used after 1898 in Java, and naphthol dyes became available in 1926. Other synthetic dyes used today include synthetic indigo, reactive, and Indrathrene dyes, which are easy to maintain and use and do not require the long preparation of natural dyes. Synthetic dyes made possible the pastel tints and jeweled tones so characteristic of north-coast Javanese batiks.

After dyeing is completed and the last of the wax is either scraped or boiled from the cloth, the finished

Wax is boiled from the cloth to prepare it for the next waxing and final wash.

After its final wash, the batik is laid out to dry, as in this Sura-karta cooperative, which dyes and dries cloth for local batik manufacturers.

batik is draped over bamboo racks or laid on the ground to dry. It is then folded and put under a press for "ironing." If the batik is destined for Chinese customers, another process takes place before the cloth leaves the factory: shells are rubbed across the surface of the cloth to give it a chintzlike quality. After a thorough rubbing —usually done by two men who sit on a bench facing each other with the batik between them—the piece is shiny and crinkly, a Chinese preference when buying "new" cloth. Numerous washings will eventually remove this chintzlike surface.

When the batik is finally ready for packaging, each piece is folded and wrapped in cellophane. Five pieces are bound together by pattern, not color, and counted by *kodi*. Special *tulis* pieces are always boxed or wrapped individually, while yardage goods are normally rolled on tubes.

◆

Let us now look at the spectacular works of art created in the late nineteenth and twentieth centuries by this intricate process. Here is a visual archive of the geographic and historic forces that have pressed upon Java for centuries. Batik was recast by the coastal Javanese eye into a vibrant cloth with a diverse artistic vocabulary. The following pages chronicle some of the finest examples.

II. BATIK IN THE ROYAL COURTS

The kraton of Cirebon.

Looming over the lush green flatlands of central Java stands a mountain that spews a wispy stream of smoke. Its name is Merapi—"mountain of fire"—and within it, so local legend has it, dwells a spirit that must be humored, honored, and generally reckoned with. In Javanese culture there is a fifth direction, in addition to the usual four. That direction is the center, and the center is the mountain, the dwelling place of the gods. From the center all other directions begin. Because Merapi is just such a spiritual landmark, it is a good place to start a journey tracing the mysteries of batik.

Central Java is about two hundred miles from the island's north coast—about a five-hour drive these days on bumpy roads. For centuries the people of central Java have been farmers, tilling soil that is among the richest in the world; for hundreds of years they have paid fealty to their various rulers. Near the volcano Merapi, farmers still follow their ancient ways, plowing with oxen, sculpting the land row by row, and preparing it for the planting of rice, coffee, and other crops. Harvesting the crops women carry baskets tied to their bodies by long pieces of batik or cradled in a woven fabric slung around their shoulders.

Agriculture has always been vital to the economy of the region, but it was in the ancient royal courts of Yogyakarta and Surakarta that the arts and culture of central Java were nurtured, subsidized, and developed. Today Yogyakarta has a population of half a million and its university is the educational center of Indonesia. Surakarta, a city of similar size some thirty miles away, is a bustling business town. In both, the ancient art of batik making survives.

The sultans still reign, and at the center of Yogyakarta and Surakarta the old courts, or *kratons*, still stand. Surrounded by high white walls and graced at the entrance by banyan trees, each *kraton* overlooks a square common called the *alun-alun*. Every day at eleven and four o'clock, ladies of the court, carrying bronze pots and yellow umbrellas, parade to the center of the *kraton*'s dirt courtyard for the traditional tea ceremony. And in a dozen or so low buildings, work and prayer go on as they have for centuries.

As one stands in an old *kraton* today, it is easy to conjure up images of the graceful noble life of yore, when all art forms flourished. There was music, in the gentle dissonance of the chimelike *gamelan*. There was classical dancing, derived from ancient Indian movements. There was diversion in the theater of shadow puppets, the *wayang kulit*, created by the court puppeteer, the *dalang*. There was the making of the mystical dagger (the *keris*), as well as literary composition, sewing, and gilding.

And, of course, there was the making of batik—regarded as one of the highest arts. More than a fine art,

At the kraton *of Yogyakarta in central Java, courtiers bring the Sultan his tea twice a day from a pavilion especially built for this purpose. (Left)*

The shadow puppet has always played an important role in ancient and modern Javanese culture. (Above)

MYSTERIES OF CENTRAL JAVA

in fact, batik came to have an inner meaning for some people. As the twentieth-century classicist K.R.T. Hadjonagoro explained:

> [Batik] was a vehicle for meditation, a process which gave birth to an uncommonly elevated sublimity in man. Truly realized beings in the social fabric of the Javanese community all made batik—from queens to commoners . . . it is almost inconceivable that in those days batik had any commercial objective. People batiked for family and ceremonial purposes, in devotion to God Almighty, in each man's endeavor to know God and draw near his spirit.

The batik of central Java has always had a style of its own: orderly, controlled, usually geometric. Its colors run to somber tones of indigo blue and *soga* brown, often combined with black on a background of cream or white. Although a natural red dye was available on the coast as early as 1817, the batik artisans of central Java did not use it. Isolated as they were from goods streaming into the northern ports from overseas, they were probably unaware of the new tint; or perhaps they were forbidden by the strict feudal court to introduce so radical a color.

To this day members of the sultan's court of Yogyakarta are forbidden to wear north-coast batik to court functions. But for all the restrictions, and despite the rather critical view the central Javanese took of their cosmopolitan brethren to the north, there was no stopping the influence of the coast and its lusty approach to life. Intermarriage was not uncommon among the people of the two areas—and so it was in their arts as well. Often the brighter colors and freer designs of north-coast batik would be reworked in central Java and then brought back to the north in altered forms.

Two hundred years ago, most central Javanese batik was made for family use. On three separate occasions —in 1769, 1784, and 1790—the ruler of Surakarta reserved specific patterns for his family. The sultan and his family, of course, were the most important personages, and for them, aristocratic women in the *kraton* traditionally made the finest batik—much as the noble young ladies of the middle ages in Europe

The full panoply of royal life in Yogyakarta's court, ca. 1900. The Dutch commissioner, resplendent in gold braid and buttons, offers his arm to the Sultan, fashionably dressed in a velvet morning coat and dodot.

Symbols of Java's courtly life (umbrellas and retainers) and Dutch colonialism (police with swords) characterize the tenuous relationship between the ruled and the rulers.

used to stitch exquisite embroidery for their families and their lords.

There were economic as well as aesthetic reasons for these Javanese women of noble birth to make batik. Among their men there was fierce competition for positions as courtiers to the sultan. These jobs, however, paid badly, and other members of the family —wives in particular—were forced to find additional sources of income, usually from the sale of homemade batik. In this way, the sultan was served and the courtiers' families were able to survive.

◆

Hinduism and Buddhism were central to the philosophical and religious life of the ancient courts of central Java; they also left their imprint on all the arts. The temple of Borobudur is one striking example. Built on a plateau overlooking the surrounding hills not far from Yogyakarta, Borobudur contains 2 million cubic feet of stone, more than five hundred images of Buddha, and represents the "mountain of the accumulation of virtue." On Borobudur's six ascending square terraces, reliefs depict the life of Buddha as he rises from the delights and damnation of the physical world to the higher sphere of total enlightenment and detachment.

Rivaling Borobudur, and not far away, is the colos-

Borobudur was built in the ninth century. Its six ascending terraces and reliefs depict the life of Buddha and his rise from the physical world to enlightenment.

A relief found at Borobudur resembles the kawung, *later found as a motif in batik design. (Top)*

A Cirebon batik illustrates an episode of the Mahabharata epic from the wayang *puppet repertoire. (Right) 9*

sal monument of Prambanan, also known as Lara Jonggrang, which was built to honor the Hindu trinity of Śiva, Viṣṇu (Vishnu), and Brahma. This tenth-century shrine, designed on a huge square plane and surrounded by four walls with four gates, is a cosmic mountain. Stone reliefs and panels illustrate Hindu classics, especially the *Ramayana.* Here the ruler and his followers were expected to practice asceticism, the form of worship most acceptable to Śiva.

These Buddhist and Hindu temples suggest that the ancient Javanese saw the world in religious, not secular, terms. In that feudal society the ruler "had achieved union with god in his lifetime." His subjects yearned for a share of this immortality. Quite likely some Hindu and Buddhist temple motifs such as the lotuslike *kawung* are representations of a sacred, regulated universe. This sense of order was mirrored in the structure of the ancient courts, the siting and orientation of homes and temples, and the code of conduct which enjoined every man of means to learn the fine arts, including horsemanship, the management of an elephant, and how to drive away "all women of loose character."

In addition to the rich Hindu-Buddhist traditions, a number of indigenous customs and beliefs also brought mystery and meaning to the forms and uses of batik. It was believed, for example, that the sarong, often sewn, lacked the mystical powers of the *kain panjang,* a length of unsewn batik of about two and a half yards. Central Java's nobility never wore the lowly sarong; not only was it lacking in magic but it had originated elsewhere, in coastal Malaya and other parts of the Indies.

The Javanese endowed their batik forms with all sorts of magical properties, beliefs which endure to this day. If a baby cries, its mother has only to wipe its face with the bottom corner of her *kain panjang* and almost instantly the baby will calm down. If a child is sick, placing a *kain panjang,* possibly with special designs, upon its head will effect a cure. And if a child is well, the *kain* will keep disease away.

The *inding,* a special batik that central Javanese women wear when menstruating, has a magic of its own. To keep a husband from straying, the wife puts her *inding* on his head; to attract another man, she places her *inding* on the unsuspecting target of her desire. And when a young girl first menstruates, she will be protected from evil if she puts a piece of her *inding* in an amulet and wears it around her neck.

These ancient ritual uses of batik have survived all the religious, cultural, and political upheavals imposed on Java by outsiders through the years.

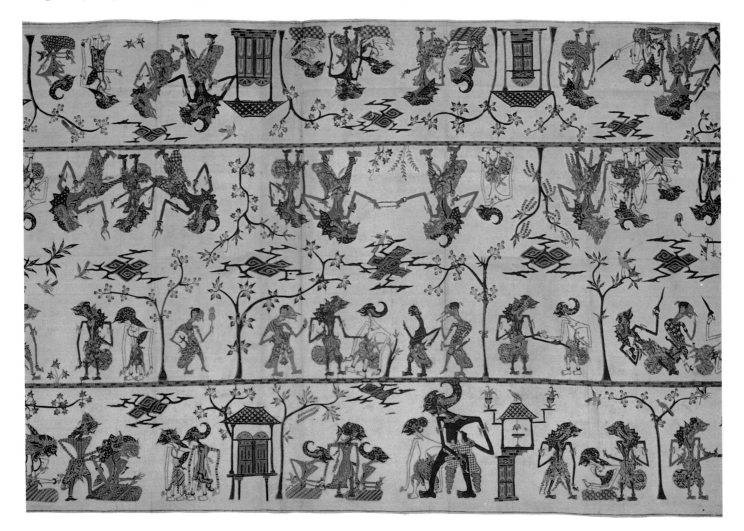

8 FORBIDDEN PATTERNS

The sultans of Yogyakarta and Surakarta decreed in the eighteenth century that certain patterns were forbidden to commoners. Even within the royal family, some batik patterns were reserved for the crown prince, while others could be worn only by his less royal cousins.

Although many people, especially those on the north coast, paid little attention to such decrees, within the hierarchical and strict court etiquette the proper use of the forbidden patterns by the "right" people at the "right" time was taken seriously. But while the patterns originally were full of meaning, eventually they became designs with no particular significance except for their beauty. Eight of the best-known forbidden patterns are illustrated here.

Kawung resembles the cross section of the aren-palm fruit, with the crosses in the center of each oval suggesting the seeds of the fruit. It also looks like a four-petaled blossom, a simplified lotus. The motif may have evolved from fish scales. *Kawung* is an old design, part of the *ceplok* category of patterns based on repeating squares, rectangles, ovals, and stars. Designs in the *ceplok* group reflect the Javanese belief in a structured universe; the cross in the center is thought to represent a universal source of energy.

Parang, the sword pattern, implies power and growth and was worn by rulers. This pattern had to be faultlessly executed. A flaw would destroy the magic power [of] the cloth. *Parang* means "broken dagger," and it is probably related to the dagger, or *keris*, "universally worn by all classes" in early nineteenth-century Java. Legends emphasize the supernatural power of the *keris*: it made heroes in war, brought good luck to the unfortunate, and healed the sick.

Parang rusak is an elegant, diagonal variation of the *parang* pattern. *Rusak* means "damaged or destroyed" and with *parang* it could mean "enemy destroying." The mythical significance of this design is similar to that of the *parang*.

Cemukiran is a raylike pattern similar to *parang* that probably owes its origin to the lotus. *Cemukiran* often borders a plain-colored centerpiece called the *modang*; the *modang* was worn only by royalty.

Sawat, or "large wings," represents the *garuda*, according to legend, a birdlike creature with the body and limbs of a man and the beak and talons of an eagle. In Hindu-Javanese mythology the *garuda* carried Viṣṇu through the heavens.

Udan liris, or "light rain," combines a variety of designs and natural shapes within parallel diagonal lines. Most likely *udan liris* is a fertility symbol related to agriculture.

Semen, which may be related to the same word in English, means "to sprout" or "to grow." The *semen* design is so full of symbolism that it may represent the worship of fertility as well as the Javanese belief in a cosmic order. Mountains suggest holy places of the gods; temples and pavilions represent places to meditate; wings provide a means by which to move into the spiritual realm; animals represent the earth; birds, Father Heaven (especially *garuda*); and the snake *(naga)* symbolizes Mother Earth, the underworld, and creatures of the sea.

Alasalasan or "virgin wood" is similar to the *semen* design and may have been its precursor. It lacks the pavilions and gateways but presents a multitude of animals and plants against a solid background. The flora and fauna suggest that *alasalasan* encouraged productivity and protection of the crops. This pattern often is applied to cloth in gold outline.

Kawung

Parang

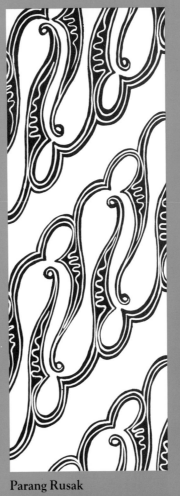

Parang Rusak

Cemukiran

Sawat

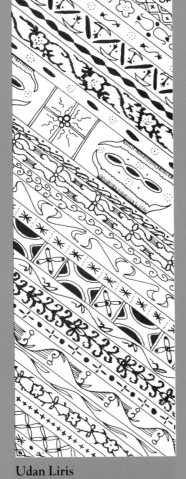

Udan Liris

Semen

Alasalasan

A ceremonial kain dodot, probably from the court of Surakarta. Its mauve center is bordered by the elegant gold-leaf alasalasan design. (Detail) 10

A splendid representation of a
once-royal pattern with a large
rectangular center field. This
kain dodot, ca. 1900, is bordered
by a parang and semen motif,
highlighted by gold leaf. (Detail) 11

Just as the courts in central Java played a key role in the development of that region's batik, so it was on the north coast—but with a difference. The difference was geography. Compared to the relative isolation and provincialism of the interior, the coastal areas were linked by traders from the sea and also served as way stations for people and goods coming from the mountains inland. The architecture of the northern courts reflected all this coming and going, as did their spiritual values, their social order, and their arts, especially their batik.

Of all the towns on Java's north coast, the ancient city of Cirebon was unique: it was the only city where a strong court culture exerted both spiritual and artistic force. From the courts of Cirebon, and from the nearby towns, especially Indramayu, where the batik artists lived and worked, came bright new accents in the development of batik.

Cirebon was founded in 1378 by a Muslim ruler with strong Hindu ties. Within a hundred years, it had become one of Java's most venerated Muslim states. Because of its fine harbor, Cirebon also became a leader in trade, with ships from the South China Sea and the Indian Ocean dropping anchor there.

Today's Cirebon is a city of about three hundred fifty thousand people, many of whom make their living from the sea. The pungent smell of drying fish is everywhere, and it is not by chance that Cirebon is called "Shrimp City": *rebon* means "small shrimp." Two of its *kratons*, dating from the sixteenth century, still exist. They are called Kasepuhan and Kanoman, and to enter their gates is to be engulfed by the spirit and artifacts of many different cultures.

The Cirebon courts are quite unlike the staid and stately courts of central Java. The terra-cotta color of their stepped walls evokes Hindu east Java; the decorative inlaid tiles and eighteenth-century Delft plates embedded in the walls call up memories of Dutch rule. Inside Cirebon's *kratons*, Hindu and Muslim influences can be seen in the monochromatic brown wood carvings and in the rock and cloud motifs of the architecture. The Chinese have also left their mark, with ornate phoenixes, peonies, and cranes. Carved tigers guard the front gates.

NOBILITY OF CIREBON
by
PARAMITA ABDURACHMAN

Cirebon has access to the Java Sea via gentle waterways such as these. From here, boats set out on daily fishing expeditions.

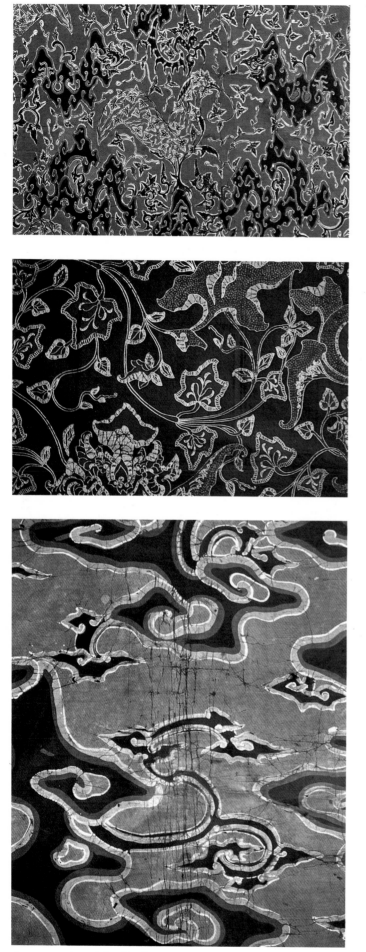

A rare version of the Cirebon cloud motif, or megamendung, is combined with roosters hidden among a tracery of leaves and vines. (Detail, top) 12

Graceful vines and leaf tendrils spiral around monstrous abstract creatures on this striking example of an early Cirebon kain panjang. (Detail, center) 13

Megamendung, as a design motif, probably suggested rain and, therefore, fertility and life. (Detail, bottom) 14

Like the Sultan's chariot, the design of this batik is inspired by mythical beast motifs combining aspects of the lion, dragon, and bird. Cloud motifs linger in the background in this 1900 kain panjang. (Detail) 15

The chariot of Cirebon's sultan in the royal court of Kasepuhan.

The batik of Cirebon, like that of the interior, was affected by wave after wave of just such different religions and cultures—Hindu, Muslim, Chinese, and European. Javanese itinerants also played a special role. Some seven hundred years ago, in the Hindu kingdom of Kediri in eastern Java, a group of artists' guilds began to send painters, musicians, and other artists along the coastal area. These guilds decreed that all their traveling artists must be male. Cirebon thus came to be one of the few places where men, not women, drew and painted cloth. As a result, the batik of this area has a strong masculine style that emphasizes bold forms, minimizes fussy detail, and projects a feeling of space quite unlike the work of either central Java or other coastal areas.

Villagers in Indramayu mend their nets.

The Old Faith

In Cirebon, as elsewhere, batik evolved as a multilayered art that blended indigenous forms, motifs, and colors with many outside influences—the first of which was Hinduism.

Before the thirteenth century, Hindu west Java had its own unique symbols that interwove pre-Hindu with Hindu concepts. These included glorious animals—the elephant (liman), the lion (singa), the dragon or the snake (naga). Vines (lianes) represented vigor, strength, and tenacity, and other forms portrayed the sea, so vital to the life of Cirebon. One of the precursors of batik—the tulisan or painted scroll that was unrolled by a narrator telling tales of Hindu lore to the accompaniment of music—reveals the use of such forms and motifs. One such twelfth-century scroll, the wayang beber, survives, and a close look suggests that the forms of batik that developed over the last three hundred years may have had roots in its painted motifs.

Java's Hindu temples may well have been the source of various designs for the batik art. The temples were built to Viṣṇu who was represented by a snail or conch shell, a motif known as çanga. Another recurrent theme were the wadas, or rock shapes, along with a body of water symbolizing meditation and the source of life. Sometimes the rocks were stretched out to blend with the conch-shell motif, sweeping up into a final curl of clouds. Megamendung, or dark clouds, suggested rain, and therefore life, for an often parched land.

An ancient banyan tree in a walled court.

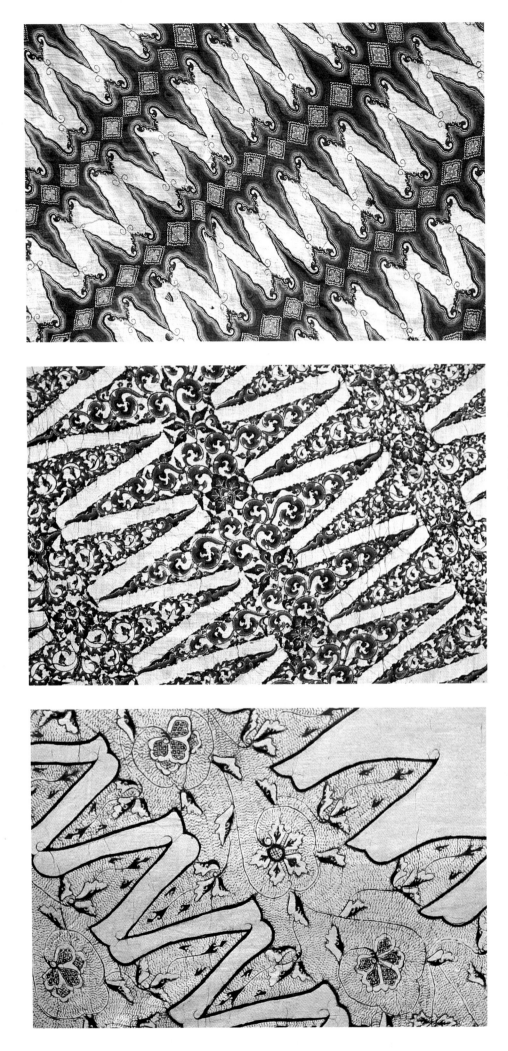

Although these Cirebon pieces resemble each other, they differ in usage and style. The kain dodot suggests Indian trade textiles and resembles a parang rusak motif, (top), while the kain panjang has flowering tendrils providing a background for the diagonals (center). A selendang has triangular shapes pointing toward the center of the cloth. (Bottom) 16, 17, 18

Batik headcloths (iket kepala)
are made in many designs. In
these examples from Cirebon,
made about eighty years ago,
male artists expressed themselves
freely, with motifs ranging from
arabesque shapes to fanciful
animals. 19, 20, 21

The New Faith

By the sixteenth century, Islam was taking hold in Java, and Sunan Gunung Jati became the Muslim ruler of Cirebon. A prominent religious leader of the period, he was one of the *Wali Sanga,* or Nine Walis, who were teachers of the Islamic faith. Sunan Gunung Jati had little interest in Cirebon as a political force. Instead, he established the city as a religious and artistic center. He built a college to train the teachers, artisans, and artists of Islam; he and his eight fellow *walis* embraced and supported the artists in particular and enlisted them to teach the Islamic faith through their art.

From Cirebon the Muslim artisans spread the new faith, making their way along the coast, mingling with existing communities and founding new ones. To the folkloric Hindu repertoire of the painted scrolls was added the leather puppet (*wayang kulit*) and the wooden puppet (*wayang golek*), characters who spun tales from the life of the Prophet, as well as stories about the Nine Walis and other heroes of Islamic lore.

New visual forms also developed as the Muslim artists experimented with painting on glass and wood, and especially on cloth. Motifs from Muslim Middle Eastern and Mogul art began to blend and coexist with Hindu and pre-Hindu designs. The rooster, traditionally a symbol of strength and vigor, now came to represent the greatness of the godhead and to herald the dawn of Islam. The Hindu lion assumed the shape of the Persian lion—the symbol of Ali, nephew of the Prophet and protector of the mystic Muslim brotherhood. There were peacocks and phoenixes guarding the gates of paradise. The *peksinagaliman*—a combination of the phoenix, the dragon, and the elephant—became the *bouraq,* half bird, half human, and the *bouraq* in turn replaced the *garuda.* In Hindu lore, it was the *garuda*

that had carried Viṣṇu to heaven; now the *bouraq* carried the Muslims' Prophet to paradise.

Arabic calligraphy was another new element that began to adorn religious banners and decorate the homes of religious and artistic leaders. Tales of Hindu deities were now written in Arabic. Because of Cirebon's all-male painting tradition, the work was masculine and bold; the artists continued to express themselves freely.

Towns such as Trusmi, Kalitengah, Plered, and Arjawinangun, which had a working relationship with the Cirebon courts, were also centers of the arts. But the focal point was a loosely knit community of three towns, Dermayu, Pauman, and Sindang. These did not come under the domain of any kingdom, but remained independent under their own chiefs. The artisans of this area regarded all motifs as their common heritage.

In time, the towns were incorporated into the single town of Indramayu. There, a particular style of batik was developed. Indramayu batik is distinguished by a restrained terra-cotta or Turkish-red color and by the traditional dark blue indigo. Perhaps the repeated use of red and blue in batik from this area was encouraged by the Chinese, for whom red symbolized fertility, happiness, good luck; blue meant sadness, mourning, and death.

The batik makers of Indramayu also developed a penchant for filling their background spaces with tiny dots. (This same technique probably developed simultaneously hundreds of miles to the east, in the coastal town of Lasem.) It was a beautiful innovation, but eventually these backgrounds became so intricate, with their lines, circlets, and little stars, that the central motif tended to disappear.

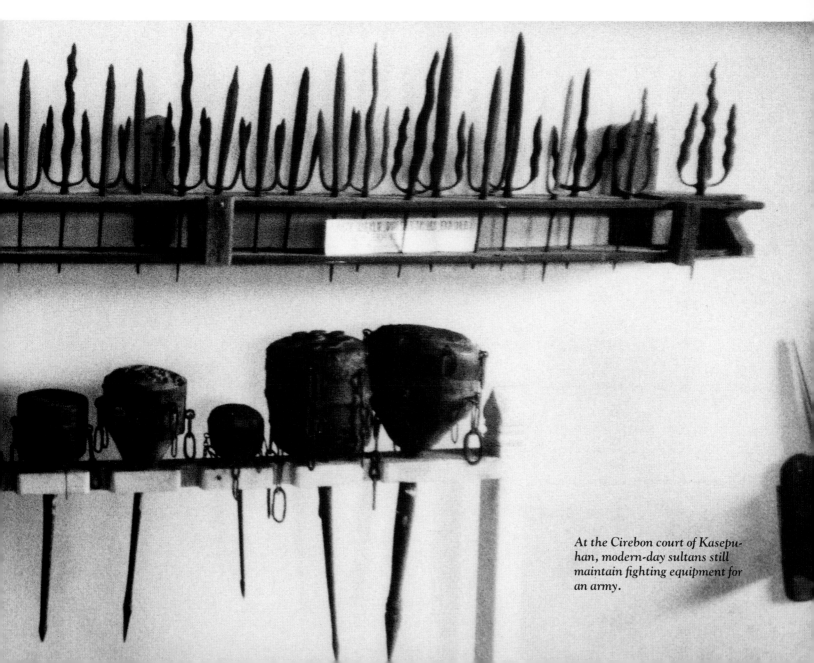

At the Cirebon court of Kasepuhan, modern-day sultans still maintain fighting equipment for an army.

PRADA—GOLD FOR THE WEALTHY

When a batik has been enriched with gold leaf, it is usually associated with ceremony and wealth. This gilded batik is called a *prada* or *pinarada mas* (*pinar* means "worked with gold thread"; *mas* means "gold"). Even in seventeenth-century Java, *pradas* were coveted and people of fashion wore calico decorated with gold flowers or gold streaks.

In the courts of central Java *pradas* were sacred and used only for the most auspicious events such as royal marriages, special court ceremonies, and court dances; in Bali, silk *prada* still clothed the statues of the gods. To the Chinese of the north coast, a *prada* presented at the wedding of a favorite child meant good luck.

Usually only the very finest *tulis* batik was chosen to be gold leafed; such a piece would take anywhere from six months to a year to finish, with the gold leaf applied as the last step. On the north coast, gold dust was mixed with linseed oil and resin to ensure that the gold would adhere firmly to the cloth. In central Java much the same method was used, except that albumen from the white of an egg was the bonding agent used to mix with the gold.

Gold was expensive, and to save both time and money, it was applied only to that part of the cloth that would show when worn. Gold was never applied, for example, to an upper edge that might later be tucked in or to an end that was covered when wrapped around the body. Despite such shortcuts, the application of gold to a batik might take up to forty-five days. ☐

Gold kain panjangs *often imitated weaving, as in this* Nitik *design. (Detail) 22*

Geometric prada *made in Surabaya displays* ceplok *and* banji *patterns. (Detail) 23*

From Lasem, ca. 1910, came
this spectacular prada called
bang-biru, meaning red and blue.
(Detail, top) 24

A sarong made in Cirebon, ca.
1900. Bold ships embellished
with gold are the major motif.
(Detail, above) 25

Status Symbols for Aristocrats

Like royalty everywhere, the Muslim kingdom of Cirebon, with its courts and dignitaries and bureaucrats, surrounded itself with the paraphernalia of status. The leading families invited artists to design crests and patterns for their sole use. The royal house of Cirebon took for its crest the white tiger that had once guarded Silwangi, a famous Hindu ruler, thus symbolically linking the new Muslim court with its Hindu forebears.

The former court of Pakungwati also became a batik motif, with its garden of artfully arranged rocks, trees, and a pond where sultans would go for rest and contemplation. There they achieved the state of *sunya ragi* (*sunya* means "zero" or "infinity," *ragi* means "soul"), the state of spiritual void in which the soul merges with the universe. Yet another crest developed, a blending of many motifs including the rooster and the rocks, each of them carrying metaphysical messages.

All these status symbols became nearly meaningless when, at the end of the seventeenth century, the Sultan of Cirebon came under the domination of the Dutch East India Company, and later the Dutch government. The Dutch achieved a monopoly on imports of cotton and opium, as well as exports of pepper, wood, sugar, rice, and any other products. They dominated Cirebon for more than a century, not to the benefit of the local people.

While gold was used by the wealthy, the poor continued to live much as they had for generations.

A Cirebon tablecloth (?) ca. 1906. The inscription reads "Long life and abundance of luck." The various animals represent longevity and prosperity. (Top) 26

A batik reminiscent of Art Nouveau, characterized by large animals, this kain panjang is called bang ungon. (Center) 27 Representations of sea creatures, united here with other animals by a spiraling vine, often found their way into north-coast batik. This tumpal semen design is typical of Cirebon as well as Pekalongan and Lasem. (Bottom and detail right) 28

An Old Court in a New Mold

With the decline of Cirebon as a spiritual force in the early nineteenth century, the making of batik for ceremonial and religious use was transformed. Batik was now made for clothing—for *kain panjangs* and sarongs—and designs of geometrics and sea life came into the marketplace. No longer was Cirebon batik the prerogative of the courts.

Some of the more traditional motifs, such as mythical animals, were still reserved for the few. They remained the heritage of particular families from the guilds or from the traditional elite; when made into apparel, the work would be done by special request and by particular artists who kept the designs a secret. When the courts finally released some of these patterns, they became so popular that most Cirebon batik today is associated with them. Lions, tigers, dragons, elephants, rocks, and clouds are repeated endlessly in all forms.

The iron fist of colonialism worked great changes in batik. In 1830 the Dutch imposed heavy taxes on agricultural acreage. This meant that men had less time to make batik, and as women slowly replaced men as makers of batik, the bold, masculine approach to design began to fade away. Never allowed to belong to the artists' guilds, the women knew neither the secrets nor the rules of traditional Cirebon batik.

In the course of their long rule, the Dutch encouraged the rise of a Chinese entrepreneurial and bureaucratic class; they even leased whole villages to Chinese who collected taxes, sold opium, and controlled the labor force. Chinese communities sprang up—Kanduran was one—and as their citizens settled in and married local people, they adopted the local style of dress, retaining their own patterns and color preferences. Chinese artifacts were regularly imported to northern Java, and the symbols of China were well known there: the *kylin*, a figure that was half dog, half lion; the *banji*, a swastikalike fretwork motif; and more common designs such as the phoenix, peony, and chrysanthemum. These Chinese motifs were eventually incorporated into the religious batik of Cirebon.

As long as one hundred years ago, these Chinese-Cirebon batiks had become popular with the Europeans, both as collectors' items and as clothing for personal use. The new styles, however, were almost never worn by the local people; the multicolored patterns were quite alien to them.

Interest in Cirebon and Indramayu batiks has revived in the past twenty years, and a clear line is now drawn between batik made for the sake of art and pieces made for the consumer. Batik artists—of whom few are left —still maintain the rules of symbolic meaning, function, and social class. Their coloring is done according to prescribed rules: light to dark ocher for the Cirebon style and variations of indigo blue and *mengkudu* red for Indramayu. The entrepreneurs, however, change dyes and/or patterns regardless of the motif's origin.

Today Cirebon's batik seems to lack the strength and dramatic sense of space of long ago. It once presented a vigorous image of a unique, dynamic culture; but that, alas, is no longer the case.

(Overleaf, details)
Two designs both of the Cirebon area, but very different. The taman arum, or the garden where a sultan would meditate amid rock formations, ponds, trees, and pavilions, is a classic motif in batik. 29
A selendang probably made for Chinese, at the turn of the century, is typical of Indramayu with its indigo color and tiny dots. 30

An early twentieth-
century wedding
portrait of a Sundanese
couple. The bride
wears a Cirebon batik,
a white kebaya, and
crown; the groom's
dress mixes styles
from both central and
west Java.

Boats line up at Jakarta's wharves.

III. JOURNEY TO PEKALONGAN

The lush hills and verdant trees of central Java gradually yield to the sandy flatlands that abut the Java Sea. There farmers, along with their wives and children and neighbors, work the flooded land, planting rice. Along the roadside lie bundles of drying onions, their pungent odor hanging heavy in the humid air. Trucks, cars, oxcarts, bicycles, and motorcycles screech to the stillness of the sea. On the horizon, weathered sailboats cast their nets, and huge tankers lumber off to other ports. This is the north coast of Java.

The colonial Dutch churches and railroad stations stand starkly alongside majestic Chinese houses whose walls and sloping roofs enclose secret inner courtyards. Brilliantly colored temples are alive with life-size carvings of mythical animals, and the smell of incense is everywhere. Five times a day, *muezzins* call Muslims to worship at mosques with Hindu minarets. The language is Bahasa, but more often than not the spoken word in the marketplace is Sundanese, Mandarin, Arabic, or Javanese. From Cirebon in the west to Surabaya in the east, the polyglot past lingers on, in art and architecture, in language and religion, and in the peoples of the place.

This dizzying mix of coastal dwellers came to be known as "beach people" (or *pesisirir*) by central Java's aristocracy. *Pesisirir* were thought to be crass, materialistic, and flamboyant, wheeler-dealers with little regard for the proprieties of a genteel life. Conversely, the coastal people viewed the inlanders as staid, conservative, and snobbish. The division between coastal and inland areas, in short, is as much cultural as it is geographic, and nowhere is this more evident than in their contrasting styles of batik.

Except in Cirebon, there were no courts or court culture on the north coast. The absence of courts meant the absence of most rules and regulations; north-coast artists were free to experiment, to let their imaginations run loose. A true folk art developed, contrasting sharply with the circumscribed patterns of Cirebon and central Java.

Nevertheless the coastal area had it own aristocratic groups, and the men often married princesses from the courts of central Java. The royal bride would bring her dancers, servants, *gamelan* players, and ladies-in-waiting, many of them well-versed in the technique of batik making, to the coast. This created yet another mix of taste, style, and motif.

Middlemen, some of mixed descent—Oriental, Arab, European—blazed the trail for the real business of batik in the last half of the nineteenth century. They engaged in the wholesale business of finished batik as well as greige goods. Family businesses were established, and—as in many other Asian homes—all members of the extended group were involved. Transactions were usually based on trust; vast amounts of money and goods changed hands without even a hint of a receipt. Traders would carry heaps of white cotton and mountains of batik piled high on their bicycles or horse carts. In some coastal towns, the areas known as "Arabic village" or "Chinatown" would turn into veritable mercantile exchanges near sundown.

In contrast to courtly central Java and Cirebon, batik in these coastal towns was not so much made for family or personal use; trade was the name of the game. Batik factories, some employing hundreds of workers, were established by entrepreneurs who catered to local and overseas tastes. The relationship of these owners of batik workshops to the workers was essentially a "master-servant" one, much like that of the feudal plantation system. Smaller ateliers would even employ household servants as their laborers.

THE FREEWHEELING NORTH COAST

Many a fortune was built on batik, mostly by north-coast Javanese employers. Labor costs were low, and there was a large population eager for work—and a great and growing demand for the product. In the 1920s, the "golden era" of batik production, thousands of people were employed in the various coastal centers. As the industry grew, the demand for skilled workers increased, and hordes of people swarmed from town to town selling their labor. But the finest batik was made in smaller factories, usually by people of mixed descent.

Java's north-coast batik illustrates much of the area's past and present. The batik is surprising and exuberant, vigorous and muted. It explodes with brilliant reds, traditional blues, and radiant yellows blending with soft pastel tints of green, lilac, and pink. The motifs—people, farm produce, fish, and animals—evoke the coast of Java in all its varied life.

A Chinese lady from Pekalongan sits for her portrait, painted in oil on wood ca. 1880.

Pekalongan is fittingly known as Batik City. Here the business of batik began around 1850 and here for nearly a century batik has been an important source of income. Most of its two hundred thousand inhabitants—Javanese, Chinese, Arab—are in some way involved in the business of batik. From early morning to late at night, pedicabs or *becaks* line up near the marketplace, heavily laden with cloth to wax, to dye, to sell. The finished batik is trucked to nearby Semarang for shipment—or, in the other direction, to Jakarta, to be sold locally or dispatched overseas.

Lying beside a lazy, muddy river, Pekalongan has a silted harbor with a few colorful fishing boats. It has its Chinatowns and its Arab sections, and until recently nearly everyone in its bustling marketplace, men and women alike, wore gaily colored batik sarongs or long checked cloths. But while batik was everywhere apparent, its sources were not. Pekalongan batik factories to this day are secreted behind closed doors, with high walls surrounding the compounds to guard against prying eyes.

The city and its environs teem with tiny *tulis* ateliers and large *cap* factories. About five miles away lies the village of Kedungwuni, known for its fine work and its many Chinese batik makers. Within a ten-mile radius there are also Javanese *kampongs* (compounds or tiny villages) that specialize either in certain types of designs or in particular techniques. Here brokers, who usually receive a commission of about ½ or 1 percent on the manufacturer's price, gather batik to sell elsewhere.

In the first half of the nineteenth century, the Dutch had exported imitation printed batik to Java, using cotton from the United States. The American Civil War stopped this traffic in the 1860s, just as an expanding Dutch colonial administration was creating a need for more cloth. To meet this demand, Chinese, Arab, Javanese, and even some Dutch factories appeared, and batik making began to progress from its cottage-industry beginnings to larger workshops. This is what happened in Pekalongan and why the town ultimately became Batik City.

Pekalongan batiks are unique in design, format, and color. Years ago, foreigners introduced such motifs as irises, daisies, chrysanthemums, swans, hummingbirds, and butterflies to Pekalongan. From the Victorian era came birds carrying love letters, flower wreaths, baskets tied with ribbons, and other fripperies of romanticism. The format of the sarong also changed: instead of triangles (*tumpal*) at the head (*kepala*) of the sarong, floral bouquets softened the hard geometric edges with undulating curves. Sometimes birds or a series of diagonal bands would be drawn across the *kepala*. At the turn of the century, Europeans were probably responsible for changing the top and bottom borders (*pinggir*) of the sarong to a softened scalloped edge that looked like lace, sometimes alternating with flowers or leaves.

The colors of Pekalongan batik, reflecting both European and Chinese influence, are perhaps its most distinguishing feature. Nowhere else are such colors found in such abundance or used with such abandon: rich Ming yellow, bright red, turquoise, royal blue, and green. European-influenced batik is characterized by flat areas of color with minimal detailing and by solid backgrounds with simple repeating shapes. Chinese designs are more dimensional—an effect achieved by using many shades of a single color and intricately filling the motif with tiny dots.

PEKALONGAN— BATIK CITY

A polyclinic organized by the Progress of Women Association prior to World War II. The women use selendangs to carry their babies and wear pesisiran (beach) designs typical of northern Java.

In overpopulated Java, one kampung, or village, abuts another. These often unnamed villages sometimes specialize in a particular aspect of batik making, such as waxing or dyeing.

TAMBAL—
PATCHWORK BATIK

Javanese patchwork batik, or *tambal,* is a clue to the history of the art. Patchwork was first suggested by the Indians, with motifs finding their way to central Java via the north coast. Later these very same designs were retranslated by the northerners onto sarongs with still more motifs and colors.

The idea of making a length of cloth from small patches is probably as old as cloth itself, necessity being the mother of invention. *Tambal* is a design whose geometric shapes—squares, rectangles, ovals, and triangles, all filled with rich motifs—make it look as if the cloth were indeed patched together. *Tambal,* meaning "beggar's cloth," was in fact originally patched clothing, worn only by monks and the poorest of the poor.

In central Java, *tambal* motifs assume ceremonial and magical functions. A simple check design *(belah ketupat),* for example, may be used to ward off evil. Another equally simple square *(poleng)* bestows fertility. A sultan in Yogykarta might wear a *tambal* to protect his country and his subjects from evil, and babies might wear *tambals* around their necks for good luck.

North-coast *tambals* are usually decorative, not symbolic, and their place of origin is easy to detect. A *tambal* from Cirebon, for instance, will have triangles patterned with sea life, animals, flowers, and geometric motifs set against clean, clear backgrounds. A later *tambal* from Pekalongan reflects that town's preference for bright colors and intricately filled backgrounds. ☐

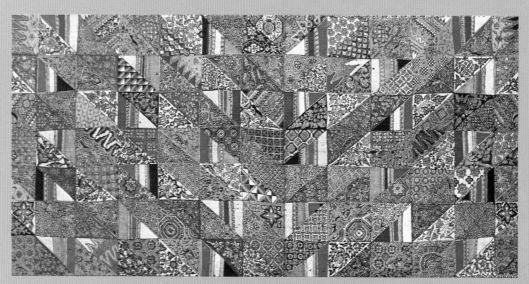

Unusual and rare kain panjang patchwork from Cirebon, made about 1890. Its overall chevron design mimics Indian block- *printed patchworks even though it contains at least twelve old Javanese batik patterns. (Detail, right)* 31

An unusually bold 1900 patchwork in the form of a sarong.
Although made in Pekalongan,
its motifs are similar to those of
Cirebon. (Detail, left) 32
A selendang from Cirebon made
at the turn of the century. The
patchwork, in shades of blue,
surrounds a central lozenge
shape. (Detail, bottom) 33

Both tulis and cap were used on
this graphic tambal from Cirebon, made about 1930. (Top) 34

An Unusual Group of Women

The story of batik in Pekalongan is largely the story of the female entrepreneur. In Javanese villages, it was not unbecoming for women to have their own sources of income, usually from produce they had themselves planted and harvested. European women—usually from Holland—were in a different situation. In a colonial society, they had enough money, many servants, and no need to work. Not surprisingly, the more enterprising batik workshops were founded neither by the uncomfortably situated Javanese nor by the affluent Dutch, but by another group altogether.

In a stratified society such as Java's, there was room for yet another class. The diversity of Java, spurred by its overpopulation and the freewheeling mercantile life of the north coast, spawned an ethnic group known as *Indische.* The word *Indische* has no English equivalent: it referred to people of European or European/Asian origin who had lived in the East Indies for a long time. As a rule, they were part Dutch and part Javanese, but they could also be Chinese or Arab (combined with any Eu-

ropean nationality), or part Chinese, part Javanese—or even pure Dutch who had lived for generations in Java and thus were "native" to the Indies.

It is not surprising that the *Indische* came to be influential designers of commercial batik (but not the biggest entrepreneurs; that distinction belonged to the Javanese). The *Indische* were mostly middle class. They had a fairly good education and could speak and read Dutch, the official language. But, unlike most Europeans, they also spoke and read the local languages and perhaps even a smattering of Chinese and Arabic as well. Whatever their origin, these women and men had separated themselves from Dutch colonial society; by their life style and intermarriage they had broken the colonial rules and were not about to be shackled by tradition and rank.

While in many ways "outsiders," the *Indische* had connections to parts of Javanese society that were inaccessible to others. They were also good at business. Recognizing that there was a market for batik within

Instead of the more common garudas, cuprds fly in this early twentieth-century sarong made in Pekalongan by Mrs. A. Simonet, a Chinese batik maker married to a Frenchman. (Left) 35 Sarongs were also made for children, such as this one from Lasem, ca. 1915. It was probably used for a circumcision ceremony. (Above) 36

On the 29th of March, 1908,
Etje Wilhem and Addy Prins,
two Dutch girls living in northern Java, were photographed
wearing kebayas and sarongs.
Each carried her doll in a
selendang.

their own group as well as among colonials, Chinese, and even upper-class Javanese, the *Indische* began to establish factories of their own.

In the 1880s most Javanese batik was made in the home; women considered that more honorable than working in a factory. At home, a woman was head of the household, but, in a factory, she was a mere wage earner, a servant. To lure women from the home to the factory, the *Indische* would advance wages against work due. This practice continues today, with the result that many batik workers are continually in debt to their bosses.

Among the *Indische* entrepreneurs were women such as Mrs. Simonet (her only known name), Lien Metze-

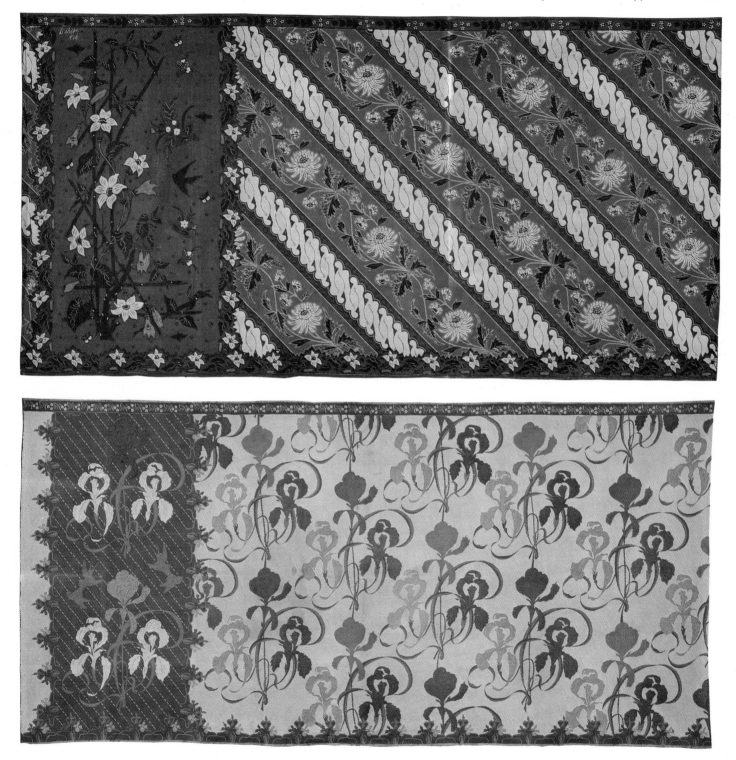

Lien Metzelaar worked in Peka-longan from about 1880 to 1920. Her batik has the typical floral border and kepala *preferred by* Indische *women. (Top) 37 Stylized irises were part of the J.*

Jans repertoire, another Indische *batik entrepreneur who catered to the wealthy at the turn of the century. This sarong, called* Buket galeran Iris, *used natural dyes and was made around*

1905. (Bottom) 38 In Pekalongan, Jans made this simple scalloped sarong, probably for a wedding. (Detail, right) 39

laar, S. E. Bower, J. Jans (also known as Widow Jans), M. de Ruyter, P. A. Toorop, and Eliza van Zuylen. In a town as small as Pekalongan, they must all have known one another, and they also knew Arab traders and other Chinese batik entrepreneurs. Among them, they created many memorable batiks.

Mrs. Simonet was Chinese-Indonesian, married to a Frenchman. She had a preference for romantic illustration, exemplified by a batik of flying cupids on a green background. Mrs. Simonet's daughter took over the atelier of Lien Metzelaar, who had worked in Pekalongan from about 1880 to 1920. This atelier was known for batik with a border of seven leaves on a straight branch, alternating with four simple flowers; Metzelaar batik is easy to recognize from this motif.

The workshop of J. Jans catered to the wealthy at the turn of the century. An early Jans sarong shows the "lace border," with delicate red scallops set against a clean, creamy background of repeated stars and flowers. The motifs changed when Art Deco was introduced in the early 1900s: stylized irises and swans in a lily patch, all combined with the typical Chinese swastika or *banji* in the background. Jans sometimes added ground betel nut and chalk to the natural dyes, to soften her colors.

Eliza van Zuylen was another fine example of the *Indische* entrepreneur. Her life spanned nearly a century, from 1863 to 1947, coinciding with the heyday of Pekalongan batik, and fortunately her life and work are well documented. Born in Jakarta, she moved to Pekalongan where she established a batik compound in 1890 at what is now a police barrack. As in other batik factories, van Zuylen's whole family was involved, with the women in charge of design and personnel and the men controlling the dyeing and fiscal matters. This work pattern persists in Java's batik factories today.

Van Zuylen batik was extraordinary. Her compound, like those of other *Indische* entrepreneurs, turned out only hand-drawn *tulis*. Few but the well-to-do could afford them. In the 1920s, the average wage of a government employee was about twenty guilders a month. A cook in a family household might earn about eight guilders a month and a farmer would subsist on less than a quarter of that. An entrepreneur who sold cloth to Mrs. van Zuylen and also marketed her batik recalled:

They were expensive—but so very beautiful. I remember that in the 1920s I paid between twelve and fourteen guilders, a vast sum in those days, for one van Zuylen batik. Most of her customers were Chinese ladies, not Europeans. Mrs. van Zuylen was marvelous, a well-liked businesswoman.

Van Zuylen designs probably came from Dutch horticultural books and sometimes even from postcards, but certainly not from any indigenous Javanese flowers. Eliza van Zuylen preferred flowers with colored edges and plain white petals set against clean backgrounds, and she executed them perfectly with simple diagonal vines and solid backgrounds. These backgrounds, so cleanly delineated, were her hallmark. To achieve them, wax was boiled from the cloth after *each* dyeing. This produced razor-sharp edges, a feat that even the best batikers in central Java were unable to match.

Van Zuylen's loosely arranged floral bouquets were also popular. These ranged from small nosegays repeated several times across the cloth to larger bouquets stretching from selvage to selvage in a formal arrangement. A bird or a butterfly usually appeared to one side of the bouquet.

The colors of van Zuylen batik are memorable—soft pastels, mauve, pink, peach, light blue. All dyeing was done at the compound, with the exception of brown, which she commissioned to special dyers in a nearby village. At the beginning of the century Chinese workshops had begun using synthetic dyes, but the *Indische* factories resisted them for many years because their reputation was built on the development of their own natural and special colors.

World War II effectively halted batik production for everyone, including the van Zuylens. Many in the family were interned, and Eliza van Zuylen herself, although not jailed, died in 1947. She was eighty-three.

The *Indische* group was highly influential and productive for about seventy years in Pekalongan and in other northern towns. At the same time, another group of Chinese men and women became equally important. Less scholarship has been devoted to them, but their designs and techniques and extraordinary colors have earned them an equal place in the history of batik.

The only natural dye Eliza van Zuylen did not prepare herself was soga brown. Instead she sent the batik to a local village for its final brown dye, as in this ca. 1910 kain panjang. (Detail) 40

Here is an early Eliza van Zuylen sarong, ca. 1900, unusual because the flowers are arranged very loosely. (Detail, left) 41
Other early van Zuylen pieces are this sarong filled with cashew-nut flowers (detail, top far left); and a geometric sarong called Dlorong Buket. (Detail, bottom far left) 42, 43
Van Zuylen's hallmark was her clean background accentuated by simple lines diagonally drawn across the badan. (Detail, top) 44

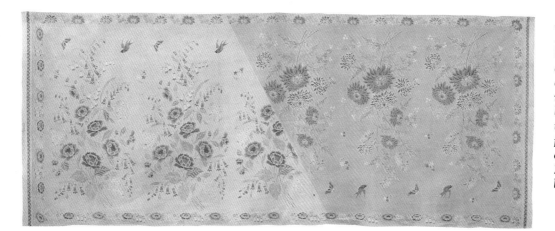

Since there are few Eliza van Zuylen pagi-sores, this signed batik is rare for its format as well as its spectacular use of synthetic dyes. Made about 1930, the mauves, pinks, peaches, and light blues soften the design of the chrysanthemums and poppies. Plain white petals with colored edges were another van Zuylen trademark. (Details below and right) 45

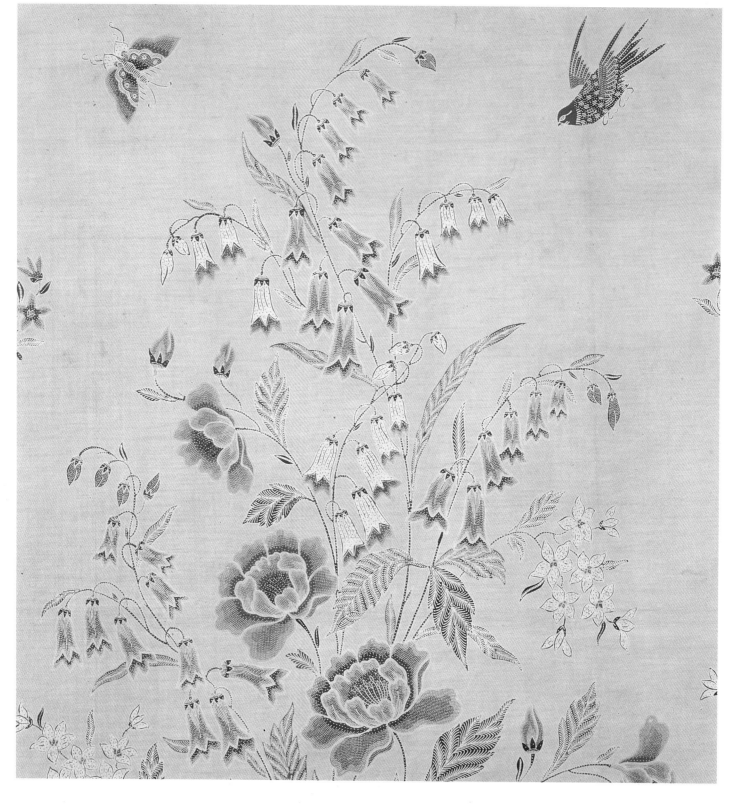

BATIK PANTS

A pair of pants belonging to a child, ca. 1930, made in Peka-longan. (Above) 46
Flowers create an overall pattern on pants from Lasem that are edged with cloud motif and banji. (Right) 47

Both the Dutch and the Chinese regarded batik as something colorful, exotic, and cool. Relaxing at home, in the morning, or at night, men wore pants that were secured by a string or a belt at the waist. An extra piece of plain cloth was added to the pants if the wearer was especially tall. Most batik pants were cut and sewn from a kain panjang; others were first cut and then batiked. Here, a seller of batik pants plies his trade, ca. 1870.

Dhlorong Khewan *pants design,
with diagonals.* 48
Pants, *ca. 1910, made from a*
kain panjang, *depicting the Lombok wars.* 49

Indigo is the only color in these
Cirebon-style *pants, made about
seventy years ago.* 50
Bang-biru Khewan *design, ca.
1905, with serpent running
along outer leg.* 51

The bottom of each pant leg is
bordered with imitation fringe,
vines, and a cloud motif. 52
*Pants made from design called
Modang.* 53

(Overleaf, detail) The daily life
of the Chinese is richly detailed
on a Semarang *sarong made in
the 1860s. Four zigzag bands are
filled with processions of people;
a fifth shows Europeans viewing
a party with gamelan players.
Domestic scenes, such as a
woman cooking rice, are represented in the triangles at the
edges.* 54

The Chinese Heritage

By the time Pekalongan began to launch its booming batik business in the 1850s, a strong Chinese middle class had already existed for more than a century and a half. Along the coast, every town had its Chinatown with tiled houses, temples, and Chinese languages. Then, as now, the Chinese were intimately involved in the design, production, and wearing of batik. In Pekalongan, the most significant designers were The Tie Siet, Oey Soen King, Oey Kok Sing, Liem Siok Hien, Lim Boe In, and Liem Boen Gan; in Kedungwuni, Oey Soe Tjoen was the most important.

By Chinese custom, age had a lot to do with who wore what. Light pinks and blues were worn by younger girls, blue and red by middle-aged women, while the elders wore a combination of blue, brown, purple, and green on an off-white ground. If the father in a family died, his wife, children, and grandchildren traditionally wore blue-and-white sarongs for two years as a sign of mourning. Red symbolized good luck, and if a baby was expected, a gift of a red carryall, or *selendang*, was presented to the parents. If the family was especially rich, a *selendang* decorated with gold would be ordered to celebrate the birth of a firstborn son.

Beautifully made *tulis* batik was often part of a bride's dowry. There was even a special batik, the *cempaka-mulya*, that was made to be worn by the parents of both bride and groom at the wedding ceremony. A week after the wedding, the bride was presented with her own *cempakamulya* batik. (*Cempaka* is a gardenia, and *mulya* means "virgin.") The circular flower of this design has a pointed petal often combined with a diagonal *parang menang* in the background, symbolizing wisdom. Sometimes the pattern includes a curved, continuous vine, signifying long life.

Batik made by the Pekalongan Chinese has two distinctive appearances. Pre-1910 Chinese batik resembles traditional north-coast batik: the rich natural colors of indigo blue and *mengkudu* red are set on cream and tan grounds. Usually these pre-1910 textiles were made at home, for family or ceremonial use. Motifs were drawn from Chinese art and applied to the traditional layout of the *kain panjang*. In the town of Lasem, the Chinese made similar batik, and it is often difficult to distinguish between those of Lasem and those of Pekalongan.

In these pre-1910 batiks, the head (or *kepala*) of the

On a street lined with Chinese homes in Pekalongan, pedicabs heavily laden with cloth to dye, wax, and sell, line up from early morning to late at night.

This special sarong, called Cempakmulya parang menang, was often part of a bride's dowry. It was made by Liem Giok Kwie of Kedungwuni about 1930. (Detail) 55

sarong was usually split: red on one half and black (red overdyed with indigo blue) on the other. An elongated triangle shape or *tumpal* was set against red and blue medallion motifs, edged top and bottom by borders that seem to evoke India more than Java or China. Often the body of the cloth contained diagonal stripes, snake motifs, or phoenixlike birds and lotus flowers, reflecting its Chinese origins.

After 1910, Chinese Pekalongan batik burst into full color with a panoply of flowers, multicolored shadings, and tiny textures of intricate filling (*isén*) for both the designs themselves and the backgrounds. This artistic explosion coincided with the introduction of synthetic dyes, which the Chinese used much earlier than the *Indische*.

Chinese batik altered dramatically after 1910 in part because of the new synthetic dyes, in part because of a new political situation. The Chinese had lived in Java for more than two hundred years. While mostly middle class, they were not citizens, nor could they own land or enjoy other prerogatives of the Dutch. All this changed in 1910 when a new law—called *Gelijkgesteld,*

meaning "to equalize"—decreed that every child born in the East Indies of Chinese parents would be considered a Dutch subject, albeit not a Dutch citizen.

The effect on batik was immediate. Javanese society was acutely conscious of class, and the Chinese were now suddenly raised to a "higher" social order. This meant that they could now wear—and make—"European" batik. European designs became a symbol of rank, a manifestation of the Chinese ascent in society; but as always with batik, motifs melded. The Dutch tulip, for instance, was soon transformed into the Chinese lotus.

The batik of Pekalongan's The Tie Siet clearly shows his Chinese heritage. He brilliantly used orange and royal blue, sometimes aqua, weaving these nontraditional colors into such age-old motifs as peacocks and birds. Although The made sure to fill each leaf with a multitude of detail, the backgrounds were usually plain with vivid Art Deco borders. In a carnival of batik, the works of The Tie Siet are always recognizable. Like most of the Chinese batik made after 1910, The's was for public sale, not family use.

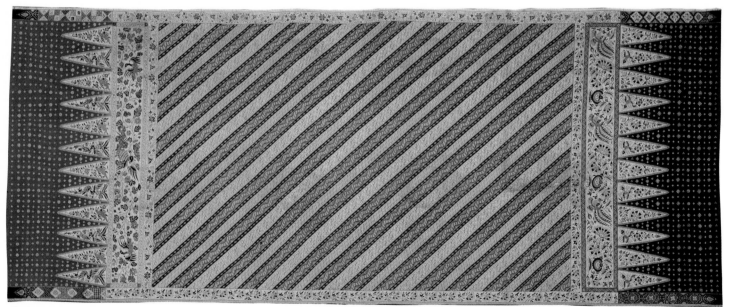

Before the advent of synthetic dyes, kain panjangs *such as this one of 1880 were typical of northern Java. Its diagonals, medallion shapes, and insect motifs are mixed on a half-red/half-black* kepala. *(Detail, right)* 56

Three Generations

In one Pekalongan house, the women of the family have been making batik for three generations. Inlaid blackwood furniture sits safely away from the sun and rain of the tropics. The floors are tiled, a small organ stands in one corner, and on the walls, above the potted plants, are family photographs. It is not unusual to find three generations of batik makers in a family business, but it is exceedingly uncommon for each generation to have brought such changes and vitality to the craft as has this family.

The grandmother, Oey Soen King (née Liem Loan Nio), was born in 1861. Cloud motifs, serpents, dragons, lotus flowers, and bats—the latter a sign of good fortune—were characteristic of her batik. Although she lived until 1942, she always used natural red and blue dyes in classic layouts typical of the late nineteenth century. Oey Soen King's pieces were all unsigned, since signatures were not yet in vogue.

Her daughter, Oey Kok Sing (née Kho Tjing Nio), was born about 1896 and died in 1966. Oey Kok Sing chose a different palette and new motifs, but displayed the same control and grace as her mother. She used vibrant synthetic colors to enliven her "European" bouquets. A secondary patterning characterizes the work of Oey Kok Sing: the cloth is packed with a background of intricate work that seems to echo the foreground motifs. Oey Kok Sing left many cloths to which she had signed her name.

Oey Kok Sing's own daughter, Liem Siok Hien, was born in 1929 and is still working. Not satisfied with the typical Dutch bouquet, she chose to lace flowers through her intricate batik paintings, introducing new combinations of exotic birds, rock formations, and mythical animals set on clean, cream grounds. Her soft backgrounds always have a surprise element: tiny castles and kernels of rice add texture and shape to the batik. The *tulis* work is so fine that it often takes Liem Siok Hien fourteen months to complete a *kain panjang*. Even her discards—she will write "rejected" in pencil on the batik—are more imaginative and of finer quality

Oey Soen King (1861–1942) was the first of three generations of batik makers in Pekalongan. Oey Soen King's batik used late-nineteenth-century classic layouts—graceful animals, garuda wings, flowers, and cloud formations—and natural dyes, as in this kain panjang. *(Detail) 57*

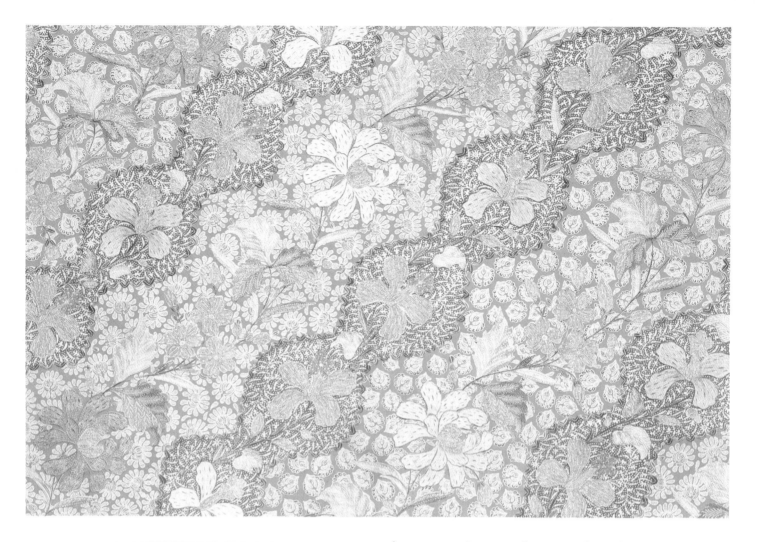

than many "accepted" pieces by other artists. Liem Siok Hien has always mixed her own colors, achieving a spectrum not found in the batik of her mother or grandmother.

Cataloguing the work of Liem Siok Hien illustrates the difficulty of tracing batik to its maker. Her maiden name was Oey Djien Nio, but her first signature was Liem Siok Hien—her Chinese married name. To this she added the town of Pekalongan where she was living. But if the batik was in the "style" of Kudus, she would write "Kudus" instead of "Pekalongan," thereby leading to further confusion. Then, in 1965, Liem Siok Hien began signing her Indonesian name, Jane Hendromartono, by which she is still known.

Oey Kok Sing (1896–1966) was the second-generation batik artist in her family. Unlike her mother, she signed her pieces and used synthetic dyes. Made for clients in Semarang about 1925, this sarong epitomizes Oey Kok Sing's preference for European bouquets and bright, synthetic colors. (Detail, top) 58

A buket tanahan (bouquet of flowers) sarong made about 1930. Oey Kok Sing filled the design with detail, while a secondary background motif gives depth to the drawing. (Detail, right) 59

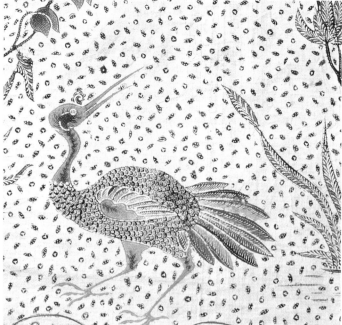

Jane Hendromartono (née Liem Siok Hien), the third generation of batik artists, was born in 1929. Her work is quite distinct from that of either her mother or grandmother. Her soft back-grounds always have a surprise element, such as this menagerie of animals including a spotted beast and a peacock. (Top left and right) 60

Scattered stones evoke a rich pattern in an off-white background. This Hendromartono pagi-sore is both subtle and stylish. (Detail, right) 61

SIGNATURES

Signed batik, like designer clothing, is sometimes a symbol of status and high quality. The practice of signing batik was introduced by the *Indische* at the turn of the century, then later adopted by the Chinese. Because traditional works were customarily anonymous, the batik of central Java is not signed.

Most likely, signatures were first introduced not as a status symbol but to protect the designs. For similar reasons, a stamp indicating the name and sometimes the address of the workshop will often appear on a piece of batik. This stamp protects owners from theft when villagers take the cloth home for batiking; it also serves as an advertisement. Often there are numbers indicating the pattern, so that customers can order batik more easily.

The signature, usually found in the *kepala* of a sarong, or in the corner of a *kain panjang,* is waxed and dyed into the cloth—by *cap* or *tulis*—just like the rest of the design. It is sometimes framed like a label by a border of contrasting color.

Quality control was important in the early workshops. Batik workers needed approval after the initial waxing, and the owner would acknowledge the work by signing her name in pencil, which was later retraced in wax. There is always some variation in the signature from one piece to another, just as there is when one is signing several checks, one after the other.

Even though there are many signed batiks—for reasons of pride, copyright, and advertisement—some of the finest examples are not identified, their makers lost to history. □

  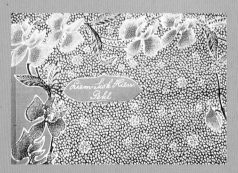

The Finest Workmanship

Chinese batik and its makers would be easier to understand if one knew English, Dutch, Javanese, and Mandarin. Few are so fortunate. However, some Chinese signed their batik, and through oral histories the role of other artists can be deciphered.

In the village of Kedungwuni, six miles from Pekalongan, lives a Chinese family whose members for many years have made the finest batik in Java. Said one admirer:

> They were the best batik one could buy. Every year I saved my money and bought one batik from Eliza van Zuylen and one batik from Oey Soe Tjoen.

Oey Soe Tjoen was known for his craftsmanship, his attention to detail—and his attention to the taste of his clientele. Unlike van Zuylen, Oey Soe Tjoen did not use plain pastel colors; his family did not think them appropriate for their largely Chinese clientele.

Oey Soe Tjoen, who died in 1975 at the age of seventy-four, came from a Kedungwuni batik family that was not related to the Oeys of Pekalongan. His wife, Netty Kwee, born in 1905 in Batang, also came from a batik-making family. They were married in 1925 and their business is still run today by Netty Kwee, along with a son who has the Indonesian name of Muljadi Widjaya, and his wife, Istyandi Setiono, who came from Yogyakarta.

Settling in Kedungwuni shortly after their marriage, the Oeys opened a batik workshop. The first piece of cloth they purchased cost five guilders; from it they made six *kain panjangs*, and resold each for twenty-two guilders. From that auspicious beginning, the Oeys built a factory that within twenty years employed one hundred and fifty workers—more than were ever employed at the van Zuylen compound. The Oey factory once produced about thirty to thirty-five pieces per month. Today, the compound, with only twenty-four workers, produces less batik than it did in 1939.

Oey Soe Tjoen numbered many of his patterns: it was easier for customers to order that way. He also signed all his pieces, usually making sure to include the name of his village, Kedungwuni.

What and who inspired the designs of Oey Soe Tjoen? Some designs came from Pekalongan, where the family would buy artwork and then adapt the patterns and colors to suit their clients. Others came from a book of flowers, a gift from a Dutch dye company. These floral motifs were usually brightly recolored in typical Chinese fashion.

Although most of the Oeys' early customers were Chinese, an increasing number of Javanese began buying from them. Some central Javanese motifs were no doubt incorporated at a client's request, but there may have been other sources of inspiration as well. One of these was perhaps Princess A. A. Ario Soerio (b. 1901) who took it upon herself to "teach" the north-coast batikers something about "real" batik. An energetic lady, she traveled to northern Java accompanied by the best batikers from the royal courts of Yogyakarta and Surakarta, demonstrating how to make *isén* (textured filling) instead of the usual dots, how to incorporate the royal crests, and how to mix *soga* brown. There is a certain irony in a noblewoman from central Java traveling north to teach about *isén*, royal crests, and *soga* brown, since these techniques, dyes, and motifs all probably originated on the north coast.

By Chinese standards at least, the Oey family of Kedungwuni was late in switching to synthetic dyes, which they did in 1928. For each new color, the cloth was immersed in a dye bath; unlike the practice of some Pekalongan workshops, color was never painted on the cloth, even for the tiniest details. Prior to 1942, as in the van Zuylen factory, *Tjap Sen* cloth—imported from Holland—was used for batiking.

After World War II, the Oeys continued their business, concentrating on their superb craftsmanship. As before, sales were generally left to middlemen, and the designs changed little except by customers' requests. To this day, the batik of Oey Soe Tjoen is considered the very finest.

An early example of a sarong made by Oey Soe Tjoen about 1930, the design is called Ganggong Tanahan. (Detail) 62

By Chinese custom, blue is the color of mourning. This sarong was made by Mrs. Oey Soe Tjoen's mother about 1920, and worn when her mother died. (Detail, top) 63

Oey Soe Tjoen of Kedungwuni was known for his fine workmanship. (Far left)

Mrs. Oey Soe Tjoen, in her eighth decade, continues to run her husband's workshop and make batik. (Left)

A pagi-sore made after World War II for customers in Semarang by Oey Soe Tjoen shows his extraordinary eye for detail. (Detail, right) 64

IV. JOURNEY TO GRESIK

Village women in eastern Java harvesting rice.

DIVERSITY
IN EASTERN JAVA

Islamic Kingdoms

As one travels eastward on winding roads from Semarang, the ocean, which can be glimpsed easily from Cirebon, suddenly disappears. Demak, once a proud seafaring kingdom, today lies nearly eight miles from the sea, its harbor long ago filled with silt. Five hundred years ago, Sunan Kalijaga—who is buried nearby and was one of the Nine Prophets of Islam—encouraged the art of batik making in Demak. While few batik makers can be found in Demak today, the town still retains a strong Muslim heritage.

Java's oldest mosque, built in 1478, stands in the center of Demak. Its architectural style combines Hindu-Javanese as well as Islamic elements, reflecting the transition of this once Hindu kingdom to Islam. The Demak mosque is so holy that Muslims consider seven pilgrimages there to equal one pilgrimage to Mecca.

Arab tradition, not the Koran itself, has long discouraged the depiction of living beings in Muslim art. This stricture had an important effect on the design of batik, and Muslim custom affected its use. In Demak, and farther east in Kudus, special batik was made for prayer shawls and headcloths, to be used locally and also exported to Muslim countries around the world. One type of Muslim-inspired batik is known as "Jambi" because it was exported from the north coast to Palembang, the capital of the Sumatran province of Jambi. These Jambi pieces have the traditional *tumpal* with borders of red and/or black, and an overall background motif.

The art of batik was encouraged by Sunan Kalijaga, one of Islam's Nine Prophets, and here in Demak the faithful continue to worship according to the laws of Islam.
A selendang, probably made in Cirebon for export to Sumatra about 1900, was used to cover the bride and groom during a wedding ceremony. (Detail, opposite) 65

Voyaging eastward from Demak, the batik of the north coast changes color. It becomes darker, with golden brown backgrounds and accents of rich creams, tans, reds, and indigos, often overdyed to add dark green and black. All this suggests that it was related, long ago, to the batik of central Java.

Batik from this region often devotes its entire surface to what looks like an abstract geometric. It is, in fact, covered with the *shahada*, written in Arabic. The *shahada* is the basic statement of Islamic belief: There is no God but Allah and Muhammad is His messenger. Even though only two color schemes are used—dark blue and cream or, more rarely, red and gold—this batik is probably the most graphic of all north-coast fabrics. Curi-

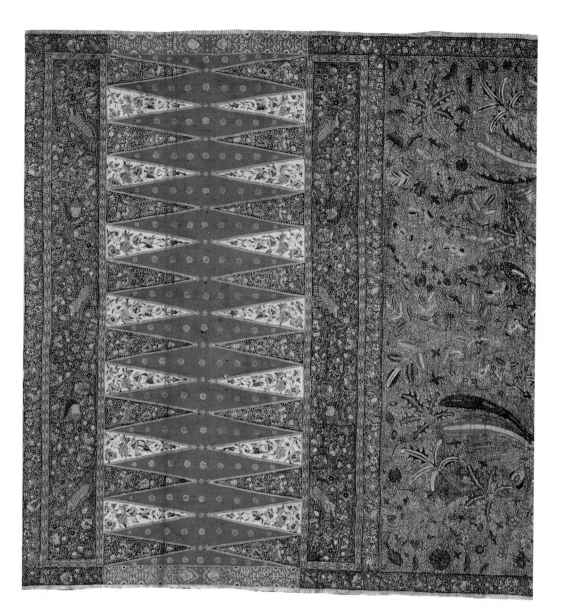

Although this sarong was made in Demak in 1900 with rich natural dyes, the kepala (top left) was sent to two other towns for finishing, which undoubtedly gave it its design name Kepala Pasang Tiga Negeri. (Detail, right) 66

The four hand-sewn borders suggest that this typical "Jambi" batik, ca. 1920, was used as a tablecloth. A motif resembling birds is hidden in a textural overall pattern. Although made in Lasem, batik of this type was frequently exported to Sumatra. (Left) 67

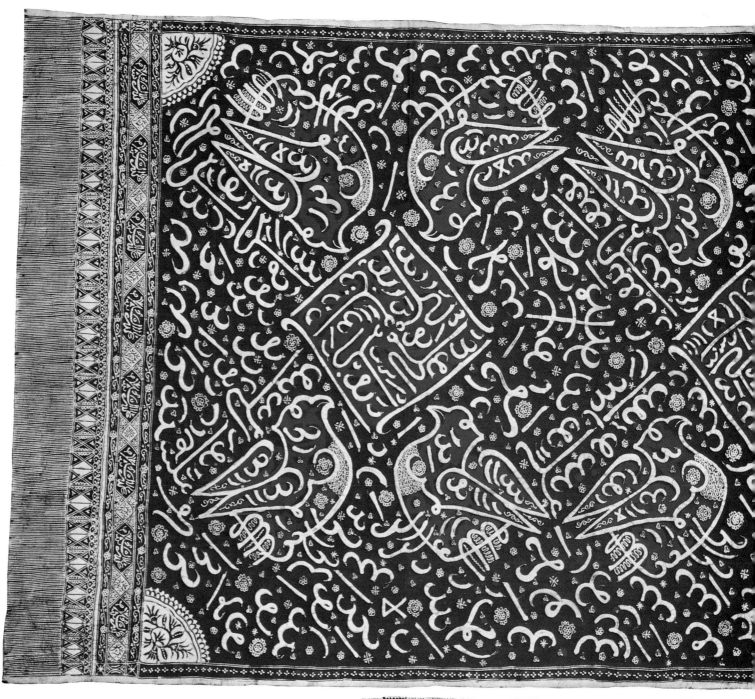

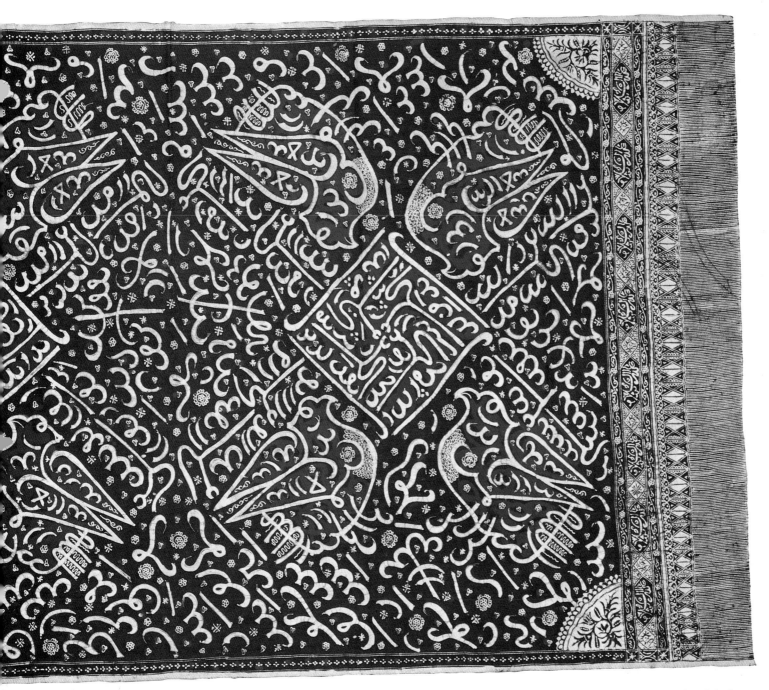

Since Arab custom discourages the use of animate objects in decoration, the shahada—or basic Islamic belief stating that there is no God but Allah and Muhammad is his messenger—is often used as a design motif. These and other words take many forms on batik, and is known as batik arab. This batik arab was made in the early twentieth century with calligraphic and bird motifs. (Top) 68

An iket kepala or headcloth, with the shahada inscription. (Far left) 69
A keris as well as Javanese writing intended to prevent bad luck are batiked onto this curious iket kepala. (Left) 70

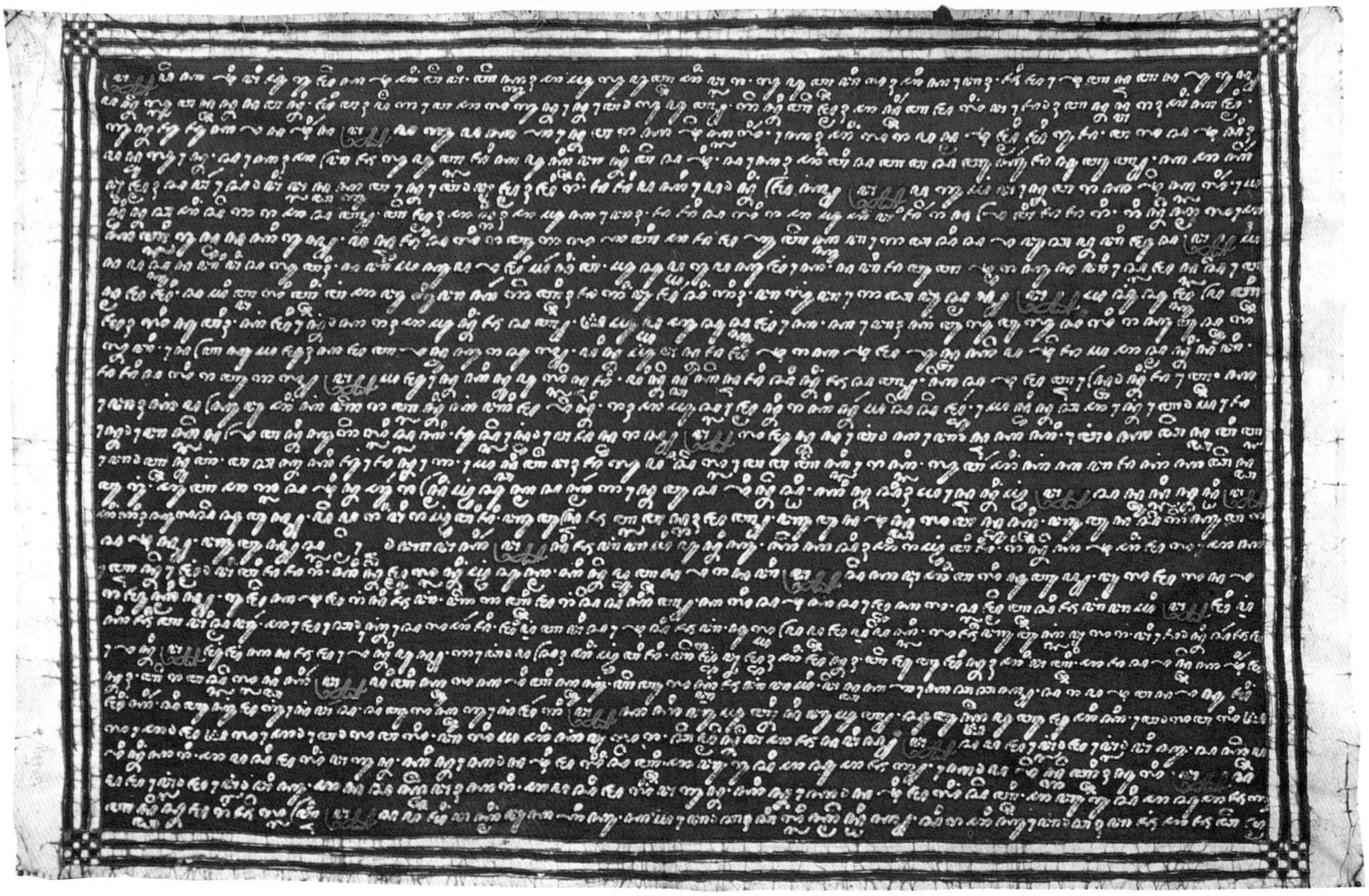

Rare headcloth decorated with
fifteenth-century Javanese
script. (Above) 72

This early twentieth-century
batik was used as a wall hanging
or perhaps as a large ceremonial
piece to cover a tray laden with
wedding gifts. (Top and right) 71

ously, the Muslim batik makers who originated these cloths never used more than two colors, even though they were surrounded by a plethora of bright Chinese colors.

Kudus, another ancient Islamic kingdom lying twenty miles east of Demak, exemplifies the mysterious Muslim colors and illustrates how the batik of Java became so richly layered by tradition, style, and religion.

To many of its eighty thousand inhabitants, the sixteenth-century mosque of Kudus is a talisman of yet another great Muslim teacher, Sunan Bonang, who is buried there. The minaret of this mosque is not like a traditional Arabic tower. Rather, it resembles the Hindu watchtowers that were erected in the fields of Java to warn rice farmers of impending catastrophes. Clashing with the *muezzin*'s call is the commercial cacophony of modern Kudus, which among other things boasts the largest clove cigarette factory in Indonesia.

From Kudus two very distinct and spectacular styles of batik emerged. The first—unmistakably the work of one hand, from one workshop—is unsigned and of unknown origin. Perhaps the batik was made farther east, in Juana; we do not know. What characterizes this style is its vigor: the scale is large, sometimes overwhelming, and the hand is free. Huge flowers are rendered simply against detailed backgrounds of continuous vines and rice patterning; large leaves are evenly and boldly portrayed with rich textural veins and saturated colors. The work is *tulis*. Even though the detailing is very fine, the whole is reminiscent of some of the earlier Cirebon batik, which was drawn by men, or of an early example of an eastern Javanese *selendang* with overblown butterflies.

The dark colors of these vivid batiks would seem to be more characteristic of Kudus than is the second style, which features colorful floral motifs set against the most intricate background to be found on the entire north coast. Almost certainly the products of Chinese workshops, these brilliantly colored pieces resemble Pekalongan batik, but no designer in Pekalongan—except for Jane Hendromartono—did such detailed work.

Undoubtedly, the economy of Kudus had something to do with the complicated, *isén* backgrounds of its batik. Fifty years ago, a few of Kudus's "cigarette barons" hired the best Pekalongan batikers and transported them sixty miles by taxi each way. The barons could afford the best; and to them the best meant batik with the most complicated backgrounds, produced by the most highly paid workers. Luxury and snobbism were at the heart of this rather amazing enterprise.

The most famous batik makers in this "Chinese" style were Lie Eng Soen and Lie Boen In. There are those who prize the batik of Lie Boen In even more highly than that of Eliza van Zuylen and Oey Soe Tjoen. This may be because so few of Lie's works exist today. Lie created most of his batik for family use, even though from 1930 to 1963 he operated a small factory in Kudus which produced exquisite batik for a limited clientele.

The batik from Demak and Kudus is as varied as that of Java's north coast—from Arabic calligraphy to muted colors to enlarged motifs and minute renderings in a glorious palette. It is a tribute to the artistic energies of these people that so many different styles emerged from a relatively small area within a two-hundred-year period.

Early twentieth-century tulis piece in natural dyes of indigo and soga brown from Juana or Kudus. It is possible that this, and the pieces on pages 146 and 147 were made by the same (unknown) artist in the same (unknown) workshop. (Detail, right) 73

Dlorong Buket Brasmawar design shows a strength of color as well as boldness of design. (Detail, far left) 74
Simple large flowers, probably lilies, are boldly rendered in this kain panjang, *made just after the turn of the century. (Below) 75*

147

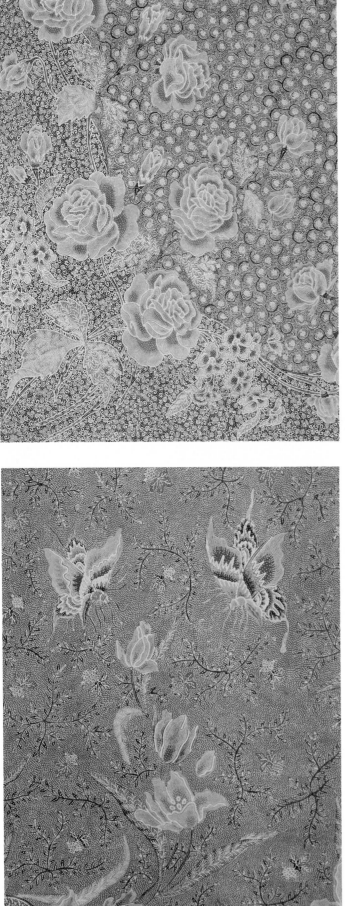

The bright colors of tulips and roses in full bloom (details) explode against a rich brown background of swimming goldfish. Made in Pekalongan by Liem Siok Hien, a third-generation batik maker, in 1950, it was signed "Kudus" because its design more closely resembled that area. (Top and above) 76 Kudus has a history of making complex batik designs. This sarong (details) was made about 1920, with vertical brushes of blue and gold against a diamond background. (Top and above) 77 This pagi-sore, signed by Lie Eng Soen, was made shortly after World War I in Kudus. The batik is richly detailed with carnations and cornflowers; its deep brown background color is common to Kudus. (Detail, right) 78

THE PRESTIGE OF SILK

Trade between China and Java goes back more than two thousand years. Although silk is not indigenous to Java, it is woven there from Chinese thread; the Javanese consider silk a luxury. Juana on the north coast (as well as Gresik in the southeast) are centers of silk weaving and silk batik. In Juana, about seventeen miles east of Kudus, silk is batiked for local and overseas customers. In the 1920s Juana silk batik was sent to Bali, Hong Kong, and Shanghai. Today it is still exported, especially to Bali.

Batik on silk, like batik covered with gold (*prada*), is a sign of wealth and prestige. Probably no batik is more significant than a silk that has been dyed yellow to be used as a religious banner or in a shadow puppet play. Yellow is the most difficult color to dye, hence the most sought after. It is the color of royalty. A yellow carryall (*selendang*) from Juana, when wrapped around a puppet during a *wayang* performance, indicates that the puppet represents Batara Guru, the Father of All, Java's most important deity.

Silk batik comes in many other colors and shapes. One type, called *lokcan*, was made in Juana in the 1920s by Tan Kian Poen, who patterned the silk with small flowers and animals, in reds, blues, browns, and yellows. These silk (*can*) batik pieces were often dominated by a shade of blue (*lok*)—hence the name, *lokcan*. Unfortunately fine silk batik is rare and most of it has long since succumbed to Southeast Asia's hot and humid climate. □

Silk selendang *probably from* Indramayu *with phoenix and* wayang *figures.* 79

A rare silk sarong from Gresik or Rembang combines plangi and tulis techniques. Made about 1900, its brilliant colors combine with the sarong's textural pattern. (Detail, top left) 80 Knotted silk fringe was attached to the end of this yellow selendang. Probably made in the 1920s, it was worn draped over one shoulder. (Above) 81 Weaving silk in Gresik. (Left)

Lasem—a Walled City

Lasem's high walls shroud this once-bustling batik city, hiding its majestic houses.

For a thousand years and more Lasem was a thriving port; today there are few reminders of the city's nautical and mercantile past. Its proud harbor no longer exists; only small fishing boats ply its desolate shore, never venturing far.

High white plaster walls border Lasem's winding dirt roads, giving the town a sense of eerie quiet and secrecy. The walls hide all but the most majestic tiled roofs of Lasem's many Chinese houses. At one time, most of the town's fifty thousand people were involved in the business of making and selling batik, but today they are mainly engaged in the trading of tobacco, rice, corn, and peanuts.

In 1870, the production of Lasem batik was in the hands of Chinese, and by the turn of the century there was a booming business in both batik *tulis* and *cap*. By 1942, there were more than a hundred small batik workshops; today there are fewer than twenty. Lasem's high walls were useful when the batik business was competitive and booming: they protected workshop owners from competitors who might copy their techniques.

For nearly a century the business of batik was profitable in Lasem, but success was bought at the expense of the workers. A Dutch report in 1930 described labor abuses in the workshops of Lasem and nearby Rembang, with accompanying photographs of starving laborers. Workers—sometimes as many as forty of them—were often crammed day and night in dark and smoky sheds, locked up from the outside world behind thick, heavy doors. Wages were low even for batikers: one-quarter to one-half those paid a common field laborer.

Today the batik makers of Lasem are often third- or fourth-generation craftsmen, running their workshops in the courtyards of their large homes. These houses, although now slightly seedy and faded, are decorated with ornate mirrors and intricately worked altar cloths, and their finely crafted Chinese beds suggest the fortunes that must have been made long ago from batik.

Many styles characterize Lasem batik, but two are most distinctive. The first, for lack of any more definitive name, is called "Cirebonese-Indramayu" because it looks as if it were made in western, not eastern, Java. Possibly these patterns were introduced by the wandering artisans of the twelfth century who also found their way west to Cirebon.

The colors are usually blue with cream or white, or red with cream or white. The red of Lasem and eastern Java is a blood red of such depth that it resembles no other color on the north coast. Motifs of these "Cirebonese-Indramayu" pieces usually consist of squiggly imaginary beasts. Unlike Pekalongan batik, the Lasem backgrounds are fairly simple, sometimes containing flowers and birds.

The second, and much more easily identifiable Lasem batik, features red, blue, and cream. Sometimes, instead of cream, the background is tan, and often a green dye is added. The *bang biru*—literally "red-blue" —batik is also characterized by its motifs of lotus flowers, pomegranates, a solid background, and often includes drawings of happy people. In the old days, *bang biru* batik was prized on the north coast and gilded for ceremonial occasions.

Behind the high walls of Lasem lie the secrets of its variegated batiks. Why the blood-red color? Why such a resemblance to Cirebon batiks? We do not know the many designers, only the history of their sweatshops and their mercantile fleet—and the legacy of their art.

With its intricate patchwork kepala, this sarong resembles batik made in Lasem, although it was probably made in Pekalongan about 1890. (Detail) 82

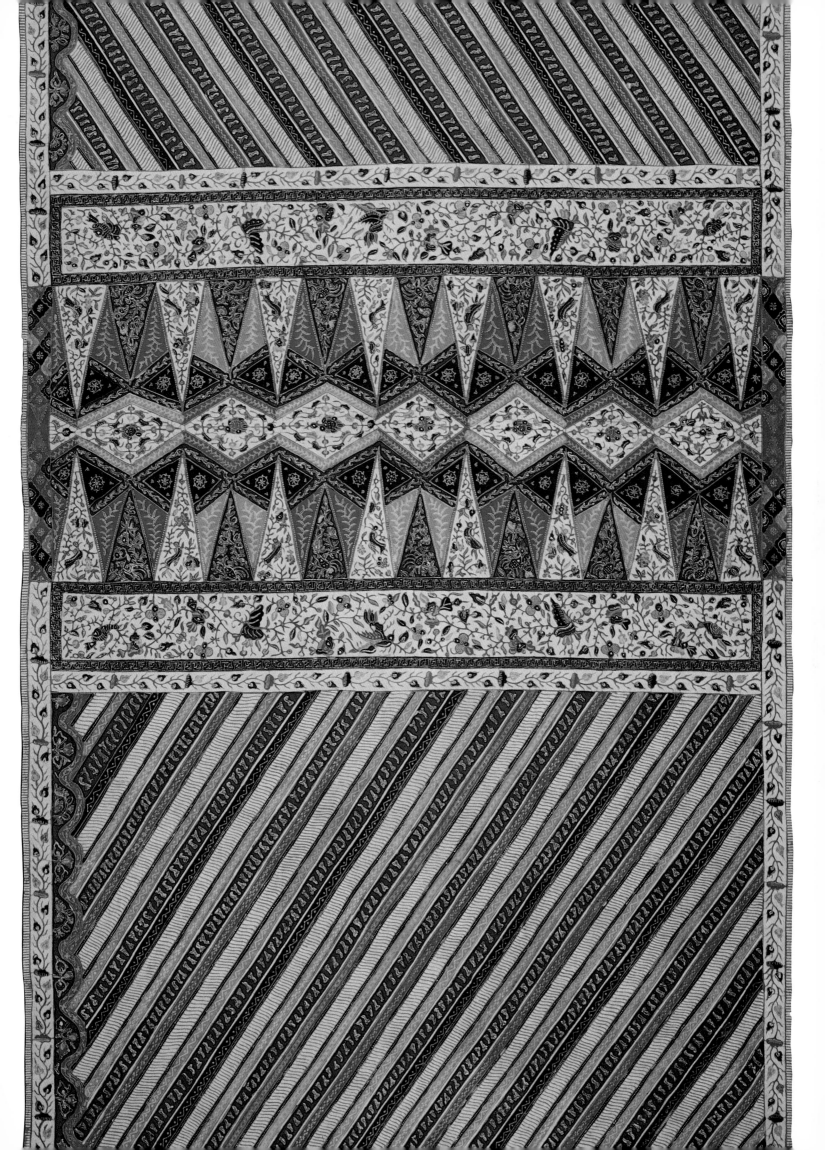

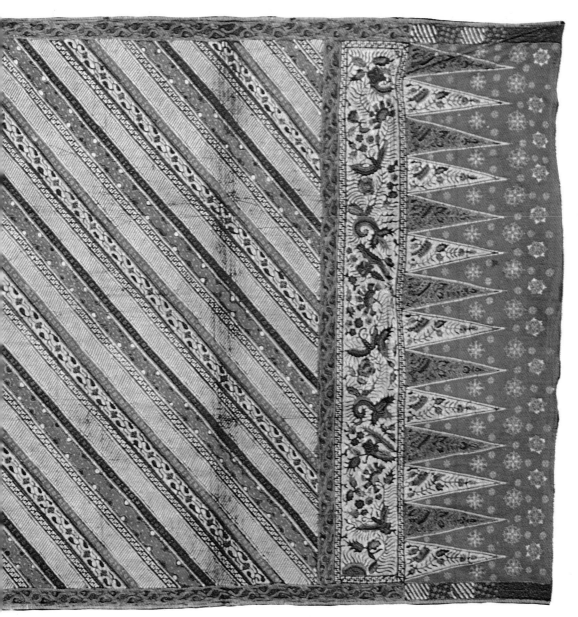

This unusual pagi-sore is divided vertically, not diagonally, resulting in half kepalas at each end. It was probably made in Lasem for export to Sumatra about 1880. 83

A baby carrier, or kain gendongan, with life-size butterflies and a deep, natural red color characteristic of eastern Java, was made in Lasem about 1900. Never used, perhaps because the awaited baby died, its chintzlike finish was achieved by rubbing shells across the fabric. 84

This 1920s Lasem sarong, with its bold banji or swastika design, utilizes all the traditional elements of north-coast batik: kepala with tumpal, and pinggir borders. (Detail, left) 85

A selendang depicting Pangeran Diponegoro, prince of Yogyakarta and hero of Javanese resistance during the 1821–1836 wars against the Dutch. In portraits such as this 1900 Lasem batik, he was usually shown on horseback, dressed in Islamic robes, and carrying a sword or banner. (Detail, right) 86

Chinese-style animals—frogs, turtles, peacocks, birds, and centipedes—all thought to have mystical powers that could be imparted to anyone wearing the cloth, are depicted here. Venomous creatures, such as the centipede, often represented strength and power; and the chickens that surround them were the only animals with the power to counteract their poisonous bites. With its symbols, this Lasem sarong of 1900 was probably worn by an adult male who had overcome many of life's difficulties. (Detail, far left) 87

An imaginative arrangement of mythical animals, birds, and flowers, this Cirebon-style bedcover from Lasem, ca. 1910, draws heavily on Chinese art and religious symbols. (Detail, top and left) 88

ALTAR CLOTHS

For more than fourteen hundred years, altars and their decorative cloths have been important to Buddhist temples and homes around the world. An altar is a sanctuary where offerings of respect and devotion are made to Buddha and other spiritual beings. Its covering is a cloth of paradise, symbolizing the *kusha* grass placed on Buddha's throne. Often elaborate, the altar cloth is a statement of perfection, of the purity of nature, and of true enlightenment.

The north coast of Java is studded with Chinese temples, whose brilliant red façades and carved and painted wooden panels speak of other worlds, of incense and of offerings. At home, most Chinese have their own altars; the wealthier the household, the more elaborate the altar.

Traditionally, altar cloths were made of silk, finely embroidered in deep rich colors. Java's climate is not kind to great silks, however, and because the Chinese were heavily involved in batik making, altar cloths came to be made of cotton. Batik, not embroidery, provided the design.

Altar cloths still are produced by the Chinese for the Chinese market throughout the north coast. Regional differences are often apparent. The design of an altar cloth, which is usually square, is normally contained in two rectangular areas, one about a quarter the size of the other. The larger part hangs over the end of the altar, the smaller usually lies on top. Sometimes ties are added to make the fastening more secure. Favorite designs include Chinese processions, dragons, mythical animals, real people, and other themes reflecting the nature of Buddhism. □

A Chinese north-coast temple with batik altar cloth.

Cirebon batik showing dragon with Tao T'ieh face. 89

Chi'lin means prosperity, the phoenix, long life. 90

A parade with lanterns outside a Chinese temple. 91

A Thok Wie design ca. 1900, and richly colored. 92

An Indian-influenced altar cloth from Lasem. 93

Bang ajo cloth depicts various Chinese symbols. 94

Village Batik

The former glory of Tuban is difficult to perceive. Like Cirebon to the west, Tuban was once a mighty seaport but is now reduced to a handful of fishing boats, a few paved streets, and a tumble of Chinese temples. This flat town with its main road running along the beach bears no resemblance to the great port of Surabaya to the southeast or Semarang to the west. And, although Tuban may share a history with Demak and Lasem, the batik from its villages is different both in style and in the method of production.

Tuban batik production is vertical and integrated: cotton is grown, spun, woven, and batiked all in the immediate vicinity. Instead of spreading the labor among the people of several towns, Tuban's "village" batik is all made in one place, within a given period of time. It usually takes ten to twelve weeks between the harvesting of the cotton and a finished batik.

What is colloquially known as "Tuban batik" is actually batik made in nearby villages such as Kerek and Bejagung. The primitive nature of production in this locale is evident in Kerek, about thirteen miles southwest of Tuban. Devoid of electricity and running water, and typical of thousands of Java's tiny enclaves, Kerek is a town of about three thousand people. It is governed by agricultural cycles and economic priorities: batik is made only when the women are not in the fields plant-

Tuban, once a mighty kingdom, is now reduced to a minor seaport with only a handful of fishing boats.

This selendang's overall semen design includes wings, pavilions, and a mountain range. It was made around 1900 in the Tuban area. (Detail) 95

A dodot made near Tuban
includes a large variety of design
forms: a pair of wings, mountains, a temple, palm trees, deer,
crocodiles, birds, and foliage. 96

In the village of Kerek, about thirteen miles from Tuban, batik is made from locally grown and homespun cotton. Except in the rainy season, most women here make batik outdoors. (Above)

ing or harvesting crops. (The women receive 10 percent of the yield for harvesting, 33 percent if they help with both the planting and harvesting.)

Between agricultural cycles, the women weave cotton into a coarse homespun on the ten primitive looms in Kerek's small thatched houses, the *clack-clack-bang-bang* of shuttles shattering the quiet of village life. After the cotton is woven, it is batiked.

For the batik process itself, Kerek workers have the luxury, at least in good weather, of sitting out-of-doors. Women stoop in front of their thatched huts, chewing betel nuts, while drawing patterns freehand onto the fabric. When finished, they dye the cloth with common natural indigo or *mengkudu* red and, more and more these days, with synthetic dyes.

When a batik is finished, the *kepala desa* (village head) often takes it to his home to sell. Sometimes he may try to sell it in other villages, but he rarely ventures as far as Tuban, because there is little transport. A sarong, which takes about three months for a woman to complete, costs the equivalent of fifteen U.S. dollars. This may seem like a bargain to outsiders, but whatever share the batiker receives—undoubtedly the village head takes a cut—it is probably more than she would have earned from planting and harvesting the crops.

The batik of Kerek and other nearby villages resembles mid-nineteenth-century batik from the Cirebon area. Both employ homespun cotton; both use either natural red or blue dyes; in both the motifs are simple: geometrics and birds and flowers drawn from nature. Dots are primitively applied to the background—as in Indramayu batiks—but in Kerek, instead of using a *cemplogen*, the wax is punctured with a palmetto thorn.

The resemblance of Tuban batik to Cirebon batik—and to some of those from Lasem—may not be entirely coincidental. If the artisans from Kediri and Japara wandered as far west as Cirebon seven hundred years ago, it is reasonable to assume that they also may have gone east, to Lasem and thence to Tuban. But while Cirebon and Lasem were vigorous towns whose batik underwent dramatic changes over the years, Tuban and its environs seem almost to have faded from the map of northern Java. The batik of Tuban remained primitive.

Farther east, on the island of Madura, the same simple method of making batik holds sway. About ninety miles long and eighteen miles wide, Madura is dotted with harbors and small villages. In Telago Bira, a shipbuilding community of about twenty-five hundred people, cotton is loomed in the village, and women freely draw designs and later batik the cloth in their homes. Their husbands sell the pieces when they go off to sea.

The color red characterizes the batik of eastern Java and so does the *naga* or snake, portrayed usually in bold *mengkudu* red and sometimes even in indigo blue. Instead of spidery vines weaving intricate circles, the *naga*—somewhat like a tree of life—appears forcefully, thrusting itself upon the cloth, proclaiming in no uncertain terms its masculinity and vigor.

Traveling south from Tuban or Madura, the batik becomes darker in color and less recognizable as a group. Traditionally, the two east-coast batik centers were Gresik and Sidoarjo, but these towns are now mere suburbs of modern Surabaya. Little is known of the old makers, although in Sidoarjo a group of Muslims, called Kaoman, made batik in the Arab quarter near the mosque. Other batik from nearby Gresik, where cement and silk are made today, has a freer form, sometimes resembling the batik of western Java with its floating leaves and simple backgrounds.

In the last two hundred years, both Gresik and Sidoarjo have been influenced by their proximity to Surabaya, Indonesia's second largest city and the hub of trading in eastern Java since the fourteenth century. A town immortalized by the lyrics of Bertolt Brecht, Surabaya is not a particularly romantic city; like Jakarta and Semarang it swarms with people jostling to make a sale or strike a bargain. Little batik originated here. Instead, Surabaya's Chinese and Arab traders combed Gresik, Sidoarjo, and other coastal towns and villages for their batik, selling the cloth but seldom making it.

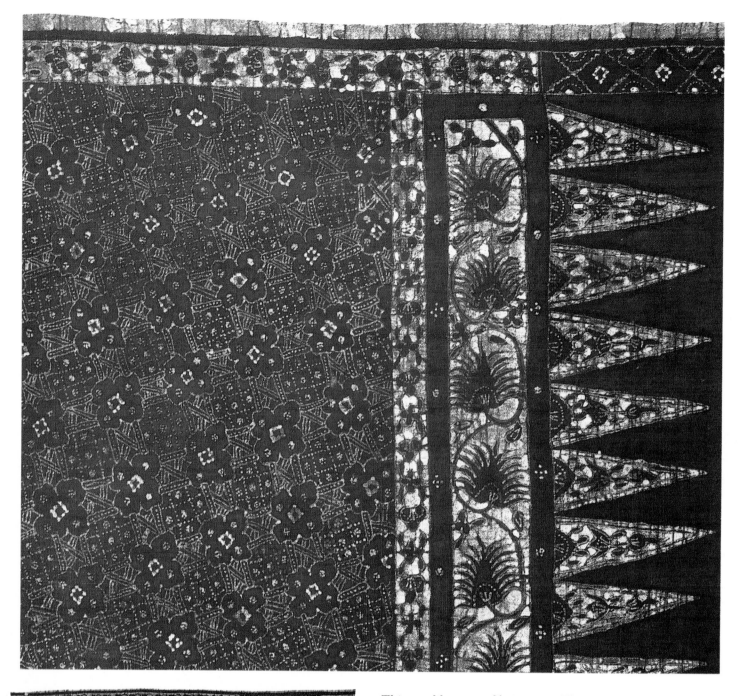

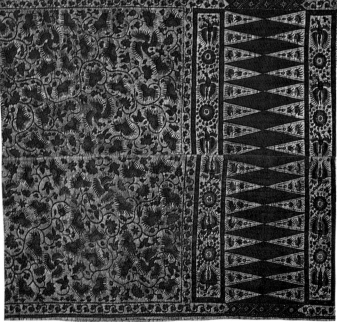

This roughly textured kain panjang is simply designed and
batiked by Kerek women in a
rich, natural indigo blue.
(Top) 97
Because of the narrow cloth (95
cm.), this Tuban sarong is
most likely an early example of
village batik. The small blue
background dots were made by
puncturing the wax with the
thorn of the palmetto before
dyeing. (Detail, left) 98

The snakelike forms of this
sarong end in stylized flowers. Its
deep red color, characteristic of
east Java and Madura, symbolizes fertility. (Detail, right) 99

Strength in Numbers

Several batik forms are referred to as "two countries"(*dua negeri*) and "three countries" (*tiga negeri*), and these combined the best styles and colors from several Javanese batik-making towns, all of which participated in their production. *Dua/tiga* batik spread along the northern coast of Java, extending east to Surabaya and south to the central highlands. Motifs and colors of *dua negeri* and *tiga negeri* batik are usually so distinctive that the origin of each piece can be easily traced. Usually the first waxing and dyeing was done in a north-coast town, the second waxing and final dyeing in central Java. "Three countries" batik was expensive because it traveled farthest and was thought to combine the best of all Javanese styles, making the "perfect" batik.

This cooperative method of production developed for economic reasons. Quite simply, certain dyes, designs, and batikers were indigenous to certain towns, and if the market called for those particular combinations, the producer would have to obtain them.

A *dua negeri* sarong, for example, might originate in Pekalongan where the head (*kepala*) and border (*pinggir*) were waxed and dyed red before the cloth was sent on to Surakarta where the body (*badan*) would receive *garuda* wings and other central Javanese motifs before being dyed *soga* brown. A three-country batik might originate in Lasem where pomegranates and vines, the main designs, were waxed and dyed red; it then might go to Kudus for these motifs to be filled and dyed blue; and it might end in Yogyakarta where *parang* motifs would be added to the background and the final color, *soga* brown, would be applied. The combinations of towns, styles, and dyes in these batiks were almost infinite.

Dua and *tiga negeri* batik was made for about fifty years, until World War II effectively halted its production.

◆

Time, taste, and people mixed to form the great variety of Java's north-coast batik—from the elegant courts of Cirebon to the dusty village of Kerek, from coarse handspun to the finest combed cotton, from monochromatic work to batik with fifteen colors, from *Indische* businesswomen to Chinese and Arab entrepreneurs, from *tulis* to *cap.*

The influence of Java's north coast on batik continued through times of national struggle, war, misery, and poverty. The Javanese had bound themselves into an organization called *Sarekat Islam* to protect themselves against Chinese batik competition. It was this very same group that became a cornerstone of the independence movement. And through it all, as we shall see, Java's unique art form emerged not entirely unscathed, but enriched by new experience.

An example of tiga negeri *("three countries") sarong from Lasem. The red flowers and border were applied in Pekalongan, the blue in a second north-coast town, and the brown border made in Surakarta. (Detail, opposite top left)* 100

A pagi-sore illustrating "three countries." Most likely the diagonal pattern and final dyeing were done in Surakarta. (Detail, opposite top right) 101

A sarong from Pacitan, ca. 1915, is a perfect example of dua negeri *("two countries"), combining the best designs from two batik centers. (Detail, opposite bottom left)* 102

Tiga Negeri *sarong ca. 1910. An unusual diagonal* kepala *is combined with a patchwork* badan. *(Detail, opposite bottom right)* 5

(Overleaf, detail left) The bold leaves of this Latar Ireng *design, made in Gresik about 1920, are filled with large grains of rice.* 103

(Overleaf, detail right) The motifs of this sarong from Sidoarjo were made using a square, not round, canting. 104

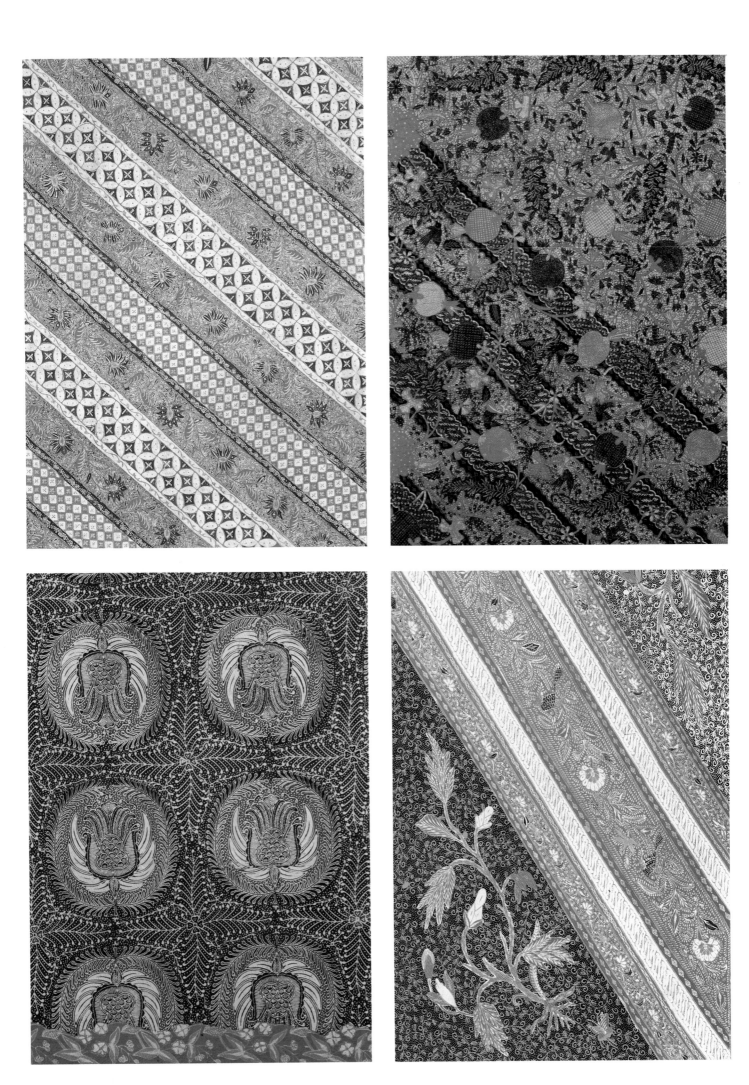

V. MODERN BATIK

Making batik by the yard

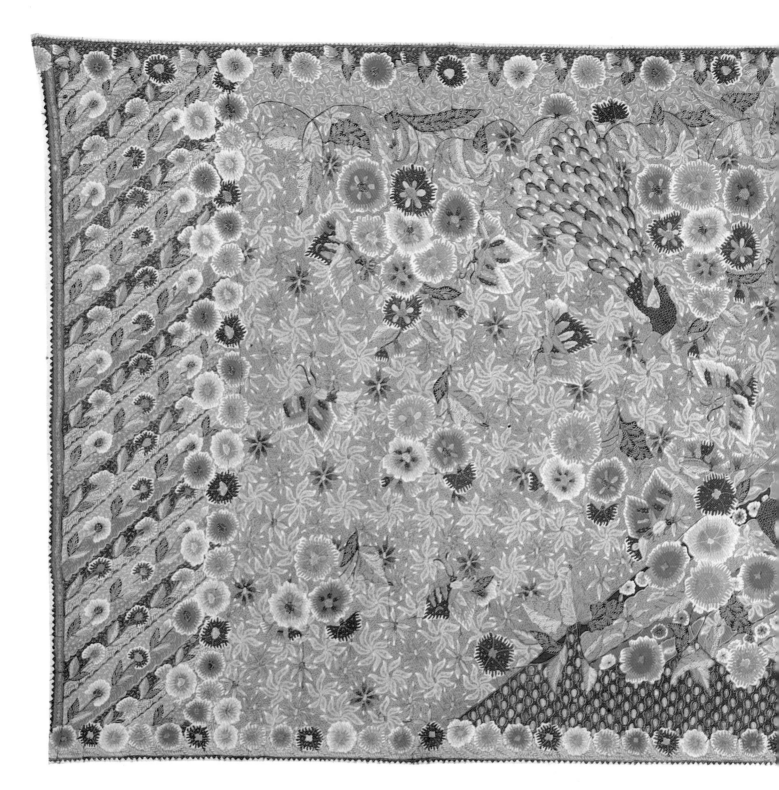

TRAUMA AND A
NEW SOCIETY

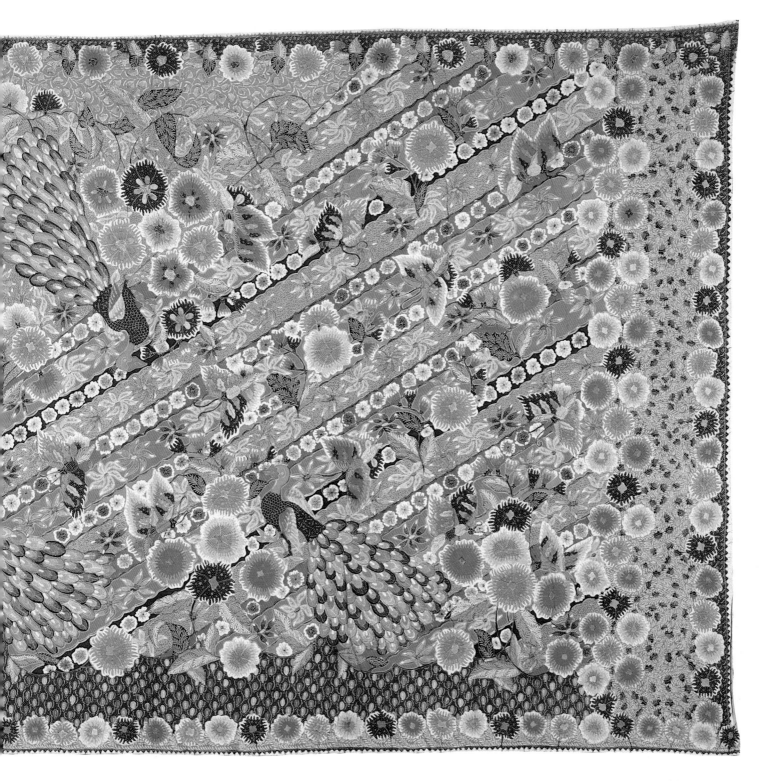

Typical batik made during the Japanese occupation of Java during World War II. 105

Cloth of War

The golden age of Javanese batik came to an abrupt halt when the Japanese invaded the Dutch East Indies in 1942. At first welcomed as liberators—especially by those who for decades had struggled against Dutch colonialism—the Japanese promised freedom from Dutch rule. They also introduced a simple, single language, Bahasa Indonesia, in an effort to unite the polyglot islands. But the "liberators" proved to be harsh overlords. Thousands of Javanese were conscripted and deported to other islands; Europeans, Chinese, and Indians shared a similar fate, many never to be seen again.

The ensuing economic upheaval affected all areas of life including the business of batik. During the Japanese occupation, numerous batik factories were closed. One batik maker remembers that just as the Japanese soldiers entered her compound, she grabbed several cherished sarongs drying on her clothesline, saving them for posterity. Everything else was confiscated. Many factories closed permanently, their valuable tools forever lost. Fine Dutch cotton was no longer imported, and cloth of any quality was virtually unobtainable.

Nevertheless a new colorful batik, known as *Hokokai,* developed in war-torn Java. Its name derived from politics, not art, and it was to be Java's last colonial batik. The Japanese, in an effort to mobilize resources for the war effort, established *Djawa* (Java) *Hokokai,* a people's loyalty organization ostensibly to serve the occupied country itself. Under the aegis of the vast bureaucracy of *Djawa Hokokai,* the Japanese organized the conscription of labor, athletic events, even the assembling of batik exhibits. The word *Hokokai* stuck as the name for wartime Javanese batik. The vibrancy of *Hokokai* batik presents a strange counterpoint to the suffering of the Javanese in those years.

Because cotton was scarce in war-torn Java, every inch of cloth was used for patterning: *Hokokai* batik is intricate, with fine details marching endlessly across the cloth. A single batik could take twelve months to make, so delicate was the work. Undoubtedly, the exuberant colors reflected the influence of Japan. Not even the richest Chinese colors of Pekalongan could match those of *Hokokai* batik with their intense shades of yellow, turquoise, fuchsia, purple, red, and pink.

Hokokai batik was made all along the north coast, especially in the Pekalongan area. While the flowers retained their regional styles, most towns used similar backgrounds and colors, making it difficult to ascertain exactly who made which batik; few *Hokokai* pieces are signed or stamped. Perhaps some batik makers, designing in the "Japanese" style, preferred to remain anonymous, for fear of being accused of collaboration with the enemy.

Rarely does one encounter a *Hokokai* sarong. Instead, morning/evening pieces (*pagi-sore*), which use more cloth than either a sarong or a *kain panjang*, were

For decades the Javanese had fought for national unity against the Dutch. Here Javanese revolutionaries, armed mostly with bamboo spears, meet to demand independence in 1946, after Japan's defeat. (Right)
Java is an overcrowded island. A policy of "transmigration" has made deep inroads into the batik business, and has also been used as a political tool. (Left)

(Overleaf, detail left) This unsigned Hokokai kain panjang makes an elegant statement in its formality of design and subtlety of color. 106
(Overleaf, detail right) A controlled abandon shows in this pagi-sore, made between 1942 and 1945 on the Javanese north coast. 107

produced. Given the cotton shortage, this was surprising: it may be that *Hokokai* was commissioned on *pagi-sores* because the Japanese thought that batik could best be displayed on such lengths; or perhaps the Japanese used *pagi-sores* for other, unknown, purposes. *Obis,* the sashes tied around kimonos, were also batiked during this period.

Visually, *Hokokai* was a natural follower of some of the Chinese-inspired batik. The bright colors remained, but the combinations changed during the war. No other era in batik history is as specifically delineated and as brief as *Hokokai.* But as with many other things in the world of style and design, *Hokokai* batik was revived in later years.

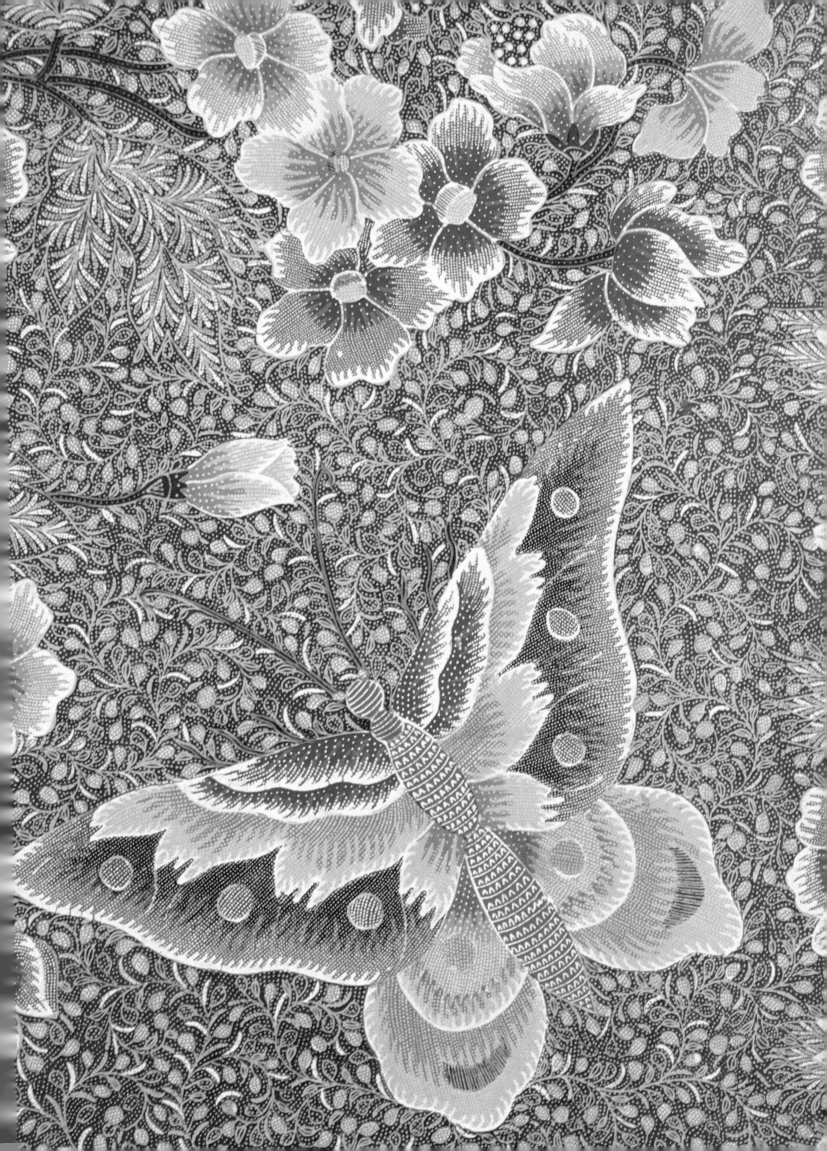

Batik Indonesia

The early part of this century saw the beginnings of a national movement that was both anti-Dutch and pro-nationalist. Sukarno emerged as its leader after being exiled by the Dutch to the island of Flores. There, prophetically, he sold batik to make a living; it was Sukarno who would be instrumental in making batik a symbol of a free and united Indonesia.

The aftermath of World War II brought new upheavals to the island of Java as it made its tumultuous passage toward nationalism. Finally, after four years of bloody battles and negotiations with Britain and Holland, a free country was established in the winter of 1949. Sukarno seized power as president and eventually became military dictator. Two decades of political confusion and economic turmoil ensued.

These years of internal and external struggle had a devastating effect on the art and industry of batik. The war and the fight for independence had disrupted Javanese feudal life, changed the power structure, destroyed the aristocracy, and forever altered the lives of the peasants. Batik workers, mostly women—who had always been poorly paid and were considered unskilled labor—looked for more lucrative jobs.

There were other profound changes. Traditionally, the consumers of batik had also been the producers of batik. Either that or they were members of the Javanese feudal aristocracy and of rich Chinese trading families who held an exclusionary view of batik and preferred to have *their* batik made in *their* backyards by *their* servants.

Centuries of cultural and artistic tradition were threatened when batik became primarily a commercial enterprise. *Cap,* and much later screenprinting, became predominant; they were more efficient and more profitable processes than *tulis.* Design was now determined by producers and middlemen who did not come from Java's prewar feudal society, which had imposed its restrictive tastes and rules on the making of batik.

After 1945 fashion in Java favored Western dress; batik as a costume virtually ceased to exist in the larger urban areas. Producers struggled to market their batik —usually unsuccessfully. Some attempted to produce batik by the yard, which was difficult because until then only *kain panjangs* of two and a half yards had been made; most turned to mass-produced "batik"—patterned screenprints.

Government regulations were not particularly helpful either. A policy of imposed transmigration, to alleviate Java's overpopulation, encouraged emigration to other islands; those batik workers who left did not carry on their craft. Export and import restrictions did little to encourage either the art or the industry. Because Indonesia was not producing its own fine cotton for batik, the cloth had to be imported, usually from the People's Republic of China. Duty had to be paid on the cotton, even though much of the finished batik would eventually be exported. A manufacturer could not export without an export license, and an export license was virtually unobtainable unless one had the right connections. Without a license and connections, a batik maker could export goods only by paying the government the cash value of his shipment, which would be returned later, less financial charges. Few batik makers could afford this roundabout transaction.

Finally, the political and economic emergence of nearby Malaysia and Singapore produced a competitive batik industry. Malaysia made "Javanese" batik, often more cheaply than Indonesia, and exported it to Southeast Asia and ports around the world. Singapore, because of its free-trade policies and the zeal of numerous Chinese and Arab middlemen, bought and sold both Malaysian and Indonesian batik. This trade was so successful that eventually it became easier and cheaper to buy Indonesian batik from Singapore dealers than directly from batik manufacturers in Java.

Sukarno, destined to become Indonesia's first president, honors his mother in this 1946 photo. After three years of civil war, Indonesia became independent in 1949.

SPECIAL BATIK FOR SPECIAL EVENTS

Batik was often made to commemorate special events. War was an especially popular subject, but so was the opening of a new railroad line, the flight of a new airplane, or the launching of a steamship. Sometimes entire fairy tales—*Cinderella, Snow White, Sleeping Beauty*—were illustrated. Often the subject was not a story, but merely the depiction of simple playing cards or dominoes.

There was nothing particularly magical about these special designs; they were more *kitsch* than art. Nevertheless, these special batiks for special events tell us what people were thinking at the time. They were popular in the same way as black-bordered mourning handkerchiefs, sold throughout the British Empire for Queen Victoria's funeral, or T-shirts emblazoned with slogans touting women's rights worn today by fashionable New York ladies.

Many of the commemorative batik pieces are associated with the workshops of *Indische* women who made them for the colonial market in Java, sometimes using *cap*, sometimes *tulis*. If nothing else, these special batik clearly show once again the many outside influences that came to bear on batik design. □

A sarong found in Sumatra but made in Java, charmingly displays a childlike affection for modern-age transport. (Detail, above) 108

Dominoes and playing cards are important forms of relaxation. Both these signed sarongs are from north-coast Java. (Details, top right) 109, 110

Arab influence is clear in this sarong, which was drawn in Pekalongan and dyed in Semarang. (Detail, right) 111

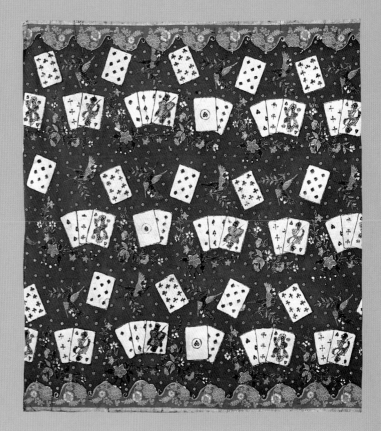

In spite of the ravages of war, the destruction of the class system, and strong competition, the batik of Java—like the arts and crafts of many another newly independent nation—reemerged as a symbol of nationhood. Under Sukarno, the Indonesian government helped the batik industry by establishing a huge system of cooperatives known as GKBI (*Gabungan Koperasi Batik Indonesia*). Since 1955, GKBI has been the single major importer and distributor of cotton cloth. Each of Java's major cities has at least one batik cooperative; Pekalongan has six. GKBI continues to be an important force in the business of batik.

The postwar renaissance of batik can be credited, most of all, to the efforts of two men of very different backgrounds. They were responsible for *Batik Indonesia*, a movement that brought back almost forgotten traditional patterns in a brilliant harmony of color. Surabaya-born Sukarno, president of Indonesia, publicly encouraged the batik movement, and Surakarta's K.R.T. Hardjonagoro, a formidable scholar of Chinese descent, made modern batik a viable art. *Batik Indonesia* combined central Javanese patterns from Surakarta and Yogyakarta with north-coast colors and techniques. Royal patterns from the courts of Cirebon underwent a metamorphosis, and Hardjonagoro even incorporated woven Balinese motifs into batik designs.

K.R.T. Hardjonagoro was a student at the university in Jakarta, interested in Javanese philosophy, history, and culture—especially dance—when he first met Sukarno. Indonesia's president encouraged the young scholar to return to Surakarta to revive postwar batik making. After all, Hardjonagoro came from a family that had made batik—*cap* only—for three generations. He had studied with Mrs. Bintang Sudibyo, who had been instrumental in developing indigenous Indonesian taste by using green and purple rather than the colors preferred by the Europeans and Chinese.

Hardjonagoro was skeptical about Sukarno's enthusiasm; nevertheless he set off on an indirect route to central Java. He traveled along the north coast and from there went to Bali with his Jakarta professor, Dr. Tjan Tjoe Siem. In Bali, at the home of the German painter Walter Spies, Hardjonagoro was inspired to marry the techniques and colors of north-coast batik with those of central Java.

Returning to Surakarta, Hardjonagoro established his own small *tulis* batik factory, experimenting with new and old design motifs. When President Sukarno saw this new *Batik Indonesia*, he was delighted, announcing publicly that he would personally buy every piece. *Batik Indonesia* became the rage. Entrepreneurs, eager to make quick money, copied the new style indiscriminately. Most copies were *cap*, and their garish colors screamed for attention: they lacked Hardjonagoro's beauty of design and subtlety of hues. But they did have the virtue of bearing the name *Batik Indonesia*.

Hardjonagoro's fertile mind continued to adapt, reinvent, and experiment with ideas. For example, he mixed natural indigo and *soga* dyes with chemical dyes to prevent fading. The more he learned about Javanese philosophy, the more his batik came to reflect central Java. Hardjonagoro became court adviser for cultural affairs and founded the museum of the *kraton* in Surakarta in 1963. Sixteen years later he was recognized as a cultural leader in Javanese life when he was elevated to *Bupati Sepuh* or Senior Regent, an unprecedented honor for a non-Javanese.

Both his lofty honor and his learning have been important to the way Hardjonagoro operates his batik factory. Unlike other owners, Hardjonagoro explains to his workers the significance of motifs. Working for a nobleman apparently gives his batikers a special status: "The product satisfies them . . . they're working for someone highly exposed to culture and the outside world." Without the hard work and inspiration of Hardjonagoro and the will of Sukarno, *Batik Indonesia* would never have become a reality. Others were to follow in their footsteps, but not before Indonesia had endured more suffering.

The process of independence and nationalization under Sukarno was dramatic. As Sukarno increasingly usurped power in the years from 1958 to 1968, the country found itself in turmoil: an attempted Communist coup, the execution of nearly seven hundred fifty thousand people (mostly Chinese), massive student riots. Twenty years later, it is estimated that 10 million people have been persecuted and one hundred thousand are believed still to be held prisoner.

Suharto, a general in the army, toppled Sukarno in 1968 and set about unifying Indonesia's many nationalities, religions, and political factions. "Unity in Diversity" described the national goal, and with Suharto came a new elite.

At the center of the elite were the new president and

his wife, who attempted to make batik a part of Indonesian life. They did this in two ways. In the first instance, Suharto decreed that black tie was out for evening wear, batik was in. Henceforth at formal occasions, men would wear open batik shirts, not the confining dinner jackets of the West. The shirts instantly caught on among the international set, as well as with the locals.

Secondly, Mrs. Suharto began a new fashion in batik design. Born in central Java, she was raised at the court of Prince Mangkunegara in Surakarta. Mrs. Suharto preferred the brown batik made exclusively for royalty by the small workshop of Princess Ayu Harjowiratmo. These pieces were distinguished more by their color than by their motifs. The batik was yellowish brown, a color that probably came from the high calcium content in the water of Wonogiri, a town south of Surakarta where the dyeing was done. North-coast manufacturers made *cap* copies of Wonogiri batik as long as the fashion lasted.

A period of relative prosperity for Java followed. Despite continuing problems of overpopulation, poverty, and illiteracy, petrodollars bought new highways, hotels, and office buildings. Diversity of design and technique, no longer hobbled by geographic distance or rigid custom, now encouraged the development of Java's modern batik artists—but in some cases paved a perilous road to bad design.

Suharto, who became president of Indonesia in 1968, encouraged the use of batik in formal dress. Here he wears an iket kepala.

K.R.T. Hardjonagoro revived traditional batik designs during the 1950s. Batik Indonesia combined designs and colors from the north coast and central Java.

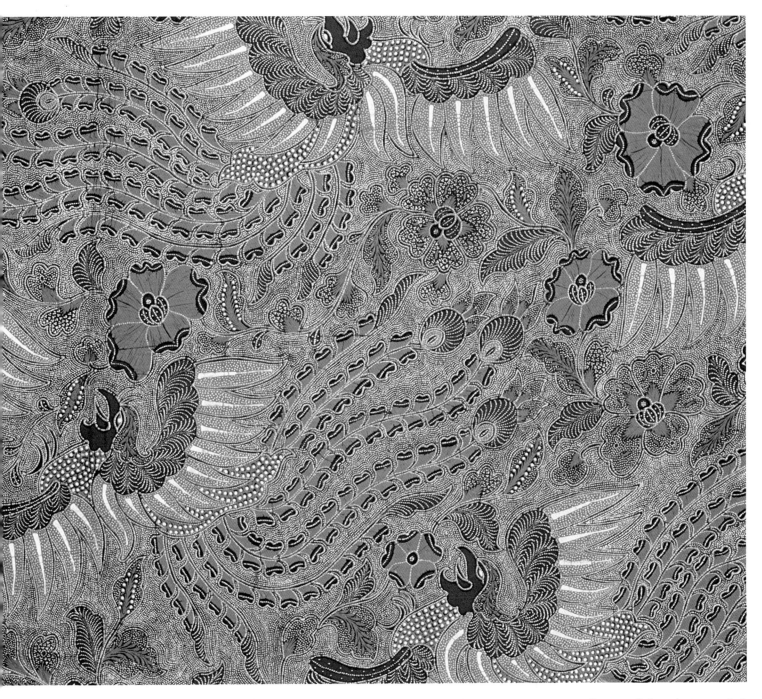

Sawung Galing *design made by K.R.T. Hardjonagono about 1970. The dyes are natural and synthetic, the technique tulis. (Above)* 112

Ardiyanto Pranata experiments with new designs, often blending them with older batik techniques, as in this silk selendang. (Detail, far left) 113

A modern version of the classic parang *pattern is enlivened by the irregular width of its diagonals. (Detail, left)* 114

Modern Trends

Batik Indonesia and Hardjonagoro's efforts rekindled an interest in the ancient art. Designers were intrigued by Hardjonagoro's ability to unify both north-coast and central-Javanese designs as well as his dramatic enlargement of traditional patterns. Ardiyanto Pranata was one who elaborated on north-coast batik in his wall hangings.

There were many changes in batik during this period. Cloth for batiking was traditionally, at most, forty inches wide. Not until the late 1960s did batik motifs explode—when Jakarta's Iwan Tirta began to use cotton that was fifty-eight inches wide. Tirta went one step further: he used these wide batiks with their massive figures of dragons and lions for women's clothing. It was a break with tradition, for while large motifs had been worn by men in Javanese high society prior to World War II, women were always more modestly clad in *kain panjangs* of smaller, more delicate designs.

Unlike Hardjonagoro, Iwan Tirta did not come from a batik family. Born in 1935 in Blora, central Java, he was educated as a lawyer at the University of Indonesia and at Yale Law School. In the late 1960s, Tirta began studying the sacred dances of the court of Surakarta. Surrounded by Javanese courtiers and stimulated by the rich cultural environment, he decided to embark on a career in batik, launching his own Jakarta-based company in 1970.

Tirta's batik attracted a great deal of attention in the international fashion world because of his innovative use of materials—including silk—and his unusual designs. Although few batik workers today are capable of fine work, they can quite easily wax Tirta's large, bold designs. Tirta pioneered in several ways: he enlarged traditional patterns with a few bold colors, he made batik for both clothing and home furnishings, and he experimented with *cap* batik by the yard.

Pekalongan's Achmad Yahya is another leading maker of modern-day batik. A devout Muslim and a third-generation batik maker, he is one of the few Javanese involved in design who owns his own factory. Born in 1929 to a Pekalongan family that owned the largest batik compound at the turn of the century, Yahya did not become interested in batik until 1955 when his parents died. He inherited some of his grandfather's *caps*, bought some more, and began to work with both *tulis* and *cap*. But business to Yahya was always secondary to the teachings of the Koran. A rare employer by any standard, Yahya's concern for others was shown when he built houses for his workers and offered them medical care.

Yahya and his Cirebon-born wife exemplify how batikers have adapted to consumer demand, rather than slavishly following old influences. Fourteen years ago he produced only sarongs and *kain panjangs*, which were sold locally. Within two years he had learned to make batik by the yard with complicated motifs, using both *tulis* and *cap*. New design configurations were drawn and special tables for waxing were erected. After mastering batik by the yard, he then learned about dyeing so that he could achieve a pastel palette on yard goods.

Two minutes by bicycle from Yahya's compound, behind a wall topped by glass shards to keep away intruders, lies the house and factory of eighty-three-year-old Achmad Said, a truly original batik artist and manufacturer whose family came to Surabaya in the fifteenth century. Members of the family intermarried with Ja-

The secretive walls of Lasem.

vanese and for hundreds of years continued to travel back and forth between Arabia and Java.

Said's great-grandmother made batik in Surabaya, but until Achmad Said set up shop in 1935, no one else in the family had been interested in batik. Said had made frequent trips to Pekalongan buying the batik of Jans, van Zuylen, and Oey Soe Tjoen, among others, to sell in Surabaya. It was in Pekalongan, where he eventually settled, that Said found his great gift for color and pattern. He also discovered a talent for business. Today Said exports to Dubai, Malaysia, Singapore, and Thailand. He is able to produce only a quarter of the pieces that are ordered each month.

The workmanship of Said is not especially distinguished; he makes only *cap* batik, but it is the wildly extravagant patterns that make his work distinctive.

A cacophony of image and sound in Tegal.

Working on primissima, a fine cotton ground, Said splashes his sarongs and *kain panjangs* with a bold array of geometric backgrounds on which bouquets of flowers are superimposed, creating a two- or three-layered effect. No one else has put geometry, nature, and color to such imaginative use.

Thirty-eight miles to the east, in Cirebon, H. Mohammed Masina, fifty-nine, and his wife have revived some of the sacred royal patterns of the court of Cirebon. It was not the Masinas, but another couple, the Madmils, who first unearthed some of the noble Cirebon designs. Because the batik work of the Masinas was so extraordinarily fine, they are given the credit for this renaissance. Iwan Tirta, too, was important in this development because he popularized the large royal lions on oversize cotton sheets, sometimes even commissioning the Masinas to batik his designs.

Both Masinas are third-generation batik makers who use traditional browns on cream or tan grounds. Chinese blues and reds characterize their palette as well. There are few north-coast batikers these days who produce Cirebon batiks in *tulis* as well as the Masinas; indeed, had it not been for the Masinas's fine technique, there would not have been anyone to carry on the Cirebon batik tradition. The Masinas are fortunate: three of their children are in the batik business.

In the four decades since 1945, batik has become more Indonesian—even international—than strictly Javanese. It is now almost impossible to recognize the locale where modern motifs originated, much less the designer. What is interesting about these modern trends and designers is that their distinctive styles are adapted from all parts of Java, especially the north coast. Their roots are as diverse as their batik.

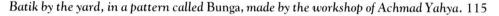

Batik by the yard, in a pattern called Bunga, *made by the workshop of Achmad Yahya.* 115

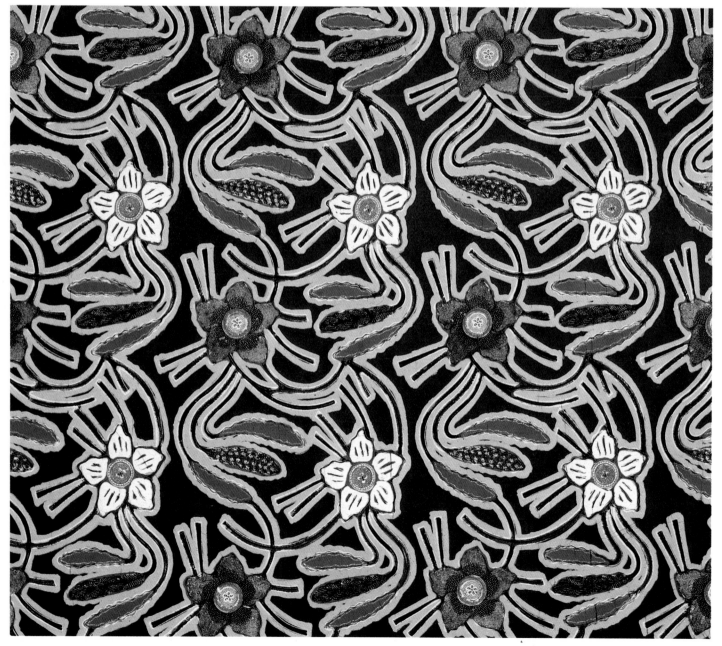

Achmad Yahya, a designer and entrepreneur, stands before an unfinished batik.

H. Mohammed Masina and his wife revived many of the sacred royal patterns of Cirebon.

Iwan Tirta is shown with a classic example of a dodot in his Jakarta shop.

Kain panjang *made in the Masina workshop uses the traditional browns and blues on a cream and tan ground.* 116

Batik for Clothing—and Home

Javanese wear batik clothing less frequently these days. In smaller villages, one can still see both men and women wearing sarongs and *kain panjangs*, and servants of the wealthy are encouraged to wear traditional batik. But in larger urban centers most people wear Western-style clothing, even though women's dresses of synthetic fibers are not as appropriate as batiked cotton to the Javanese climate.

In the late 1960s, yet another revolution in batik production occurred—akin to the introduction of the *cap* more than a century before. An enterprising couple in Jakarta discovered that by changing the equipment for dyeing, waxing, and drying, they were able to batik pieces much longer than the traditional two- or three-yard lengths. Yardage batik meant that it could be used in a variety of new ways—for home furnishings such as draperies, upholstery, and even wallcovering, as well as in the manufacture of Western-style shirts, skirts, and dresses. At first the traditional narrow cotton was used; later wider and heavier groundcloths were preferred.

The pioneering factory in this type of batik was Curcuma, in Jakarta. Perhaps some techniques were learned from the Dutch in eastern Holland, who had mastered waxing and dyeing batik yardage years earlier; the origin of the inspiration is unknown. Curcuma made *cap* batik, producing two-color cloth in thirty-two-yard bolts. Unfortunately, the factory soon folded, but the idea was brought to other batik manufacturers in Jakarta and Pekalongan. Longer tables were built for waxing, rollers and racks were installed to handle the waxed cloth so it would not crack, and larger tubs were built for dyeing and washing.

It was possible, by 1974, to produce running yardage in eight colors, combining both *cap* and *tulis* techniques. The more complicated the design and the more colors required, however, the shorter the yardage. Thus, to guarantee quality, no more than ten to sixteen yards could be produced at one time. Even with fewer colors and only the use of *cap*, it was difficult to make one bolt exactly match another.

Batik by the yard spread throughout Java and to countries around the world, attracting a greater audience than ever before. Nevertheless, the very nature of the batik-making process still limits its quantity and quality. If every yard must mimic exactly the yard before and after, the batik process cannot be used. For batik, despite its cooperative production, is a highly individual art that defies exact reproduction.

Modern townspeople of Pekalongan sometimes wear traditional batik, although this custom is fast dying out.

The Future of Batik

In 1970 there were nearly seven hundred thousand batik workers on the north coast of Java, but within thirteen years their numbers had been reduced to about two hundred fifty thousand. There are many reasons for the decline of batik: the breakdown of a feudal society; the decline of batik as clothing; the policy of transmigration; the competition from Malaysia and Singapore and from "batik" screenprints; the arcane import and export policies; and the fact that Javanese women, as they became better educated, sought other careers.

Unlike many other parts of Southeast Asia, in the four decades since World War II there has been little evidence of entrepreneurial fervor in the Indonesian textile industry. The Javanese are still probably the largest dealers in batik, although not necessarily the most influential. High interest rates, government intervention, and a limited appetite for work are not particularly conducive to a healthy business. "A swollen and ill-paid bureaucracy" offers little help to the factory owner who may need a loan. To add further to his woes, the sale of batik fluctuates wildly: the largest local sales always come before major holidays or ceremonies such as weddings and birthdays.

The textile industry is the only major industry in modern Indonesia that is based on imported raw materials; it is "not competitive enough to prevent substantial textile imports." The irony here is that in a nation that is fiercely overpopulated and has a low per-capita income, batik *should* be a thriving business because the process is labor intensive and the need for capital is minimal. But sadly, because of overwhelmingly adverse economic factors, batik probably will never become more than a major cottage industry.

Economics is not the whole story. Batik is a cooperative art. No single artist—no Leonardo da Vinci, no Manet, no Picasso—has evolved from batik because the production of a piece of cloth involves everyone from designer to entrepreneur, from waxer to dyer to *tulis* craftsman. In such an enterprise, few individuals receive much recognition. Their reasons for making batik are as varied as mankind itself: beauty, devotion, habit, need—even greed.

Recalling Cirebon court motifs, this modern wall hanging was designed by Iwan Tirta and made by the Masinas on a king-size sheet. The peksinagaliman *flanking each side of a cave is derived from Hindu mythology; the lotus is a sign of royalty.* 117

Some Javanese take a particularly snobbish view of batik, believing that form and function should be as one; that batik should convey symbolic information; that mere visual beauty is worthless unless accompanied by aesthetics, ethics, and religion. To these sticklers, modern batik has become a lowly decorative art rather than the realization of philosophic ideas.

The problem with such an exclusionary view is its definition of beauty. A batik may be full of meaning and still not be a work of art. Or, a batik may be beautiful without having a philosophy behind it. Similarly, just because a batik is old does not mean that it is beautiful or useful; and just because it is new does not mean that it is ugly or useless.

The aesthetic questions about batik are simple. Does a piece inspire? Does it provoke? Does it explode with energy?

Modern batik designers are aware that theirs is an art whose heyday is past. They search for new inspirations in their roots and in new techniques. By the twenty-

first century, *cap* batik will probably give way almost entirely to screenprinting; *tulis* will continue in limited quantity for a rich clientele. Rather than representing aspects of Javanese life, culture, and religion, batik will be more and more the inspiration of particular designers. No doubt their best work will be seen as art, used for wall hangings or perhaps even for ceremonial and religious occasions. Ironically, this was the original use of the cloth. After more than two hundred years, batik will have come full circle.

Achmad Yahya's workshop developed a method for making tulis and cap batik by the yard. Women sit by smoldering wax, drawing tulis designs onto the already block-printed batik. (Opposite)
In the backyard of his house where Achmad Said has his batik factory, young girls enliven each design with handpainting. (Below)

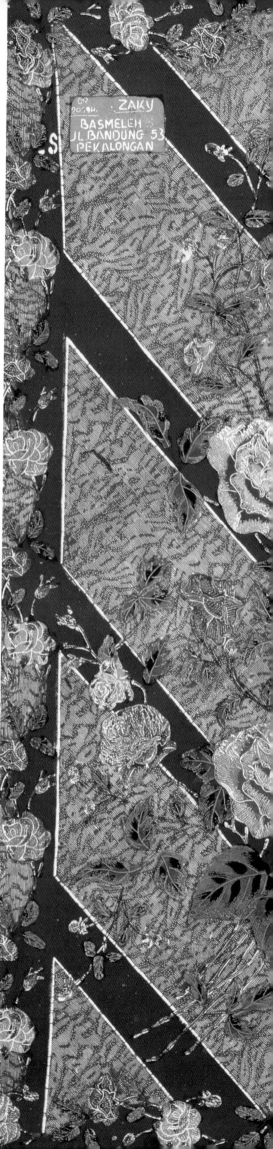

Achmad Said, 83, sold and bought batik throughout northern Java until he settled in Pekalongan. Of Arab origin, he makes and sells his vivid sarongs worldwide.
Colorful sarongs with bold geometric backgrounds and floral bouquets are a specialty of Said's batik factory. (Detail, below) 118
"ZAKY" is the signature of Said's batik. There is no mistaking his hand or his address in the unusual sarong on the right. (Detail) 119

GLOSSARY

The pronunciation of the Indonesian language is basically phonetic: vowels are short (fAther, Ebb, chIlly, ShOck, pUt) and the consonants are hard (G as in grill, J as in jail, T as in take, etc.). Some peculiarities are that the letter C is pronounced as "ch" (the Indonesian word CAP, therefore, sounds like "chop") and the letter combination NY is much the same as the Spanish ñ, as in mañana.

Alasalasan: Motif depicting flora and fauna, suggesting productivity and protection of crops.

Alun-Alun: Grassy common in the center of each Javanese town.

Analine Dye: Synthetic, nonorganic dye; a colorless, oily liquid.

Badan: Body of a sarong, about three-quarters the length of entire cloth.

Bahasa Indonesia: National *lingua franca* of Indonesia since 1942.

Banji: Chinese swastika-like symbol often used in batik.

Bang Biru: Literally, red blue.

Becaks: Pedicab-tricycles used everywhere in Java as transportation.

Belah Ketupat: Simple check design.

Biron: From *biru*, meaning blue.

Borobudur: Ninth-century Buddhist temple in central Java.

Çanga: Snail or conch shell motif representing Visṇu.

Canting: Basic tool with which hand-drawn *tulis* batik is made.

Cap: Copper block used to apply wax to cloth. Sometimes written *tjap*.

Cempakamulya: Special batik worn by parents of both bride and groom at Chinese wedding.

Cemukiran: Raylike pattern similar to *parang*.

Ceplok: Category of patterns based on repeating squares, rectangles, ovals, and stars.

Dodot: Batik made by sewing two *kain panjangs* together.

Dua Negeri: "Two countries," or batik made in two cities or areas.

Garuda: Mythical beast, a symbol of God and Father Heaven.

Gringsing: Fish-scale motif found in batik.

Hokokai: Batik made during World War II and name of Japanese political organization.

Iket Kepala: Batik headcloth.

Indigo: Grown everywhere, the indigo plant provides the most common color found in batik.

Indische: People of European and/or European/Asian origin who lived in the Dutch East Indies for a long time.

Inding: The batik worn by Javanese women when menstruating.

Isén: Fine "filling" or intricate patterning found within a batik motif.

Kain Panjang: "Long cloth" approximately two and a half to three yards long; entire surface is decorated, often with borders at the shorter ends.

Kampong: Compound or tiny village found throughout Indonesian archipelago.

Kawung: Four-petal blossom which, with its central element, represents Buddhism's five cardinal directions.

Kebaya: Long-sleeved blouse, usually decorated with lace and embroidery; worn with a sarong or *kain panjang*.

Kemben: Narrow batik, or breast cloth, wrapped around upper part of the body to fasten a *kain panjang* or sarong.

Kepala: "Head" of a sarong has wide perpendicular band usually in middle or end with color and pattern dissimilar to the body or *badan*.

Keris: Dagger or sword, once carried by Javanese men of all classes.

Kodi: Form of measurement; one *kodi* equals twenty batik pieces.

Kraton: Javanese court.

Liman: Elephant.

Lokcan: Particular type of silk batik.

Megamendung: Cloud motif found in batik.

Modang: Plain-colored centerpiece in batik.

Mengkudu: Natural red color derived from the *Morinda citrifolia* plant.

Naga: Dragon or snake motif.

Naphthol Dye: Also called Azoic and used on cotton and linen.

Ngregreng: The first waxing of a batik.

Pagi-Sore: "Morning-evening" cloth; longer than a *kain panjang*, usually each half has a different design and color.

Parang: "Broken-knife" motif, and a diagonal; probably related in meaning to the *keris*, or dagger.

Parang Rusak: Diagonal motif; variation of *parang*.

Pesisir: Beach, or coastal area.

Peksinagaliman: Motif combining phoenix, dragon, and elephant.

Pinarada Mas: Batik embellished with gold leaf or gold thread.

Pinggir: Borders lining selvedges of a sarong.

Plangi: Technique of tying and dyeing cloth.

Prada: Batik enriched with gold leaf.

Sarong: Waistcloth worn by Javanese and Malays; probably originated in India.

Selendang: Long narrow cloth exclusively used by women as a carryall or shawl.

Semen: Means "to sprout" or "to grow"; refers to the curling tendrils in the background pattern of batik.

Soga: Rich brown dye from bark of the *Pelthophorum ferrugineum* tree; characteristic of batik from Yogyakarta and Surakarta.

Singa: Lion.

Tambal: Patchwork batik; design looks as if cloth were patched.

Taplak: Napkin covering lap of a batik worker to protect her from hot, dripping wax.

Tengahan: Plain-colored portion in the middle of an *iket kepala*.

Tiga Negeri: "Three countries"; batik made in three regions or cities.

Tom: Javanese name for indigo.

Tulis: Hand-drawn batik.

Truntum: Geometric star-shaped design meaning "budding of love" or "happiness."

Tumpal: Two rows of equilateral triangles facing each other that run down each side of *kepala* of a sarong.

Udan Liris: "Light-rain" motif combining variety of designs within parallel diagonal lines.

Visṇu: Hindu God.

VOC: *Vereenigde Oost-Indische Compagnie*, or Dutch East India Trading Company, established in 1602 by Holland.

Wada: Rock-shape motif from Hindu art.

Wali: Prominent religious leader and Prophet of Islam.

Wayang: Puppet used in storytelling, from epic Javanese scriptures.

NOTES

1. TALES OF A TRADE ROUTE ISLAND

Pg. 22: **have been batiked:** Steinmann, 1958, 27.

Pg. 22: **batik making, appeared:** Rouffaer, 1917, 199.

Pg. 22: **sent to Sumatra:** *Ibid.*, 192.

Pg. 22: **dot, or drop:** Larsen, 1976, 77.

Pg. 22: **a "cotton printer":** Raffles, 1817, Vol. I, 164.

Pg. 23: **very unsatisfactory condition":** Cited in Lattimore, 1968, 43, from *The Travels of Fa-Hsien*, trans. by H. A. Giles.

Pg. 24: **purpose of life":** Wolters, 1974, Vol. IX, 480.

Pg. 24: **of east Java:** Steinmann, op. cit., 36.

Pg. 24: **common laborer upward":** Raffles, *op. cit.*, 308–309.

Pg. 24: **of the Indies:** Neil, 1973, 243.

Pg. 24: **thereby cleanse it:** Wolters, *op. cit.*, 481.

Pg. 24: **preservatives, and flavorings:** The spice trade resembled the lucrative opium trade. Opium was cheap to buy and easy to transport; it had a huge international market and the profits were enormous.

Pg. 25: **people in Malacca:** D.G.E. Hall, 1964, 199; and Schrieke, 1955, 18.

Pg. 25: **than thirty thousand:** Schrieke, *op. cit.*, 2.

Pg. 25: **garments and hangings":** Rawson, 1974, Vol. 17, 272.

Pg. 28: **silk to China:** Loeber, 1926, 17; according to Lattimore (*op. cit.*, 330) the Chinese regarded foreign trade more as a diplomatic gesture than as an economic necessity.

Pg. 28: **home once more:** Cited in Schrieke, *op. cit.*, 20.

Pg. 28: **magnificence and majesty:** de Bry, 1601, 29.

Pg. 28: **Chinese-born ruler:** Melink-Roelofsz, 1962, 107.

Pg. 28: **Demak, and Banten:** Mills, 1979, 75, 83.

Pg. 28: **and overseas settlement:** Mackie, 1976, 4.

Pg. 28: **married to Javanese:** Raffles, *op. cit.*, 74.

Pg. 28: **artists of thriftiness":** Nieu-hoff, 1704, 314. (Nieuhoff's diaries are dated 1653 to 1662. They were first published in Holland in 1682; the 1704 edition is the English translation.)

Pg. 30: **of Asia's riches:** Lattimore, *op. cit.*, 117–118.

page 30: **on other shores":** Schrieke, *op. cit.*, 60.

Pg. 30: **such wanton destruction:** *Ibid.*, 72.

Pg. 31: **in the world":** Cited in Raffles, *op. cit.*, 192.

Pg. 36: **five thousand years:** Neil, *op. cit.*, 164.

Pg. 36: **East Indian archipelago:** Schrieke, *op. cit.*, 13.

Pg. 36: **and eighteenth centuries:** Steinmann, *op. cit.*, 27.

Pg. 36: **be batiked garments:** Nieu-hoff, *op. cit.*, illustrations throughout both editions.

Pg. 36: **yoke of Holland:** Jonge, 1862–1909, VI, 39, 83, 101; Dagh-Register, 1877 (1677, 93) and Graff, 1935, 13.

Pg. 36: **or painted cloth":** Raffles, *op. cit.*, 87.

Pg. 36: **ignored such strictures:** *Ibid.*, 85–86.

Pg. 36: **fit for weaving":** Nieuhoff, *op. cit.*, 332–334.

Pg. 36: **traditional Javanese loom:** Palmer, 1972, 16.

Pg. 36: **mistress, or daughter:** Raffles, *op. cit.*, 86.

Pg. 36: **out of India":** Linschoten, 1598, 34.

Pg. 36: **production of batik:** Day, 1966, 125.

Pg. 38: **slaves in Java:** Raffles, *op. cit.*, 76.

Pg. 38: **were not colorfast:** Veldhuisen, 1980, 14.

Pg. 41: **Java continued grimly:** Neil, *op. cit.*, 301.

Pg. 42: **again by 1900:** *Ibid.*, 293.

Pg. 42: **styles and specialties:** Veldhuisen, *op. cit.*, 42.

Pg. 52: **its better batik:** *Ibid.*, 14.

Pg. 52: **earlier Dutch material:** Mrs. Oey Soe Tjoen, personal communication, 1982–1983.

Pg. 52: **receive the dyes:** Cited by Gittinger, 1979, 117.

Pg. 52: **to absorb wax:** Hamzuri, 1981, 11.

Pg. 52: **on the cotton:** de Raadt-Apell, 1980–1981, 85.

Pg. 52: **the batik process:** Abdurachman, personal communication, 1983.

Pg. 52: **in the world:** Steinman, *op. cit.*, 17.

Pg. 56: **ready for sale:** Ibu Praptini, 1983, field work.

Pg. 58: **even shredded chicken:** Tirta and Lau, 1966, 23.

2. BATIK IN THE ROYAL COURTS

Pg. 63: **the highest arts:** Raffles, 1817, Vol. I, 258, from the *Niti sastra*, one of the greatest Javanese moral works: "Man is pleased with the *dodot* cloth . . . and women are proud of their bosom; but a good man prefers the sacred writings, which may lead him to the life to come."

Pg. 64: **near his spirit":** Hardjonagoro, 1979, 229.

Pg. 64: **early as 1817:** Raffles, *op. cit.*, 168.

page 64: **for his family:** Rouffaer and Juynboll, 1914, 438–439.

Pg. 66: **sources of income:** Hawkins, 1961, 52.

Pg. 66: **accumulation of virtue":** Labin, 1979, 42.

Pg. 67: **in his lifetime":** Wolters, 1972, Vol. 17, 480.

Pg. 67: **of loose character":** Raffles, *op. cit.*, 255, from the *Raja Kapa-kapa*, a series of laws promulgated by the sultans.

Pg. 67: **keep disease away:** Hardjonagoro, 1983, personal communication.

Pg. 67: **around her neck;** *Ibid.*

Pg. 68: **a simplified lotus:** Solyom, *op. cit.*, 66.

Pg. 68: **[of] the cloth:** *Ibid.*, 61.

Pg. 68: **by all classes":** Raffles, *op. cit.*, 87.

page 68: **mean "enemy destroying":** Solyom, *op. cit.*, 69.

Pg. 68: **related to agriculture:** Veldhuisen-Djajasoebrata, 1979, 210.

Pg. 68: **a cosmic order:** Solyom, *op. cit.*, 249–257.

Pg. 68: **of the crops:** *Ibid.*, 258.

Pg. 82: **or gold streaks:** Nieuhoff, 1704, 301.

Pg. 82: **with the gold:** Solyom, 1977, 63.

3. JOURNEY TO PEKALONGAN

Pg. 94: **conservative, and snobbish:** Tirta, personal communication, 1983.

Pg. 94: **style, and motif:** *Ibid.*

Pg. 94: **as their laborers:** *Ibid.*

Pg. 95: **selling their labor:** *Ibid.*

Pg. 96: **for more cloth:** Veldhuisen, 1980, 29.

Pg. 96: **flowers or leaves:** *Ibid.*, 15–17.

Pg. 98: **for good luck:** Hardjonagoro, personal communication, 1983.

Pg. 102: **to the Indies:** de Raadt-Apell, 1980–1981, 92.

Pg. 106: **in a factory:** Veldhuisen, *op. cit.*, 15.

Pg. 106: **against work due:** *Ibid.*, 15.

Pg. 106: **to a Frenchman:** *Ibid.*, 39.

Pg. 106: **from this motif:** *Ibid.*, 28–29.

Pg. 106: **are well documented:** The most recent research in this area is Veldhuisen's *Blauw en Bont (Blue and White)* published in 1980; and de Raadt-Apell's *De Batkerij van Zuylen te Pekalongan* published also in 1980.

Pg. 106: **quarter of that:** Tirta, *op. cit.*

Pg. 106: **well-liked businesswoman":** Said, personal communication, 1983.

Pg. 106: **unable to match:** de Raadt-Apell, *op. cit.*, 86–87.

Pg. 106: **a nearby village:** *Ibid.*, 87.

Pg. 106: **and special colors:** Veldhuisen, *op. cit.*, 31.

Pg. 118: **the most important:** Other Chinese batik makers along the north coast whose works are memorable include in Kedungwuni: Gan Tjing Nio, Liem Ping Wio, Na Swan Hien, and Oei Sing Djuan; in Pekalongan: Gan Tjoe Liam, Oey Ghing Lim, Oei Hian Swie, Oey King Lim, and Tan It Long; and in Tegal: Tjioe Ertin. Some are still alive and working. For further

names see Veldhuisen's *Blauw en Bont.*

Pg. 118: **the wedding ceremony:** Idris, personal communication, 1983.

Pg. 118: **background symbolizing wisdom:** Mrs. Oey Soe Tjoen, personal communication, 1983.

Pg. 120: **Java or China:** Gittinger, 1982, 41.

Pg. 120: **a Dutch citizen:** Mackie, 1976, 9.

Pg. 120: **batik was immediate:** Hardjonagoro, personal communication, 1983.

Pg. 122: **yet in vogue:** Hendromartono, personal communication, 1983 to end of section unless otherwise noted.

Pg. 122: **is still working:** Liem Siok Hien married Oey Djien Nio.

Pg. 128: **is not signed:** de Raadt-Apell, 1980–1982, 86.

Pg. 128: **retraced in wax:** *Ibid.*, 86.

Pg. 130: **Oey Soe Tjoen":** Tan, personal communication, 1982.

Pg. 130: **largely Chinese clientele:** Mrs. Oey, personal communication, 1982–1983 to end of section unless otherwise noted. When Netty Kwee signed her batik she used the name of her husband, Oey Soe Tjoen.

Pg. 130: **mix *soga* brown:** Tirta, *op. cit.*

4. JOURNEY TO GRESIK

Pg. 144: **rather amazing enterprise:** *Ibid.*

Pg. 144: **a limited clientele:** *Ibid.*

Pg. 150: **Hong Kong, and Shanghai:** Kat Angelino, *op. cit.*, 258.

Pg. 150: **most important deity:** Hardjonagoro, personal communication, 1983.

Pg. 150: **Tan Kian Poen:** Tirta, *op. cit.*

Pg. 152: ***tulis* and *cap*:** Veldhuisen *op. cit.*, 29.

Pg. 152: **fewer than twenty:** Sutjahjo, personal communication, 1983.

Pg. 152: **copy their techniques:** Tirta, *op. cit.*

Pg. 152: **common field laborer:** Kat Angelino, 1930, Vol. 2, 270.

Pg. 170: **the independence movement:** Hawkins, *op. cit.*, 71.

5. MODERN BATIK

Pg. 178: **else was confiscated:** Anonymous, personal communication, 1982–1983.

Pg. 178: **of batik exhibits:** Takashi Shiraishi, personal communication, 1983. The Japanese also established a war-time *Hokokai* organization in Manchuria. Sometimes Javanese World War II batik is known as *Djawa Baru* meaning "New Java." This was meant to imply that although the Japanese occupied Java, it was free from the Dutch and a nation of its own.

Pg. 178: **signed or stamped:** Idris, personal communication, 1983.

Pg. 182: **make a living:** Neil, *op. cit.*, 309.

page 186: **of cotton cloth:** Hawkins, *op. cit.*, 55.

Pg. 186: **first met Sukarno:** Hardjonagoro was born Go Tik Swan. All that follows is personal communication 1983 except where otherwise noted.

Pg. 186: **a non-Javanese:** Veldhuisen-Djajasoebrata, 1979, 235.

Pg. 186: **the outside world":** Hardjonagoro, *op. cit.*

Pg. 186: **be held prisoner:** Cited in the *Radcliffe Quarterly*, December 1983, 19–20.

Pg. 187: **dyeing was done:** Tirta, personal communication, 1983.

Pg. 190: **his parents died:** Yahya, personal communication, 1982–1983 and all that follows unless otherwise noted.

Pg. 190: **the fifteenth century:** Said, personal communication, 1982–1983 and all that follows unless otherwise noted.

Pg. 192: **court of Cirebon:** Masina: personal communication 1983 and all that follows unless otherwise noted.

Pg. 196: **hundred fifty thousand:** Tirta, *op. cit.*

Pg. 196: **and ill-paid bureaucracy":** *Economist* Intelligence Unit, 1974, Vol. IX, 470.

Pg. 196: **substantial textile imports":** *Ibid.*, 469.

CONCORDANCE

1. *Kain Panjang Pagi-Sore,* Pekalongan, ca. 1915
Cotton, machine spun, synthetic dyes, *tulis*
Warp 252.3 cm./Weft 105 cm.
Signed: The Tie Siet Pekalongan
Collection: Inger McCabe Elliott, New York/#1126

Brilliant colors of royal blue and orange enliven traditional motifs of peacocks and birds, set against clean brilliant background colors. Synthetic dyes in combination with soft floral forms edged with elegant geometric Art Deco borders were hallmark of The Tie Siet.

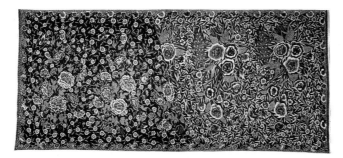

2. *Kain Panjang Pagi-Sore,* North Coast, 1942–1945
Cotton, machine spun, synthetic (possibly natural indigo) dyes, *tulis*
Warp 240.5 cm./Weft 106 cm.
Collection: Inger McCabe Elliott, New York/#1250

Probably made during the Japanese occupation of Java, this predominantly blue and green *kain* with bright accents of color is packed with details, typical of batik made during this period.

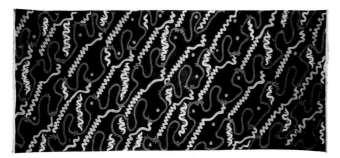

3. *Kain Panjang,* Garut (?), ca. 1900
Cotton, machine spun, natural dyes (?), *tulis*
Warp 243 cm./Weft 106 cm.
Collection: Tropen Museum, Amsterdam/Series 862/No. 9

Striking for its bold and primitive style, batik has serpentine and corkscrew-shaped figures in rich red and ivory intertwined with fish (?) and flower motifs. Batik resembles other early examples from West Java. (Tropen Museum reference no. 862/No. 10, II/4.)

4. *Tumpal Pasung Lokaan Naga* Sarong, Cirebon, ca. 1900
Cotton, machine spun, natural dyes, *tulis*
Warp 189 cm./Weft 102.5 cm.
Collection: Anita E. Spertus and Robert J. Holmgren, New York/#J126

Major motif is the *naga,* which may be interpreted as a snake, serpent, or dragon, symbolizing fertility.

5. *Tiga Negeri* Sarong, Pekalongan, 1910
Cotton, fine woven, natural dyes (?), *tulis*
Warp: 207 cm./Weft: 105.5 cm.
Collection: Inger McCabe Elliott, New York/#1152

Unusual *kepala* diagonals are combined with patchwork *badan* of classic Javanese patterns. These patterns include *parang* and *kawung.*

6. *Kain Panjang,* Kudus or Juana (?), ca. 1916
Cotton, machine spun, natural dyes, *tulis*
Warp 253 cm./Weft 104 cm.
Collection: Inger McCabe Elliott, New York/#1279

Extraordinary for its zigzag design, richly detailed background covered with oversize lilies. Natural dyes of indigo blue and *soga* brown are common to Juana and nearby Kudus. Fine *tulis* was made by unknown artist probably early twentieth century in Kudus or possibly Juana. Artistic style similar to numbers 74, 75, and 76. Possibly each piece made by same artist or workshop.

7. Sarong, Lasem (?), ca. 1910–1920
Cotton, machine spun, natural dyes, *tulis, prada*
Warp 203 cm./Weft 106.5 cm.
Collection: Lisbet Holmes and Henry Ginsburg, London

Unusual *kepala* with curvilinear *tumpal*. Gold-leaf sarong has traditional north-coast colors, *bang-biru* (red and blue). Phoenix (symbol of longevity) is interlaced between lotus (?) flowers (a symbol of purity). Sarong probably made to celebrate special occasion. *Kepala* seems influenced by earlier Indian trade textiles.

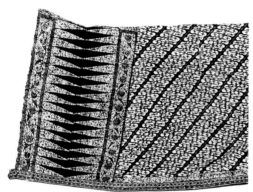

8. *Parang* Sarong (?), Java, ca. 1810–1820
Cotton, possibly handspun, natural dyes, *tulis*
Warp 220 cm./Weft 85 cm.
Collection: Museum of Mankind, London/#K75413 As 1939
A4. 119

Donated 1939 to Museum of Mankind by Mrs. J. M. Drake, granddaughter of Reverend Raffles Flint, nephew and heir of Sir Thomas Stamford Raffles. Batik probably brought to England in the early part of nineteenth century by Sir Thomas Stamford Raffles himself. One of earliest surviving examples of Javanese batik. Major motif: diagonal *parang* bordered by unusual double border on the bottom selvedge; outer of two, stitched onto batik. Two seams across width suggest that batik shortened from *kain panjang* to sarong.

9. *Mahabharata Bale Si Gala-gala* *Kain Panjang,* Cirebon, 1925
Cotton, machine spun, *tulis*
Warp 260 cm./Weft 106.5 cm.
Collection: Iwan Tirta, Jakarta

Batik tells an episode of *Mahabharata* epic from the *wayang* repertoire. *Wayang* figures drawn in two directions so cloth could be worn both ways.

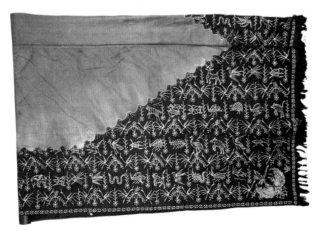

10. *Dodot Bangan Tulak Alasalasan Pinarada Mas*
Kain Dodot, Central Java, ca. 1900
Cotton, machine spun, natural dyes, *tulis, plangi, prada*
Warp 207 cm./Weft 385 cm.
Collection: Hans Siegel, Ronco/#B19

Alasalasan has plain background, unlike complicated tendril filled backgrounds of *semen*. Drawn in fine linear gold-leaf glue-work on dark blue background, rows of plant forms alternate with mythical animals. Mauve-colored central portion, achieved by *plangi*, is unusual. Scalloped edges of center portion achieved by binding and sewing cloth prior to dyeing. Pattern thought to be specific to Surakarta and used as ceremonial dress within courts. Two pieces joined together form ceremonial *dodot*; fringed at one end only. Almost identical example appears in *Indonesian Textiles,* Irene Emery Roundtable, 1979.

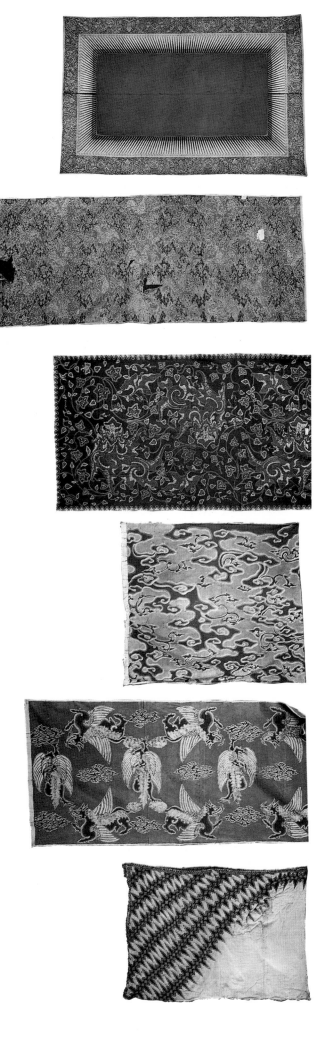

11. *Kain Dodot,* Yogyakarta, ca. 1900
Cotton, natural dyes, *tulis, prada*
Warp 320 cm./Weft 210 cm.
Collection: Smend Gallery, Cologne/#20

Splendid representation of once royal pattern and garment indicated by large rectangular solid (olive green) center field *(tenganhan).* Bordered by a knifelike variation of *parang* motif and *semen,* highlighted by *prada,* gold-leaf glue-work. *Lar* (wing) motif included in *semen* border both as single wings *(mirong)* and as double wings combined with a broad extended tail *(sawat).*

12. *Mega Soemirat Senggon Patran Ayam Alas*
Kain Panjang, Cirebon, ca. 1900–1910
Cotton, natural dyes (?), *tulis*
Warp 265 cm./Weft 105 cm.
Collection: State Museum of Yogyakarta, Sonobudoyo/#E/K 171/94

Rare batik of cloud motifs and cocks *(ayam alas)* are hidden in the delicate tracery of leafy vines *(patran).* Cock or rooster was regarded as symbol of strength, courage, and fertility, whereas vines symbolized vigor and tenacity.

13. *Singa Barong Semen* *Kain Panjang,* Cirebon, ca. 1910–1920
Cotton, machine spun, natural dyes, *tulis, prada*
Warp 265 cm./Weft 110 cm.
Collection: Museum Nasional, Jakarta/#20461

Graceful vines and leaf tendrils spiral around large abstract shapes suggesting monstrous creature *(barong).* Edged on all sides by stylized geometric borders, motifs are highlighted with gold-leaf glue-work. Batik is striking example of Cirebon style. Acquired in 1933 by the Museum Nasional.

14. *Megamendung* *Kain Panjang,* Cirebon, ca. 1900–1910
Cotton, natural dyes (?), *tulis*
Warp 236 cm./Weft 103.5 cm.
Collection: State Museum of Yogyakarta, Sonobudoyo/#E/K 170/93

Rain-cloud motifs *(megamendung)* in this classic and rare example were strongly influenced by Hindu art.

15. *Singa Barong* *Kain Panjang,* Cirebon, ca. 1900–1910
Cotton, machine spun, natural dyes (?), *tulis*
Warp 256 cm./Weft 105 cm.
Collection: Museum Nasional, Jakarta/#21739

Batik is combination of influences. Mythical beast motifs combine aspects of lion, dragon, and bird, with a cloudlike rock formation in background. Lion *(singa)* is symbolic of fertility; also wards off evil spirits. Dragon *(barong)* is symbol of underworld and fertility. Wings *(lar)* reminiscent of *garuda* wings. Museum Nasional bought batik from Thio Gwan Joe in 1936.

16. *Bangun Tulak Pilin Berganda*
Ceremonial *Kain Dodot,* Cirebon, ca. 1900
Cotton, handspun (?), fibers have a rough texture, *tulis*
Warp 280 cm./Weft 207 cm.
Collection: State Museum of Yogyakarta, Sonobudoyo/#E/K 164/87

Strong resemblance to *parang rusak* motif.

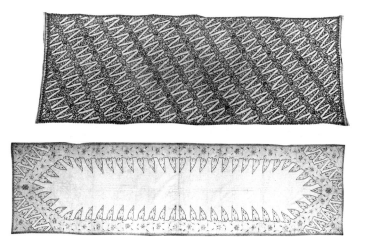

17. *Parang Kembang Ukel Kain Panjang*, Cirebon, ca. 1900
Cotton, handspun (?), (rough fibers), natural dyes (?), *tulis*
Warp 208 cm./Weft 100 cm.
Collection: State Museum of Yogyakarta, Sonobudoyo/#E/K
175/98

Flowering tendrils provide background for a diagonal *parang*.

18. *Selendang,* Cirebon, ca. 1910–1920
Cotton, natural dyes (?), *tulis* (?)
Warp 235 cm./Weft 62 cm.
Collection: State Museum of Yogyakarta, Sonobudoyo/#E/K
166/89

Clean, white center is edged with light blue border filled with delicate flowers and vines in tracery. *Tumpal*, or triangular shapes, point toward the center of cloth. Simple zigzag design resembling *parang* motif cuts diagonally through each corner of cloth. Suggests strong Indian trade influence.

19. *Iket Kepala,* Cirebon, ca. 1900–1910
Cotton, natural dyes (?), *tulis*
Warp 101 cm./Weft 98 cm.
Collection: State Museum of Yogyakarta, Sonobudoyo/#E/K
161/84

Headcloth unusual for its geometric solid indigo center (*tengahan*) softened by arabesque shapes bordering center.

20. *Iket Kepala,* Cirebon, ca. 1910–1920
Cotton, natural dyes (?), *tulis* (?)
Warp 105 cm./Weft 103 cm.
Collection: State Museum of Yogyakarta, Sonobudoyo/#E/K
238/161

Rosettes filled with flowers and leaves repeat in rich shades of indigo and red throughout headcloth.

21. *Iket Kepala,* Cirebon, ca. 1910–1920
Cotton, natural dyes (?), *tulis*
Warp 98 cm./Weft 93 cm.
Collection: State Museum of Yogyakarta, Sonobudoyo/#E/K
168/91

Headcloth with solid red diamond shape centered within cloth, edged by cloud motifs and birds. Cloth bordered on each side with *parang*-like motif.

22. *Nitik Kain Panjang,* Pekalongan, ca. 1920–1930
Cotton, machine spun, natural dyes (?), *tulis* (with square *canting*), *prada*
Warp 253 cm./Weft 103 cm.
Collection: Museum Nasional, Jakarta/#23731

Example of batik designed to resemble weaving. Powerful, bold, and rich in color.

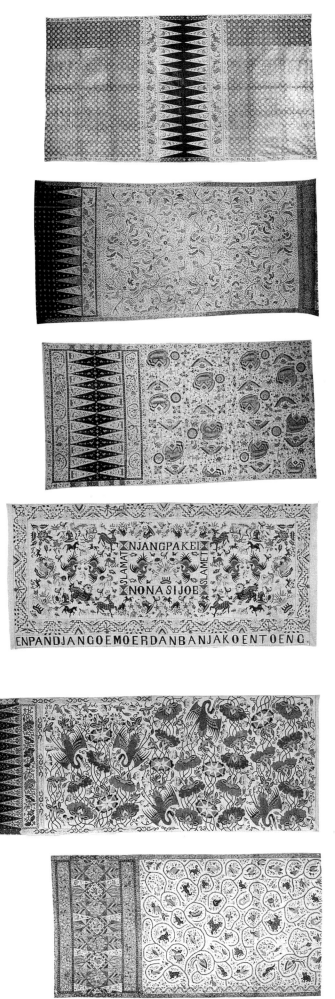

23. Sarong, Surabaya (?), ca. 1880–1900
Cotton, machine spun, natural dyes, *tulis, prada*
Warp 213 cm./Weft 110.5 cm.
Collection: Sergio Feldbauer, Milan

Overall design of *ceplok* alternating with *banji* fills body of sarong; probably used to celebrate a wedding. Gold only applied on the parts that show when worn.

24. Sarong, Lasem, ca. 1900–1910
Cotton, machine spun, natural dyes, *tulis, prada*
Warp 262 cm./Weft 108 cm.
Collection: Lisbet Holmes and Henry Ginsburg, London

Traditional north-coast sarong, in *bang-biru* (red and blue), embellished with gold-leaf glue-work, or *prada.*

25. Sarong, Cirebon, ca. 1900
Cotton, machine spun, natural dyes, *tulis, prada*
Warp 208 cm./Weft 108 cm.
Collection: Lisbet Holmes and Henry Ginsburg, London

Bold ships are major motif in body of sarong that is embellished by gold-leaf glue-work, or *prada.*

26. Tablecloth (?), Cirebon, ca. 1906
Cotton, machine spun, natural dyes, *tulis*
Warp 235 cm./Weft 105 cm.
Central Rectangle: *NJANGPAKEI SLAMAT (2) NONA SI JOE*
Border: *ENPANDJANGOEMOERDANBANJAKOENTOE*
Collection: Inger McCabe Elliott, New York/#1045

This cloth represents good luck to its owner, Nona Si Joe. *Slamat* (sometimes spelled *selamat*) means good luck; deer, longevity, and *chi'lin* indicates prosperity. Elegant geometric border probably mirrors stepped walls bordering Cirebon's royal courts. The inscription across the bottom border of this banner, "Long life and abundance of luck," sums up its meaning.

27. *Bang Ungon* *Kain Panjang,* Cirebon, ca. 1900
Cotton, machine spun, natural dyes (?), *tulis*
Warp 108.59 cm./Weft 271.78 cm.
Collection of Mary Hunt Kahlenberg and Dr. Anne Summerfield, Los Angeles/#21

Large stylized cranes and lotus flowers show considerable Chinese influence, while intertwining branches and floral forms reflect European Art Nouveau style.

28. *Tumpal Semen* Sarong, Cirebon, ca. 1910–1920
Cotton, machine spun, natural dyes (?), *tulis*
Warp 202 cm./Weft 104 cm.
Collection: Inger McCabe Elliott, New York/#1505

Gangan, the spiraling vine motif represents sea foliage; unites animals, birds, and sea life in this sarong. *Gangan* is typical of Cirebon batik, often used in Pekalongan, Lasem, and Madura batik as well. *Kepala,* with elaborate *tumpal,* is richly decorated, giving a patchwork effect.

29. *Taman Arum Sunya Ragi* *Kain Panjang*, Cirebon, ca. 1900
Cotton, machine spun, natural dyes, *tulis*
Warp 257 cm./Weft 112 cm.
Collection: Soelaeman Pringgodigdo, Jakarta

Classic design: *taman arum* is a garden found within the courts of Cirebon used by the Sultan for meditation and spiritual guidance. Cloudlike rock formations (*wadas*) along with ponds, trees, and *pendopo* (verandah or pavilion) are all elements of the garden.

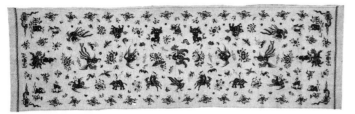

30. *Selendang,* Juana, ca. 1930–1940
Cotton, machine spun, natural dyes (?), *tulis* and *cap* (?)
Warp 213 cm./Weft 63 cm.
Collection: Jacques Gadbois

Chinese figures ride on fanciful animals—deer, lions, dragons, elephants, birds. All figures are dark indigo against pale blue background filled with small dots made by *cemplogen*. Although from Juana, batik resembles those from Indramayu region.

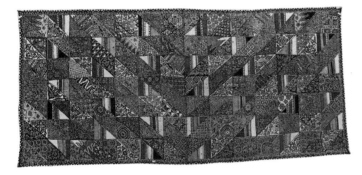

31. *Tambal Belah Ketupat*
Kain Panjang, Cirebon, ca. 1890–1900
Cotton, natural dyes (?), *tulis*
Warp 259 cm./Weft 115 cm.
Collection: State Museum of Yogyakarta, Sonobudoyo/#E/K 156/80

Unusual patchwork pattern (*tambal*) with overall chevron design, made in Cirebon. *Tambal* bordered by *seret kemodo,* a two-striped hem of another color. No visible repeat in batik. Shades of blue, black, and white used in motifs. Cloth mimics Indian block-printed patchwork samplers, even though it contains the following old Javanese patterns:

senggon serivelon	*patran jeruju*
patran manuk	*patran selukan*
patran traten	*parang rusak*
patran bunga teleng	*patran simbar*
patran simbar senggon manuk	*patran bunga jonge*
patran kanghung	*patran tunjung*

32. *Tambal* Sarong, Pekalongan, ca. 1900
Cotton, machine spun, natural dyes, *tulis*
Warp 203.5 cm./Weft 104 cm.
Collection: Anita E. Spertus and Robert J. Holmgren, New York/#J175

Patchwork squares are cut by diagonals in the *badan* forming triangles filled with finely drawn creatures such as crabs, goats, phoenixes, and turtles. Variations of the *ceplok* and *parang* also fill triangles. Undulating wavy line on one side of *badan* might represent surface of sea (?). Although made in Pekalongan, many motifs stylistically similar to examples from Cirebon.

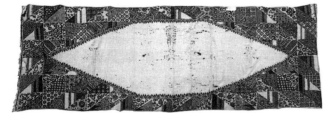

33. *Tambal* Selendang, Cirebon, ca. 1900–1910
Cotton, natural dyes (?), *tulis*
Warp 235 cm./Weft 62 cm.
Collection: State Museum of Yogyakarta, Sonobudoyo/#E/K 176/95

Lozenge shape is surrounded by *tambal* design in shades of blue on remainder of the cloth.

34. *Tambal* *Kain Panjang*, Cirebon, ca. 1930–1940
Cotton, machine spun, natural dyes (?), *tulis* and *cap*
Warp 240 cm./Weft 92 cm.
Collection: Smend Gallery, Cologne/#23

Good example of Cirebon *tambal* in shades of blue and white. Rectangles set in diagonal motion are filled with geometric and floral patterns.

35. *Bidadari Buket* Sarong, Pekalongan, ca. 1916
Cotton, machine spun, natural dyes (?), *tulis*
Warp 219.5 cm./Weft 107 cm.
Signed: Mesr. A. Simonet Pekalongan
Collection: Inger McCabe Elliott, New York/#1287

Red floral borders and *kepala* are both typical of Pekalongan, but large decorative *tumpal* in *badan* is unusual because this motif usually occurs in a *kepala*.

36. Child's Sarong, Lasem (?), ca. 1915
Cotton, natural dyes (?), *tulis*
Warp 140 cm./Weft 85 cm.
Collection: Smend Gallery, Cologne/#35

Extraordinary for its size and design, sarong was probably worn by a child for circumcision.

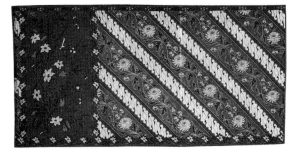

37. *Dlorong Buketan Parang Rusak*
Sarong, Pekalongan, ca. 1910–1920
Cotton, machine spun, natural dyes, *tulis*
Warp 212 cm./Weft 106 cm.
Signed: L Metz Pek
Collection: Inger McCabe Elliott, New York /#1503

Large diagonal bands of *parang rusak* alternate with floral vines. Floral borders and *kepala* are typical of Pekalongan sarongs from ateliers run by both Chinese and *Indische* women.

38. *Buket Galaran Iris* Sarong, Pekalongan, ca. 1905
Cotton, machine spun, natural dyes, *tulis*
Warp 221.5 cm./Weft 107.5 cm.
Signed: J Jans
Collection: Inger McCabe Elliott, New York /#1401

Stylized iris bouquets, reminiscent of Art Deco style, arranged diagonally across *badan*. Similar bouquets arranged in *kepala*, although set against darker background decorated by diagonal striping of fine dots.

39. Sarong, Pekalongan, ca. 1910–1920
Cotton, machine spun, natural dyes (?), *tulis*
Warp 217.5 cm./Weft 110 cm.
Signed: Fred Jans Pekalongan (according to museum records)
Collection: Tropen Museum, Amsterdam /Series 1256/No. 12

Early sarong from atelier of Jans show a "lace" border with delicate red scallops set against clean creamy background of repeated stars and flowers. Most likely this sarong was made for a wedding because repeated star motifs look like *truntum* ("budding of love") worn by relatives of bride or groom. Flowers in *kepala* include carnations, roses, and convulvus.

40. *Kain Panjang,* Pekalongan, ca. 1910–1920
Cotton, machine spun, natural dyes, *tulis*
Warp 265 cm./Weft 107 cm.
Signed: E v Zuylen
Collection: Inger McCabe Elliott, New York /#1135

Bouquet of peonies (?) in formalized layout with birds flying, common to van Zuylen batik. Peony buds border the bottom edge (*pinggir*) and rich saturated natural colors boldly fill design areas.

41. Sarong, Pekalongan, ca. 1900–1910
Cotton, machine spun, natural dyes, *tulis*
Signed: E v Zuylen
Warp 216 cm./Weft 106 cm.
Collection: Smend Gallery, Cologne /#5

Early example of sarong from van Zuylen; nosegays of flowers repeat across *badan* forming an overall pattern. Unusual for van Zuylen because her later batik show bouquets of flowers in formalized arrangement in *badan*.

42. Sarong, Pekalongan, ca. 1900
Cotton, machine spun, natural dyes (?), *tulis*
Warp 212 cm./Weft 104 cm.
Signed: E v Zuylen
Collection: Jacques Gadbois

Simple overall pattern of cashew-nut flowers fills *badan* rather than the more typical van Zuylen bouquets.

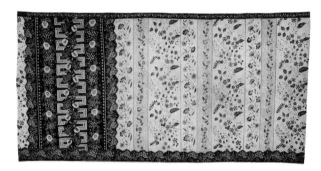

43. *Dlorong Buketan* Sarong, Pekalongan, ca. 1910–1920
Cotton, machine spun, natural dyes, *tulis*
Warp 212 cm./Weft 107 cm.
Signed: E v Zuylen
Collection: Inger McCabe Elliott, New York/#1502

Unusual example because of striped design layout. Most typical van Zuylen sarongs were filled with flower bouquets rather than geometrics.

44. Sarong, Pekalongan, ca. 1915
Cotton, machine spun, natural dyes (?), *tulis*
Warp 207 cm./Weft 105 cm.
Signed: E v Zuylen
Collection: Inger McCabe Elliott, New York/#1138

Van Zuylen's hallmark was her clean background often accentuated by simple vines diagonally drawn across *badan*. This sarong —flawlessly executed—is an excellent example of such work.

45. *Kain Panjang Pagi-Sore,* Pekalongan, ca. 1930–1940
Cotton, machine spun, synthetic dyes, *tulis*
Signed: E v Zuylen
Warp 203 cm./Weft 107 cm.
Collection: Sergio Feldbauer, Milan

Pagi-sore exhibits spectacular van Zuylen colors: pastel mauves, pinks, peaches, and light blues. Subtle color variation softens design of chrysanthemums and poppies (?). Note flowers with colored edges and plain white petals, a van Zuylen preference.

46. Pants, Pekalongan, ca. 1930–1940
Cotton, machine spun, natural (?) dyes, *tulis*
Warp 40 cm./Weft 30 cm.
Collection: Smend Gallery, Cologne/#14c

Child's pants decorated with diagonal stripes filled with *parang* motif as well as flower vines and geometrics.

47. Pants, Lasem, ca. 1930–1940
Cotton, handspun, natural (?) dyes, *tulis*
Warp 106 cm./Weft 65 cm.
Collection: Smend Gallery, Cologne/#14b

Stylized flowers create an overall pattern on pants. Hem is bordered with cloud motifs that are edged by *banji*.

48. *Dlorong Khewan* Pants, Cirebon, ca. 1890–1900
Cotton, machine spun, natural dyes, *tulis*
Warp 122 cm./Weft 68 cm. A 28 cm. band of white cotton attached at waist.
Collection: Anita E. Spertus and Robert J. Holmgren, New York/#J302

Cloud motifs alternate with diagonal stripes of stylized animals, birds, and flowers. Bottom of each hem bordered by cloud motifs edged with *banji*.

49. Pants, Cirebon, ca. 1910–1920
Cotton, machine spun, natural dyes (?), *tulis*
Warp 111.5 cm./Weft 52 cm.
Collection: Inger McCabe Elliott, New York/#1506

Pants made from *kain panjang* showing soldiers, cannons, and palanquins, a popular motif depicting the Lombok wars.

50. *Kelengan Indigo Margasatwa Alasan*
Pants, Temang Gung, ca. 1920–1930
Cotton, machine spun, natural (?) dyes, *tulis*
Warp/Weft unknown
Collection: Asmara Damais Arifin, Jakarta

Flowers, birds, and animals decorate pants made in Temang Gung in Cirebon style. *Kelengan* refers to use of only one color in design —in this example, indigo.

51. *Bang-Biru Khewan* Pants, Pekalongan, ca. 1900–1910
Cotton, machine spun, natural dyes, *tulis*
Warp 105 cm./Weft 62 cm.
Private Collection

Red and blue creatures (*bang-biru khewan*) are framed by diagonal lines forming squares with *banji* motif at each corner intersection. Influenced by Chinese art, most striking aspect of these pants is intertwining serpents running along each outer leg.

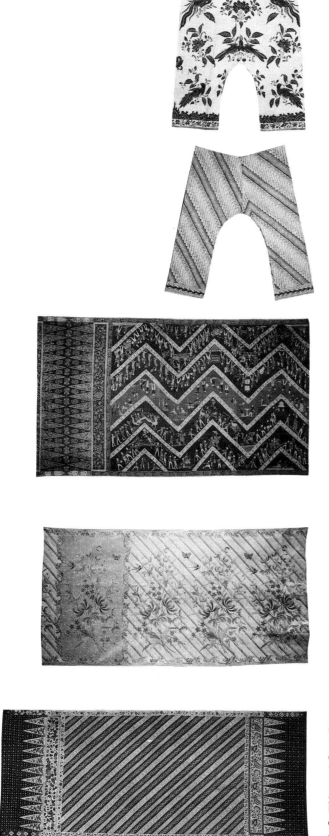

52. Pants, Pekalongan, ca. 1930–1940
Cotton, machine spun, natural (?) dyes, *tulis*
Warp 70 cm./Weft 55 cm.
Collection: Smend Gallery, Cologne/#14a

Pants with alternating flower bouquets and birds nestled in branches. Bottom of each leg is bordered by small imitation fringe, floral vine, and cloud motifs.

53. *Modang* Pants, Pekalongan, ca. 1880
Cotton, machine spun, natural dyes, *tulis*
Warp 99 cm./Weft 64 cm.
Collection: Anita E. Spertus and Robert J. Holmgren, New York/#J248

Pants made from *kain panjang* with alternating motifs of *cemukiran* and *gringsing*.

54. Sarong, Semarang, ca. 1865
Cotton, handspun, natural dyes, *tulis*
Warp 212 cm./Weft 112 cm.
Collection: Rijksmuseum voor Volkenkunde, Leiden/Series 101/ No. 22

Life of Chinese on Java's north coast is detailed in this lively sarong. Body divided by large zigzagged bands, four filled with processions of people on foot and seated on fantastic animals. *Tandak* party is represented on fifth band with *gamelan*, and Europeans shown as onlookers. Representation from daily life such as a woman cooking rice is shown in triangles on long sides. Donated to Leiden museum in 1869 by Colonial Ministry. Batik shown at Paris Exhibition in 1867.

55. *Cempakamulya Parang Menang*
Sarong, Kedungwuni, ca. 1930–1940
Cotton, machine spun, synthetic dyes, *tulis* and *cap* (?)
Warp 217 cm./Weft 110 cm.
Signed: Liem Giok Kwie Kedungwoeni
Collection: Winnifred de Groot, Leiden

Cempakamulya means "beginning to grow." Special batik, often part of bride's dowry, and sometimes worn by parents of both bride and groom. Pointed petals moving in circular motion are common to this design. The background, *parang menang*, symbolizes wisdom.

56. *Parang Tejo* Kain Panjang, Pekalongan, ca. 1880
Cotton, machine spun, natural dyes, *tulis*
Warp 261 cm./Weft 105 cm.
Collection: Anita E. Spertus and Robert J. Holmgren, New York/#J230

Alternate rows of *parang* and *naga* motifs run diagonally across body. Natural indigo blue and *mengkudu* red used against rich cream ground. *Kepala* is split: half red, the other half black. Medallion shapes, often mixed with insect motifs, fill both red and black *kepalas*, each intersected by a row of *tumpal*. Piece typical of late-nineteenth- and early-twentieth-century batik made in northern Java prior to advent of synthetic dyes.

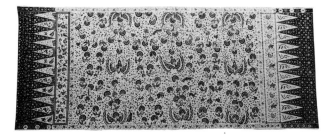

57. *Kain Panjang,* Pekalongan, ca. 1910–1920
Cotton, machine spun, natural dyes, *tulis*
Warp 262 cm./Weft 105 cm.
Artist: Oey Soen King
Collection: Jane Hendromartono, Pekalongan

Similar in format to other north-coast batik of same period, using natural red and blue on creamy tan grounds set off by split *kepalas,* half red, the other half either indigo blue or black. Imaginative, graceful animals combined with traditional *garuda* wings attached to plant forms; flowers rendered in old Chinese style. *Tumpal* decorated with traditional cloud formations as well as with centipedes. Delicately and sensitively drawn, batik combines traditional motifs with style and imagination of artist.

58. *Semarangan*-style Sarong (sewn together),
Pekalongan, ca. 1925
Cotton, machine spun, synthetic dyes, *tulis*
Warp 200 cm./Weft 105 cm.
Signed: Ny Oey Kok Sing
Collection: Inger McCabe Elliott, New York/#1229

Made for people living in Semarang about 1925 by Mrs. Oey Kok Sing. Sarong reflects her preference for "European" bouquets; brighter colors are achieved by using synthetic dyes.

59. *Buket Tanahan* Sarong (sewn together),
Pekalongan, ca. 1930
Cotton, machine spun, synthetic dyes (?), *tulis*
Warp 201 cm./Weft 105 cm.
Signed: Ny Oey Kok Sing
Collection: Inger McCabe Elliott, New York/#1536

Buket tanahan means bouquet of flowers. Pattern is packed with detail. Secondary background motif gives depth to drawing, characterizing work of Oey Kok Sing.

60. Sarong, Pekalongan, 1969
Cotton, machine spun, synthetic dyes, *tulis*
Warp 211 cm./Weft 106 cm.
Signed: Jane Hendromartono '69 Pekalongan—Java
Collection: Jane Hendromartono, Pekalongan

Unusual design with intricate work: typical Dutch bouquets, exotic birds, animals, and rock formations on cream ground. Soft background always has a surprise element; tiny castles and *berasan* (rice kernels) add texture and shape to batik.

61. Kain Panjang Pagi-Sore Pekalongan, 1972
Cotton, machine spun, synthetic dyes, *tulis*
Warp 260 cm./Weft 107 cm.
Signed: Jane Hendromartono—Java c Ind.
Collection: Jane Hendromartono, Pekalongan

Animated birds glide across a soft background of small stones (*krikilan*) on this subtle *pagi-sore*. Other images include lotus ponds, swans, fish, rocks, birds, beetles, daffodils, and cherry blossoms.

62. *Ganggong Tanahan* Sarong, Kedungwuni, ca. 1930
Cotton, machine spun, synthetic dyes, *tulis*
Warp 258 cm./Weft 106 cm.
Signed: Oey Soe Tjoen Kedungwuni 104
Collection: Smend Gallery, Cologne/#6

Early example of sarong made in workshop of Oey Soe Tjoen. Unusual for its "European" irises, sarong is striking example of Oey's delicate work.

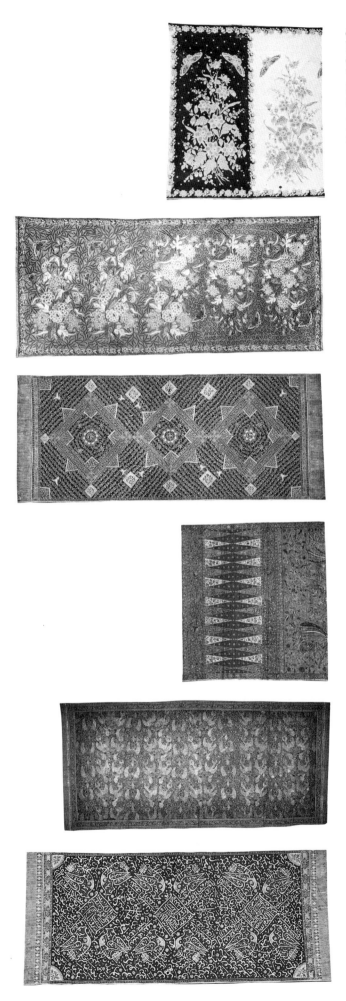

63. *Kelangan* Sarong (sewn together),
Kedungwuni, ca. 1930–1940
Cotton, machine spun, natural dyes (?), *tulis*
Warp 258 cm. (?)/Weft 106 cm. (?)
Signed: Oey Soe Tjoen 21B
Collection: Batik Art Oey Soe Tjoen, Kedungwuni

By Chinese custom, blue and white sarongs were worn for mourning. Note fine workmanship.

64. *Buket Semarangan*
Kain Panjang Pagi-Sore, Kedungwuni, 1960
Cotton, machine spun, synthetic dyes, *tulis*
Warp 250.5 cm./Weft 106.5 cm
Artist: Oey Soe Tjoen
Collection: Inger McCabe Elliott, New York/#1207

Made for people in Semarang; packed with detailing, and clearly shows fine artistic execution that made workshop of Oey Soe Tjoen famous.

65. *Asara Arab* Selendang, Cirebon, ca. 1900–1920
Cotton, machine spun, natural dyes, *tulis*
Warp 227 cm./Weft 90.5 cm.
Collection: Inger McCabe Elliott, New York/#1441

Blue and white with Arabic script was also known as *batik arab,* or *juffri.* These pieces usually made in Java were exported to Sumatra and worn in wedding ceremonies to cover heads of bride and groom. The word *Allah* is repeated throughout.

66. *Kepala Pasang Tiga Negeri* Sarong, Demak, ca. 1900–1910
Cotton, machine spun, natural dyes, *tulis*
Warp 200 cm./Weft 106 cm.
Collection: Inger McCabe Elliott, New York/#1023

Striking for its rich detail, saturated natural colors, and motifs of peacock and *semen.* The *tumpal* is in vivid counterpoint to the sarong's *badan.*

67. Tablecloth (?), Lasem, ca. 1920
Cotton, machine spun, natural dyes (?), *tulis*
Warp 206 cm./Weft 90 cm.
Collection: Inger McCabe Elliott, New York/#1231

Motif resembling birds hidden in textural all-over pattern. The hand-sewn borders on four sides suggest batik might have been used as tablecloth. Made in east Java, batik of this type was exported to Sumatra.

68. *Selendang* or *Kain Panjang,* Cirebon, ca. 1910–1920
Cotton, machine spun, natural dyes (?), *tulis*
Warp 214 cm./Weft 90 cm.
Collection: Smend Gallery, Cologne/#16

Primitively rendered birds and ornamental motifs suggest Arabic calligraphy that decorate this batik.

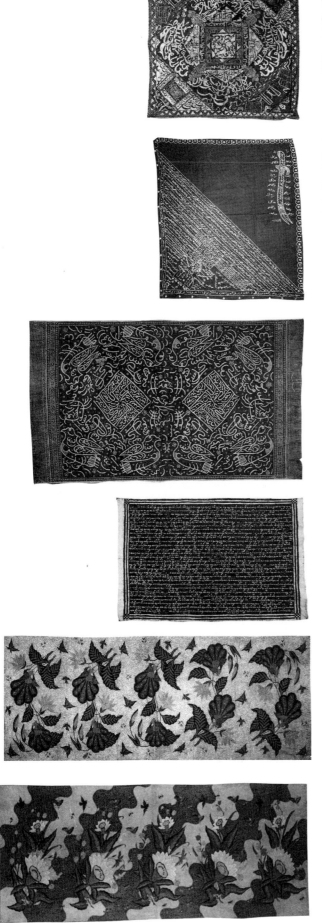

69. Iket Kepala, Cirebon (?), ca. 1910–1920
Cotton, machine spun, natural dyes (?), *tulis*
Warp 94 cm./Weft 90 cm.
Collection: State Museum of Yogyakarta, Sonobudoyo/#E/K 179/102

Arab headcloth that depicts *shahada,* or basic statement of Islamic belief: there is no God but Allah, Muhammad is his prophet.

70. Iket Kepala, Palembang (?), ca. 1930–1940
Cotton, natural dyes (?), *tulis*
Warp 110 cm./Weft 110 cm.
Collection: K.R.T. Hardjonagoro, Surakarta

Headcloth with Arabic script used to avert evil or bad luck.

71. Wall Hanging (?), Palembang (?), ca. 1910–1920
Cotton, machine spun, natural dyes (?), *tulis*
Warp 141 cm./Weft 82 cm.
Collection: Inger McCabe Elliott, New York/#1517

May be wall hanging or ceremonial piece used to cover a tray on which wedding gifts were carried.

72. Iket Kepala, Palembang (?), ca. 1910
Cotton, machine spun, natural dyes (?), *tulis*
Warp 105 cm./Weft 67 cm.
Collection: State Museum of Yogyakarta, Sonobudoyo/#E/K 178/101

Rare headcloth decorated with fifteenth-century Javanese script.

73. Kain Panjang, Kudus or Juana, ca. 1910–1920
Cotton, machine spun, natural dyes, *tulis*
Warp 250 cm./Weft 105 cm.
Collection: Smend Gallery, Cologne/#22

Large peacock feathers, flowers, and leaves boldly rendered and richly colored in dark natural tones resemble the style of numbers 6, 74, and 75. See below.

74. Dlorong Buket Brasmawar *Kain Panjang,*
Kudus or Juana ca. 1910
Cotton, machine spun, natural dyes, *tulis*
Warp 250 cm./Weft 106 cm.
Collection: Inger McCabe Elliott, New York

Bouquets of large flowers against zigzag background pattern of rice strongly resembles artistic style of numbers 6, 73, and 75. Although unsigned, all could be the work of one artist. Batik was purchased from east Javanese maker evident by dark colors.

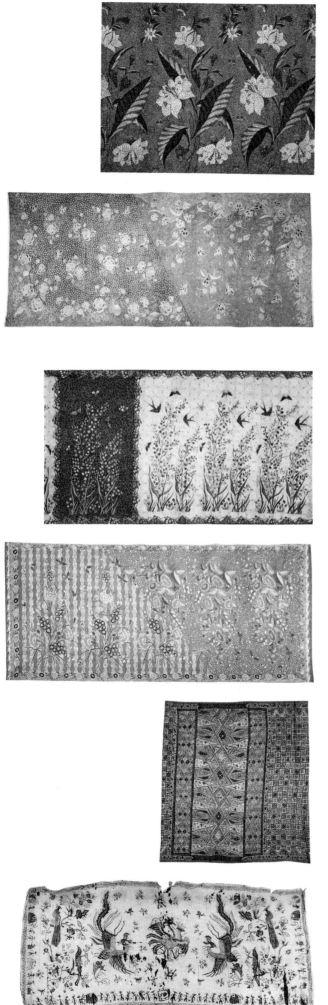

75. *Kain Panjang,* Kudus or Juana (?), ca. 1900–1910
Cotton, machine spun, natural dyes, *tulis*
Warp 250 cm./Weft 104 cm.
Collection: Smend Gallery, Cologne/#2

Simple large lilies (?) boldly rendered in rich natural color. Artistic style similar to numbers 6, 73, and 74. See above.

76. *Buket Semarangan Pagi-Sore* *Kain Panjang Pagi-Sore,*
Pekalongan, ca. 1950
Cotton, machine spun, synthetic and natural dyes (?), *tulis*
Warp 253.5 cm./Weft 106 cm.
Signed: Liem Siok Hien Kudus
Collection: Inger McCabe Elliott, New York/#1444

Roses in bright full bloom float gracefully on patterned background. Complementing design of roses are tulips on a background of swimming goldfish. Made in Pekalongan ca. 1950 by Liem Siok Hien, but signed Kudus, because artist thought design resembled Kudus-style batik.

77. *Kembang Buket Tanahan* Sarong, Kudus, ca. 1920–1930
Cotton, machine spun, natural dyes (?)
Warp 197 cm./Weft 108 cm.
Collection: Inger McCabe Elliott, New York/#1072

Vertical bushes of blue and gold set against rich background of patterned diamond shapes. *Kepala* is set apart from *badan* by contrasting dark blue color.

78. *Kain Panjang Pagi-Sore,* Kudus, ca. 1920–1930
Cotton, machine spun, synthetic and natural dyes (?), *tulis*
Warp 251 cm./Weft 107 cm.
Signed: Lie Eng Soen Kudoes
Collection: Inger McCabe Elliott, New York/#1075

Pagi-sore richly detailed with carnations and cornflowers set against scalloped, striped background. Although reminiscent of batik by Chinese makers in Pekalongan, deep brown background color is more common to Kudus area.

79. *Selendang,* Indramayu (?), ca. 1900
Silk, natural dyes, *tulis*
Warp 127 cm./Weft 53.2 cm.
Collection: Ardiyanto Pranata, Yogyakarta

Probably an example of *lokcan*; a very old piece with phoenix (?) and *wayang* figures across one side.

80. Sarong, Gresik or Rembang, ca. 1900–1910
Silk, machine woven, synthetic dyes, *tulis, plangi*
Warp 191 cm./Weft 96 cm.
Collection: Sergio Feldbauer, Milan

Rare sewn silk sarong that combines *plangi* and *tulis* techniques with rich brilliant color and textural pattern.

81. *Selendang*, Semarang (?), ca. 1920–1930
Silk, machine woven, natural dyes, *tulis*
Warp 252 cm./Weft 27 cm.
Collection: Jacques Gadbois

Unusual for its attached knotted silk fringe; probably worn draped over one shoulder.

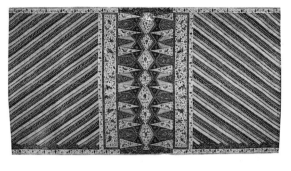

82. Sarong, Pekalongan, ca. 1890–1900
Cotton, machine spun, natural dyes, *tulis*
Warp 201 cm./Weft 105.5 cm.
Collection: Anita E. Spertus and Robert J. Holmgren, New York/#J174

Although made in Pekalongan, sarong resembles batik made in Lasem. Intricate *kepala* has patchwork effect against diagonal bands running in opposite directions on *badan.*

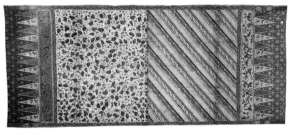

83. *Kain Panjang Pagi-Sore*, Lasem (?), ca. 1880–1890
Cotton, machine spun, natural dyes, *tulis*
Warp/Weft unknown
Collection: Mrs. H. Sa'adiah Djody, Jakarta

Found in Pandang (Sumatra) in 1975, but might have been made in Java (Lasem area) for export to south Sumatra. Unusual because a vertical, not diagonal, separates each half of cloth. Unlike other *pagi-sores*, batik has half *kepalas* at each end.

84. *Kain Gendongan*, Lasem, ca. 1900
Cotton, machine spun, natural dyes, *tulis*
Warp 336 cm./Weft 94 cm.
Collection: Jacques Gadbois

Batik has oversize butterflies and deep, natural red color, characteristic of eastern Java. Highly chintzed surface probably achieved by rubbing shells across fabric. This baby carrier was never used, possibly because the awaited baby died.

85. Sarong, Lasem, ca. 1920
Cotton, natural dyes (?), *tulis*
Warp 200 cm./Weft 107 cm.
Collection: Smend Gallery, Cologne

Batik has powerful, bold swastika throughout its body. All traditional formats of north-coast batik evident in this example, including *kepala* with *tumpal* and borders (*pinggir*).

86. *Pangeran Diponegoro* Selendang, Lasem, ca. 1900
Cotton, machine spun, natural dyes, *tulis*
Warp 296 cm./Weft 98.5 cm.
Collection: Iwan Tirta, Jakarta

Selendang depicts Pangeran Diponegoro, Prince of Yogyakarta and hero of Javanese resistance against Dutch during 1821–1836 wars. In official portraits, Pangeran Diponegoro often depicted riding on horseback, dressed in Islamic robes and turban, carrying a sword or banner in his hand.

87. Sarong, Lasem, ca. 1900
Cotton, machine spun, natural dyes, *tulis*
Warp 183 cm./Weft 106 cm.
Collection: Inger McCabe Elliott, New York/#1080

Chinese in style and color, called *bang-bangan* (red). Depicted are frogs, turtles, chickens, peacocks, birds, and centipedes. These animals have mystical powers that can be appropriated by someone wearing such a cloth. It was quite common for Chinese to represent strength and power through venomous creatures such as centipedes. Chickens surround centipedes because only they could counteract poisoned bites of these animals. Such a powerful batik probably worn only by adult male who had already overcome some of life's mystical difficulties.

88. Bedcover, Lasem, ca. 1910–1920
Cotton, machine spun, natural dyes (?), *tulis*
Warp 254.5 cm./Weft 207.5 cm.
Collection: Iwan Tirta, Jakarta

Imaginative arrangement of mythical animals, birds, flowers, and religious symbols draws heavily on Chinese art. *Chi'lin* (half-dog, half-lion) of Chinese mythology creates centerpiece, surrounded by deer, elephants, lions, and fantastic birds. Along with phoenix, roosters and peacocks are also part of outer bedcover border. Medallion shapes with ribbons point to well-known Chinese religious symbols: *mata uang* (coin) to ward off evil and *siput* (conch shell) to guarantee safe voyage. Motifs in batik combine to provide good fortune, prosperity, fertility, and longevity to its owner.

89. *Bang Bangan Naga Murka* Altar cloth,
Cirebon, ca. 1910–1920
Cotton, machine spun, natural dyes, *tulis*
Warp 108 cm./Weft 103 cm.
Collection: Inger McCabe Elliott, New York/#1418

Design incorporates *naga* (serpent or dragon) with *Tao T'ieh* face, a type of dragon. Altar cloth is bordered by Chinese swastika (*banji*) design.

90. *Bang Biru* Altar cloth, Pekalongan, ca. 1940
Cotton, machine spun, synthetic dyes, *tulis*
Warp 108 cm./Weft 90.5 cm.
Collection: Inger McCabe Elliott, New York/#1427

Bang-biru (red and blue) design has bird at its center surrounded by mythical beasts, including *chi'lin* and phoenix. *Chi'lin* symbolize prosperity and phoenix means long life.

91. Altar Cloth, Cirebon, ca. 1920–1930
Cotton, machine spun, natural dyes, *tulis*
Warp 137 cm./Weft 100 cm.
Collection: Wieneke de Groot, Jakarta

Large Chinese temple and parade of people carrying lanterns and banners fill this altar cloth. Dragons, lions, and jellyfish (squids?) are also a part of the designs. Some people still wear traditional Chinese *kunair*, or braid, at back of head.

92. _Thok Wie_ Altar cloth, North East Coast, ca. 1900
Cotton, machine spun, natural dyes (?), _tulis_
Warp 94 cm./Weft 85 cm.
Collection: Mary Hunt Kahlenberg and Dr. Anne Summerfield,
Los Angeles/#507 A-I-J

Top band depicts four Chinese characters; two imitation tassels hang from each end of band. Center medallion shows phoenix descending on floral spray. Above right and left of medallion are two figures, each making an offering; below the medallion are two lions.

93. Altar Cloth, Lasem, ca. 1900
Cotton, machine spun, natural dyes (?), _tulis_
Warp 118.11 cm./Weft 113.3 cm.
Collection: Mary Hunt Kahlenberg and Dr. Anne Summerfield,
Los Angeles/#57

Lower portion of altar cloth has two interlocking plants with pineapples and oversize blossoms. Butterfly, insects(?), and falling leaves(?) appear around plant; top has a central floral bouquet surrounded by four leaping horses, small monkeys, butterflies. Main motif strongly influenced by Indian textiles; many Indian _palempores_ (or bedcovers) were traded to Indonesia with similar voluptuous and exotic blossoms. Roots at bottom of plants characteristic of Indian textiles, while top portion more Chinese, reflected in lighter quality of drawing, more delicate flowers, and lively animals.

94. _Bang Ajo_ Altar cloth, Pekalongan, ca. 1930
Cotton, machine spun, synthetic dyes (?), _tulis_
Warp 100 cm./Weft 105 cm.
Collection: Inger McCabe Elliott, New York /#1456

Design is _bang ajo_ (red), with dragons and phoenix. Along with Chinese mythical animals, including phoenix, this altar cloth contains other symbols: a coin for warding off evil and a jar representing Buddha's stomach.

95. _Semen Gunung_ _Selendang,_ Tuban, ca. 1910
Cotton, handspun, hand-woven, natural dyes, _tulis_
Warp 294 cm./Weft 72 cm.
Collection: Inger McCabe Elliott, New York

Overall _semen_ design includes _lar_ (wings), pavilions, a series of mountains _(gunung),_ and a root system.

96. _Alasalasan_ _Dodot_ (?), Tuban (?), ca. 1910–1920
Cotton, handspun, natural dyes, _tulis_
Warp 236 cm./Weft 185.5 cm.
Collection: Mary Hunt Kahlenberg and Dr. Anne Summerfield,
Los Angeles /#0123

Overall design includes pair of _lar_ (wings), series of mountains, a temple form, a twining root system, palm trees, deer, crocodiles, birds, and variety of foliage. Batik found in Lampong area of Sumatra, but probably made on the north coast of Java.

97. _Kain Panjang,_ Kerek (a village near Tuban), 1983
Cotton, handspun, hand-woven, _tulis_
Warp 263 cm./Weft 89 cm.
Collection: Inger McCabe Elliott, New York

Recently made in Kerek of locally grown and spun cotton. Cloth batiked by village woman. Process from harvesting cotton to dyeing cloth can take up to four months. Cloth is simply designed with rich, natural indigo; quality of handspun fibers creates roughly textured cloth.

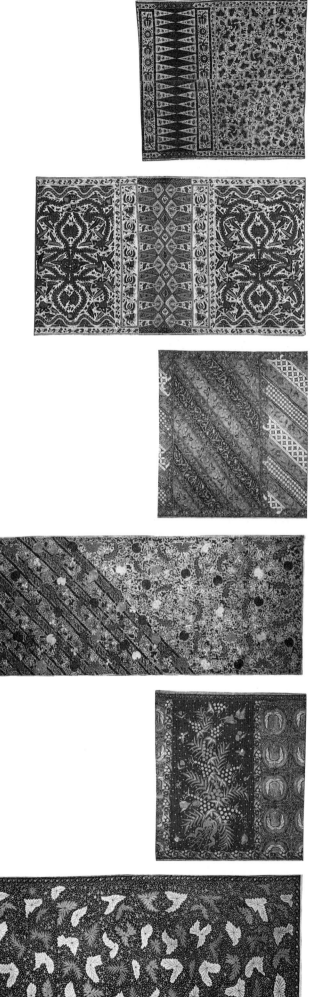

98. Sarong (sewn together), Tuban, ca. 1900
Cotton, handspun, hand-woven, *tulis*
Warp 210 cm./Weft 95 cm.
Collection: Sergio Feldbauer, Milan

Floral and bird design, typically found in villages near Tuban, inspired by nature. Design is set into traditional sarong format with *tumpal pasang* (?). Possibly an early example of village batik because of the narrow cloth. Small blue background dots made by puncturing wax with the thorn of palmetto before dyeing.

99. Sarong, Lasem (?), Madura (?), 1880–1890
Cotton, machine spun, natural dyes, *tulis*
Warp 188 cm./Weft 106.5 cm.
Collection: Jacques Gadbois

Large, rounded snake or *naga*-like forms end in stylized flowers. Deep red color symbolizes fertility. Although this batik was purchased in Lasem, its red color *(mengkudu)* is characteristic of Madura and east Java.

100. *Tiga Negeri Kepala Dlorong* Sarong (sewn together),
Lasem, ca. 1910
Cotton, machine spun, natural dyes (?), *tulis*
Warp 197 cm./Weft 106.5 cm.
Collection: Inger McCabe Elliott, New York/#1081

Diagonals of flowers and geometrics. Flowers and borders applied in Pekalongan (red); blue applied in second north-coast town; and brown border applied in Surakarta. Geometric patterns include variations of *ceplok,* one of which is *kawung* motif.

101. *Kain Panjang Pagi-Sore,* Pekalongan, 1930
Cotton, machine spun, natural dyes, *tulis*
Warp 257.5 cm./Weft 103.5 cm.
Collection: Brake-Lau, New Zealand

An example of *tiga negeri,* probably begun in Pekalongan where it received its flowers and red color. Then sent to another north-coast town where flowers were filled in and blue dye added. Finally, in Surakarta, *parang* was applied in background and entire piece dyed *soga* brown.

102. *Buket Garuda Sumping* Sarong (sewn together),
Pacitan, 1915–1920
Cotton, machine spun, natural dyes, *tulis*
Warp 192.5 cm./Weft 105 cm.
Collection: Inger McCabe Elliott, New York/#1019

Combines best designs from several batik-making towns, an example of *dua negeri* (two countries). Red floral *kepala* and borders were most likely applied in eastern Java while remainder applied at later date in Surakarta.

103. *Latar Ireng* Kain Panjang, Gresik, 1920–1930
Cotton, machine spun, natural and synthetic dyes (?), *tulis*
Warp 269 cm./Weft 109 cm.
Collection: Inger McCabe Elliott, New York/#1471

Large overall pattern of bold leaves filled in with large rice grains. Red border on edges of each side is more typical of Pekalongan than Gresik.

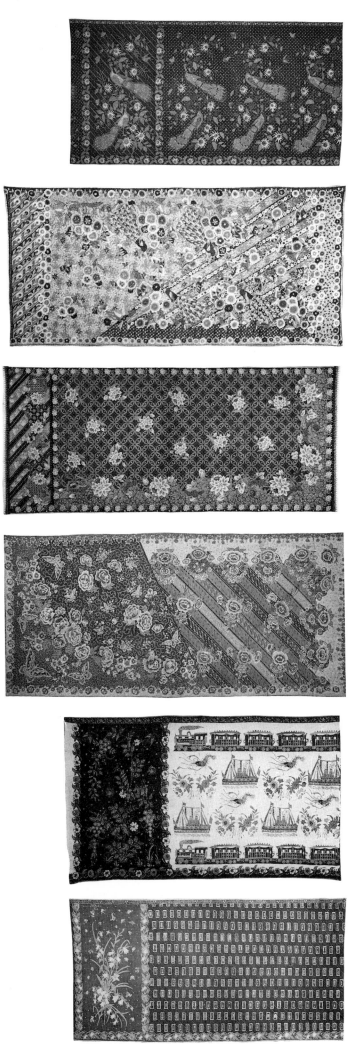

104. Sarong, Surakarta (?), 1900–1910
Cotton, machine spun, natural (?) dyes, *tulis*
Warp 202 cm./Weft 106 cm.
Signed: Ny(y)o Tan Sing Ing sola
Collection: Inger McCabe Elliott, New York/#1184

Peacock design is possibly *dua negeri* batik. Although purchased in Sidoarjo, signature reads Sola (Surakarta) in central Java. Overall background pattern is interesting because motifs are square instead of round, achieved by using *canting* with a square tip.

105. *Kain Panjang Pagi-Sore*, North Coast, 1942–1945
Cotton, machine spun, synthetic dyes, *tulis*
Warp 236 cm./Weft 109 cm.
Collection: Inger McCabe Elliott, New York/#1428

Typical of batik made during Japanese occupation of Java during World War II, called *Hokokai*. Crammed full of intricate designs of luscious peacocks, blooming flowers, and fanciful borders, *Hokokai* is known for its extraordinarily bright colors.

106. *Kain Panjang*, Pekalongan, 1942–1945
Cotton, machine spun, natural and synthetic dyes (?), *tulis*
Warp 256 cm./Weft 104 cm.
Collection: Inger McCabe Elliott, New York/#1256

Lilac-colored flowers set against a rich brown and gold geometric background; *Hokokai*.

107. *Kain Panjang Pagi-Sore*, Pekalongan, 1942–1945
Cotton, machine spun, synthetic dyes, *tulis*
Warp 230 cm./Weft 104 cm.
Collection: K.R.T. Hardjonagoro, Surakarta

An excellent example of a Javanese *Hokokai* batik.

108. Sarong, Pekalongan, ca. 1930
Cotton, machine spun, natural dyes (?), *cap*
Warp 181 cm./Weft 108 cm.
Inscription: DJSM inscribed on train
Collection: Inger McCabe Elliott, New York/#1498

Made for export to Sumatra. Sarong with airplanes and steamships was probably made to celebrate a new air link.

109. Chinese Dominoes Sarong, Pekalongan, ca. 1930–1940
Cotton, machine spun, synthetic dyes, *tulis*
Warp 211 cm./Weft 106 cm.
Signature: Unreadable
Collection: Brake-Lau, New Zealand

Pictorial representation of Chinese dominoes.

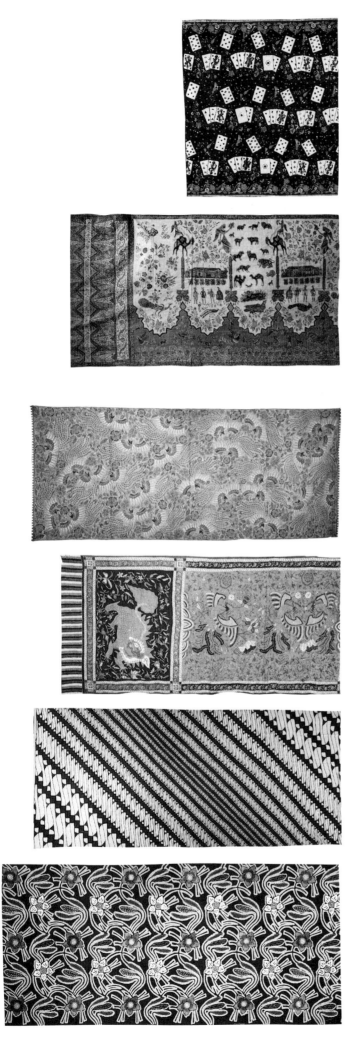

110. Playing Cards Sarong, Pekalongan (?), ca. 1930–1940
Cotton, machine spun, synthetic dyes (?), *cap*
Warp 188 cm./Weft 106 cm.
Signed: H. Ehsan
Collection: Inger McCabe Elliott, New York/#1585

Pictorial representation of playing cards.

111. Sarong, Pekalongan (drawn), Semarang (dyed),
ca. 1920–1930
Cotton, machine spun, natural dyes (?), *tulis*
Warp 222 cm./Weft 110.5 cm.
Inscribed: TABLJER (under each house)
Collection: Museum Nasional, Jakarta/#23408

Pictorial representation of daily life shows definite Arab influence. Blue area below scallops in *badan* could represent sea, or underworld. Above blue-scalloped border, creamy white ground filled with houses, people, ships, camels, angels, birds, elephants, and lions. Under each house inscription reads TABJLER. Batik purchased by Museum Nasional in 1939.

112. *Sawung Galing* *Kain Panjang*, Surakarta, ca. 1970–1980
Cotton, machine spun, natural and synthetic dyes, *tulis*
Warp 205.5 cm./Weft 104.5 cm.
Signed: K.R.T. Hardjonagoro Gotikswan
Collection: Iwan Tirta, Jakarta

Overall pattern of birds, or *sawring galing*, enlivened by bright colors typical of north coast.

113. *Selendang,* Yogyakarta, ca. 1970–1980
Silk, synthetic dyes, *tulis*
Warp 352 cm./Weft 118 cm.
Artist: Ardiyanto Pranata
Collection: Joop Avé, Jakarta

Inspired by Chinese art, *selendang* is striking for its gaily colored imitation fringe at each end.

114. *Parang* *Kain Panjang*, Surakarta, ca. 1980
Cotton, machine spun, natural and synthetic dyes, *tulis*
Warp 260 cm./Weft 105 cm.
Signed: K.R.T. Hardjonagoro Gotikswan
Collection: K.R.T. Hardjonagoro, Surakarta

Modern version of classic *parang* pattern is enlivened by irregular width of diagonals.

115. *Bunga* Yard goods, Pekalongan, 1972
Cotton, machine spun, synthetic dyes, *tulis* and *cap*
Warp ca. 7.7 meters/Weft 106 cm.
Artists: Inger McCabe Elliott and Achmad Yahya
Stamped: © China Seas, Inc.
Collection: Inger McCabe Elliott, New York

Designed and manufactured by China Seas, Inc., in the workshop of Achmad Yahya, batik sold through China Seas' showrooms worldwide. Combined *tulis* and *cap* technique difficult to achieve in long yardages without cracking the wax.

116. *Kerata Kencana* Kain Panjang, Cirebon, Trusmi, 1972
Cotton, machine spun, natural dyes, *tulis*
Warp 249 cm./Weft 105 cm.
Artist: made in the workshop of H. Masina
Collection: Brake-Lau, New Zealand

As in this example, the Masina workshop often uses traditional browns and blues on cream and tan grounds. *Kerata kencana* is a new rendition of traditional motifs that include *megamendung* motif.

117. Wall Hanging, Jakarta, 1978
Cotton, machine spun, synthetic and natural dyes (?), *tulis*
Warp 280 cm./Weft 269 cm.
Artist: Made in the workshop of H. Masina, commissioned by Iwan Tirta
Collection: Inger McCabe Elliott, New York

Typical of older batik from court of Cirebon, this modern batik is made on a king-size sheet. White tigers (*sili wangi*) are symbol of kingdom of Pajajaran and also name of kings. *Peksinagaliman* (bird, serpent, elephant) flank each side of cave motif, which is derived from the *hindu kala* or *banas pati* ornament. Lotus, symbol of royalty, is derived from both Indian and Chinese art. Pandanus tree symbolizes life.

118. Sarong, Pekalongan, 1982
Cotton, machine spun, synthetic dyes, *cap*
Warp 198 cm./Weft 107 cm.
Signed: ZAKY
Collection: Inger McCabe Elliott, New York

Brightly colored sarongs, such as this example, with bold geometric backgrounds and floral bouquets are specialty of Achmad Said workshop. Although *cap* work is quite primitive, motifs and colorings are inspired.

119. Sarong, Pekalongan, 1980
Cotton, fine woven, synthetic dyes, *cap*
Warp: 187 cm./Weft: 102 cm.
Collection: Inger McCabe Elliott, New York/#ZKIME

Modern *cap* batik made by the workshop of Achmad Said. Unusual for its *tumpal* running the width of the *badan*. Two inscriptions read: (1) "Zaky, Basmelah, Jl. Bandung 53, Pekalongan," and (2) "Sinbad, RG 63666."

Textiles not shown in full color

120. *Parang* Sarong, North Coast (?), ca. 1810–1820
Cotton, possibly handspun, natural dyes, *tulis*
Warp 206 cm./Weft 114 cm.
Collection: Museum of Mankind, London/#K 75415 As 1939 A4.120

See number 8 above. Major motif: diagonal *parang*. Two lengths of fabric sewn together lengthwise achieve the 114 cm. width.

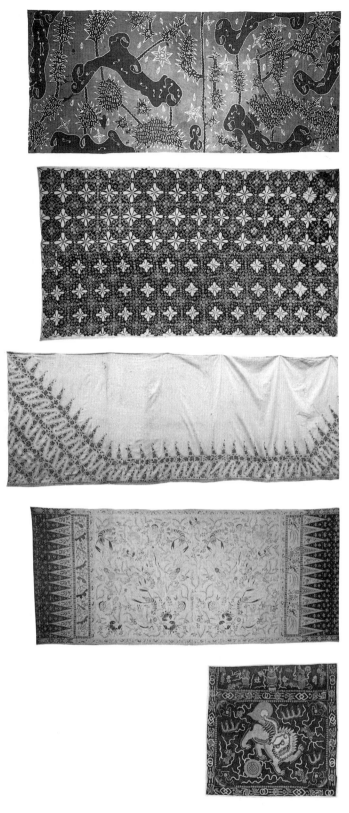

121. Kain Panjang, Tasikmalaya, ca. 1900
Cotton, machine spun, natural dyes (?), *tulis*
Warp 236 cm./Weft 104 cm.
Collection: Tropen Museum, Amsterdam/Series 862/No. 10

Donated 1934 to Tropen Museum. Batik resembles other early examples from West Java, rendered similarly in bold, masculine painterly style of batik of Cirebon. Thorny sea cucumbers, four-, five-, and seven-pointed stars, along with curvy lines set against a reddish brown background, are characteristic of early twentieth-century batik from West Java.

122. Kain Dodot, Cirebon, ca. 1900–1910
Cotton, handspun, hand-woven, natural dyes, *tulis*
Warp 290 cm. /Weft 150 cm.
Collection: Tropen Museum, Amsterdam/Series 807/No. 1

Handsome example of old Cirebon batik. Principal motif is four-leaf flower figure, *tjempaka piring* (Jasper, *Batikkunst,* pg.125, fig. 137 and 138) that spreads across the entire cloth rectangularly. Stylized flower, presumably *melati* (see Jasper, same source, fig. 137), is located in middle of rectangles formed by the joining of *tjempaka piring* and surrounded in background by small stars, *kembang tandjoeng.*

123. Kain Dodot, Cirebon, ca. 1910–1920
Cotton, natural dyes (?), *tulis* (?)
Warp 340 cm./Weft 208 cm.
Collection: State Museum of Yogyakarta, Sonobudoyo/#E/K 181/101

Clean, white center (*tengahan*) has three diagonal bands of *parang* stretching diagonally across each corner. *Tumpal,* or triangular motifs, point toward the center of the cloth. Style suggests strong Indian trade influence.

124. Taman Laut *Kain Panjang,* Cirebon, ca. 1920
Cotton, machine spun, natural dyes (?), *tulis*
Warp 251 cm./Weft 105.5 cm.
Collection: Iwan Tirta, Jakarta

Sea garden (*taman laut*) is rich with creatures: crab, shrimp, lobster, and fish are symbolic of water, underworld, and fertility. Workshop of batik is unknown, but it bears striking resemblance in style and execution to *Bank Ungon* batik (also shown in this chapter); possibly both were made by same workshop.

125. Bang Bangan Killin Altar cloth, Cirebon, ca. 1910–1920
Cotton, machine spun, natural dyes, *tulis*
Warp 95 cm./Weft 92 cm.
Collection: Inger McCabe Elliott, New York/#1436

Central motif is the *chi'lin,* or *killin* (half-dog, half-lion), of Chinese mythology that symbolizes prosperity.

126. Bang Bangan Altar cloth, Cirebon, ca. 1930
Cotton, machine spun, synthetic dyes, *tulis*
Warp 105 cm./Weft 95 cm.
Collection: Inger McCabe Elliott, New York /#1586

Chinese figures bordered by birds, *chi'lin,* and *banji.*

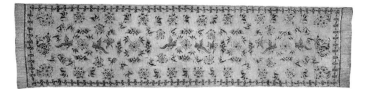

127. *Selendang,* town unknown, ca. 1920–1930
Cotton, machine spun, natural dyes, *tulis, cemplogen, prada*
Warp 212 cm./Weft 50 cm.
Collection: Lisbet Holmes and Henry Ginsburg, London

Selendang embellished by gold-leaf glue-work, or *prada,* which could have been made to celebrate the birth of first-born Chinese son. Small finely dotted background was probably made with *cemplogen,* typical of the Indramayu region.

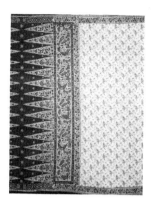

128. Sarong, Pekalongan (?), Lasem (?), ca. 1880–1890
Cotton, machine spun, natural dyes on batik portion, *tulis*
Warp 196 cm./Weft 108 cm.
Collection: Jonathan Hope, London

An extraordinary example because it combines batik and (ca. 1880) chintz fabric from Europe, sewn together to resemble a Javanese sarong.

129. Sarong, Pekalongan, ca. 1920–1930
Cotton, machine spun, natural dyes (?), *tulis*
Signed: J Jans
Warp 213 cm./Weft 109 cm.
Collection: Jacques Gadbois

Stylized swans in a lily patch set against a background of the typical Chinese swastika design, or *banji.* Probably influenced by Art Deco.

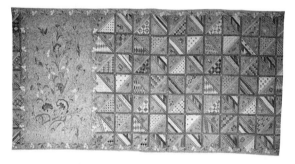

130. *Tambal* Sarong, Pekalongan, ca. 1930–1940
Cotton, machine spun, synthetic dyes, *tulis*
Warp 211 cm./Weft 108 cm.
Collection: Inger McCabe Elliott, New York/#1504

Patchwork design with large triangles filled with geometrics in alternating triangles including *ceplok* and *garis miring* (diagonal stripes). *Kepala* and alternating triangles between the geometric pattern is filled with intricate tendrils. Overall colors characteristic of Pekalongan.

131. *Kursi Goyang* Sarong, Pekalongan, ca. 1930–1940
Cotton, machine spun, synthetic dyes, *tulis*
Warp 196 cm./Weft 106 cm.
Collection: Smend Gallery, Cologne/#17

Sarong with representations of rocking chairs *(kursi goyang),* cars, bicycles, airplanes, and horses.

132. Sleeping Beauty Sarong, Pekalongan (?), ca. 1920–1930
Cotton, machine spun, natural dyes (?), *tulis* (?)
Warp 200 cm./Weft 105 cm.
Collection: Brake-Lau, New Zealand

Pictorial representation of fairy-tale characters and story of "Sleeping Beauty" that was commonly made in workshops of *Indische* women for colonial Javanese market.

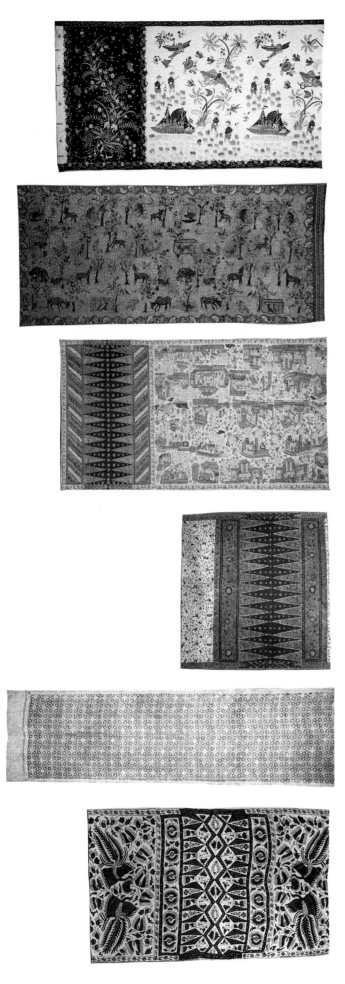

133. Sarong, Pekalongan, ca. 1920–1930
Cotton, machine spun, natural dyes (?), *tulis*
Warp 200 cm./Weft 107 cm.
Collection: Inger McCabe Elliott, New York/#1273

Airplanes, soldiers, and ships were popular subjects in batik commemorating special events, exemplified by this sarong.

134. *Kain Panjang,* Pekalongan (?), ca. 1920–1930
Cotton, machine spun, natural dyes, *tulis*
Warp 242 cm./Weft 107 cm.
Collection: Deutsches Textilmuseum Krefeld, Krefeld/#15988

A menagerie of animals of the sort one would find in a zoo.

135. Chinese Town Sarong, North Coast, ca. 1900
Cotton, machine spun, natural and synthetic dyes (?), *tulis*
Warp 200 cm./Weft 106 cm.
Collection: Smend Gallery, Cologne/#9

Daily life of Chinese town is contained within classic layout of sarong with red *kepala* framed by striking diagonals with *papan.*

136. Sarong (sewn together), Lasem, ca. 1910–1920
Cotton, machine spun, natural dyes (?), *tulis*
Warp 204 cm./Weft 104.5 cm.
Collection: Inger McCabe Elliott, New York/#1234

Overall *semen* design in the body has small scattered creatures hidden by a crackle effect with *tumpal pasang.* Batik probably made in East Java for export to Jambi in Sumatra.

137. *Selendang,* Java, ca. 1930–1940
Silk, machine woven, natural dyes (?), *tulis* (?)
Warp 257 cm./Weft 51 cm.
Collection: Soelaeman Pringgodigdo, Jakarta

Silk *selendang* with geometric pattern is unusual because most were decorated with birds and flowers. Long *selendangs,* such as this example, were tied around waist for dancing.

138. Sarong, Juana, ca. 1940–1950
Silk, machine woven, natural dyes (?), *tulis* (?)
Warp 160.5 cm./Weft 95 cm.
Collection: Inger McCabe Elliott, New York/#1572

Batik on silk, made in Java and typical of what is worn today in Bali as a waistcloth. The major motif is the phoenix.

139. Temple Banner, central Java (?), ca. 1910–1920
Silk, machine woven, natural dyes (?), *tulis*
Warp 251 cm./Weft 53 cm.
Collection: Jacques Gadbois

Whimsical Chinese people riding on animals while participating in a temple ceremony, carrying flags, umbrellas, or waving. Motifs may depict ceremonial parade to a temple. Combined with paisley border, yellow color suggests a special event.

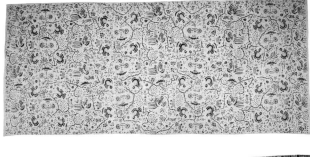

140. *Gemek Setekam* *Kain Panjang,* Lasem, ca. 1880–1890
Cotton, machine spun, natural dyes, *tulis*
Warp 202 cm./Weft 107.5 cm.
Collection: Inger McCabe Elliott, New York

Gemek setekam refers to small bird depicted in batik. Purchased from Chinese maker in Lasem, batik was made for mourning, evidenced by its blue and white colors.

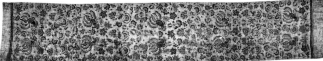

141. *Selendang,* Tuban, ca. 1900
Cotton, handspun, hand-woven, natural dyes, *tulis*
Warp 356 cm./Weft 54.5 cm.
Collection: Sergio Feldbauer, Milan

Floral and bird design is typical of those found in villages near Tuban and inspired by nature.

142. Wall Hanging, Jakarta, 1980
Cotton, machine spun, synthetic dyes, *tulis*
Warp 281 cm./Weft 284 cm.
Signed: Iwan Tirta

Using modern king-size sheet, Iwan Tirta designed his version of *Hokokai* batik: flowers and butterflies enlarged to "supergraphic" size.

143. Peacock Yard goods, Pekalongan, 1974
Cotton, machine spun, synthetic dyes, *tulis* and *cap*
Warp ca. 7.7 meters/Weft 106 cm.
Artists: Inger McCabe Elliott and Achmad Yahya
Stamped: © China Seas, Inc.
Collection: Inger McCabe Elliott, New York

Based on traditional Javanese motif, repeats made for yard goods. This particular group of colors—pastel—unusually difficult to achieve and demands precise dye measurements.

BIBLIOGRAPHY

Abdurachman, Paramita, ed., *Cerbon*, Jakarta, Indonesia: Yayasan Mitra Budaya Indonesia, 1982.
An excellent brief book about the history, economics, and batik of Cirebon. Much material by P. R. Abdurachman. Translation is facile, and the information about Cirebon batik highly informative.

Acosta, José de, *Histoire Naturael en Morael van de Westersche Indien*, Amsterdam: B. Iansz voor I. E. Cloppenburgh, 1624.
Translated by Linschoten ca. 1598. Originally published in Seville in 1590. De Acosta was a Jesuit priest.

Adam, Tassilo, "The Art of Batik in Java," *Bulletin of the Needle and Bobbin Club*, Vol. 18, Nos. 1–2, 1934, pp. 2–79.
Dye techniques plus systemized discussion of motifs by a Dutch government ethnologist. Photographs included.

Adams, Dr. Monni, *Threads of Life*, A private collection of textiles from Indonesia and Sarawak, New York: Vogue Offset Company, 1981.
Exhibition catalogue of textile exhibit shown at the Katonah Gallery in 1981 that includes ikat, plangi, and batik.

Adhyatman, Sumarah, *Keramik Kuna Yang ditemukan di Indonesia* (Antique Ceramics Found in Indonesia), The Ceramic Society of Indonesia, Jakarta: Jayakarta Agung Offset, 1981.
Excellent up-to-date discussion of Indonesian ceramics. Important to discussion of batik motifs. Profusely illustrated, color and black and white.

Allen, Oliver E., *The Pacific Navigators*, Alexandria, Va.: Time-Life Books, 1980.
Excellent brief history with superb illustrations, especially of fifteenth- and sixteenth-century explorers.

Arensberg, Susan MacMillan, *Javanese Batiks*, Yarmouth, Me.: Leether Press, undated ca. 1982.
Brief, valuable, to-the-point description of batik and batik in relation to the Museum of Fine Arts, Boston.

Barrow, Sir John, *A Voyage to Cochina 1792–1793*, London: T. Caldwell and W. Davies, 1806.
One of the earliest voyagers; interesting book.

Bastin, John, and Bea Brommer, *Nineteenth Century Prints and Illustrated Books of Indonesia*, Utrecht, Holland: Spectrum Publishers, 1979.
An important and original source for the history of Java—and batik. Color and black-and-white illustrations.

Batiks, Victoria and Albert Museum, London: Her Majesty's Stationary Office, 1969.
Brief introduction to the history of batik, although not especially accurate. Color and black-and-white illustrations.

Beal, Samuel, trans., *Travels of Fah-Hian and Sun-Yun from China to India 400 A.D. to 518 A.D.*, London: Trübner and Co., 1869.
Good general background of two intrepid travelers.

Berg, C. C., "Kidung Sunda Inleiding, tekst, Vertaling en aanteekeningen," *Bijdragen tot de Taal-Land-en Volkenkunde van Nederlandsch Indie*, Vol. 83, K.I.T.L.V., The Hague: Martinus Nijhoff, 1927.

Bijl de Vroe, C.L.M., *Rondom de Buitenzorgese Troon*, Indische Dagboek van C.L.M. Bijl de Vroe 1914–1919, Haarlem: Fibula van Dishoeck, 1980.
Diary of adjutant to governor general of Dutch East Indies. Lively, interesting, with many photographs.

Blussé, Léonard, "Chinese Trade to Batavia During the Days of the V.O.C.," *Archipel*, Vol. 18, Paris: 1979, pp. 195–213.
One of the few studies to look at trade between Java and China in the seventeenth and eighteenth centuries.

Bodine, Sarah, "Batiks Fit to Be Dyed," *Metropolis*, New York: Bellerophon Publications, 1983, pp. 22–24.

Overall description of batik technique and use with several black-and-white photographs.

Bolland, Rita, J. H. Gerlings Jager, and L. Langewis, *Batiks from Java: the Refined Beauty of an Ancient Craft*, 3 Vols., Amsterdam: Koninklijk Instituut voor de Tropen, Department of Cultural and Physical Anthropology, 1960.
Fine-quality color and black-and-white plates in each volume selected from the rich collection of the Tropical Museum, Amsterdam. Surveys patterns of Javanese principalities: central Javanese traditional and Pekalongan motifs.

Bossert, Helmuth Th., *Decorative Art of Asia and Egypt*, New York: Frederick A. Praeger, Inc., 1956.
Wonderful color plates of textiles and decorative patterns from various museums, with short introduction.

Bry, John Theodore de, *Petit Voyage*, Latin ed., Frankfurt: 1601.
Theodore de Bry, with his sons John Theodore and John Israel and two sons-in-law, published four books on their voyages—which began in 1588 —to America and the East Indies. German edition appeared in 1597, the Latin four years later. Well illustrated.

Bühler, Alfred, "Dyeing Among Primitive Peoples," *Ciba Review*, No. 68, 1948, pp. 2,478–2,512.
Description of entire dye process including natural dye sources and their preparation.

———, *Ikat Batik Plangi: Reservemusterungen auf Garn und Stoff aus Vorderasien, Zentralasien, Südosteuropa und Nordafrika*, 3 Vols., Basel, Switzerland: Pharos-Verlag Hansrudolf Schwabe, 1972.
Three volumes that describe resist techniques in Europe, North Africa, Middle East, and Central Asia. Included is a description of materials, techniques, and motifs from each area; also notes, maps, and excellent bibliography.

———, "Primitive Stoffensfesrengen," *Führer durch des Museum für*

Völkerkunde, Basel, Switzerland: 1963.
Detailed study of resist dyeing.

Dagh-Register Gehouden int Casteel Batavia vant Passerende Daer ter Plaetse als over Geheel Nederlandts India, 1624–82, Batavia: 1877.
Day book of the V.O.C. Batavian headquarters.

Daniell, William, A *Picturesque Voyage to India by Way of China*, London: Longman, Hurst, Rees and Orme, 1810.
Daniell went with his uncle, Thomas Daniell—also a painter—to the Orient. William Daniell was responsible for the aquatints in Raffles's first edition.

Day, Clive, *The Dutch in Java*, Kuala Lumpur, Malaysia, and England: Oxford University Press, 1966 (originally published 1904).
An early, most influential, liberal work about the Dutch colonial system in Indonesia.

"De batik industrie," *Djawa*, Vol. 6, 1926, pp. 157–166.
One of the many studies in the first part of the century to assess the batik industry in Java.

Donahue, Leo O., *Encyclopedia of Batik Designs*, East Brunswick, N.J.: Cornwall Books and Associated Presses, Inc., 1981.
Reference book of *cap* designs, terribly illustrated with black-and-white drawings. Poorly organized, hastily assembled work.

Economist Intelligence Unit, "Management of the [Indonesian] Economy," *Encyclopaedia Britannica*, Vol. IX, Chicago: H. H. Benton, 1974, pp. 470–471.
Excellent overview of how Indonesia is managed.

———, "Sources of [Indonesian] National Income," *Encyclopaedia Britannica*, Vol. IX, Chicago: H. H. Benton, 1974, pp. 468–470.
Up-to-date reporting, especially about the textile business.

Fischer, Joseph, *Threads of Tradition*, Berkeley, Cal.: Fidelity Savings and Loan Association for the University of California, 1979.
Exhibition catalogue of the Lowie Museum of Anthropology. Photographs and text dealing with relationship of culture and art, historical influences, and technical skills of artisans in Indonesia.

Frost, Elizabeth, "The Perilous State of Political Freedom," *Radcliffe Quarterly*, Cambridge, Mass.: December 1983, pp. 18–22.
"Transmigration" is described as a means of political imprisonment, not population control.

Gasthaus, Ruth, et al., *Museum*, Braunschweig, Germany: Westermann, 1983.
Small catalogue showing textiles from all over the world housed at Deutsches Textilmuseum. Descriptions included. Impressive collection.

Genscher, Hans-Dietrich, Prof. Mochtar Kasumaatmadja, et al., *Java und Bali*, Mainz, Germany: Verlag Philipp von Zabern, 1981.
Overall discussion of arts of Java and Bali. Profusely illustrated in color including some batik. A very good overall discussion of Indonesian arts.

Gittinger, Mattiebelle, "Indonesian Textiles," *Arts of Asia*, Kowloon, Hong Kong: Arts of Asia Publications, September–October 1980, pp. 108–123.
General overview of Indonesian textiles including description of batik and ikat.

———, ed., *Indonesian Textiles*, Irene Emery Roundtable on Museum Textiles 1979 Proceedings, Washington, D.C.: The Textile Museum, 1980.
Scholarly collection of essays dealing with all aspects of Indonesian textiles including social, religious, and technical; important book.

———, *Master Dyers to the World*, Technique and Trade in Early Indian Dyed Cotton Textiles, Washington, D.C.: The Textile Museum, 1982.
Catalogue for exhibition by the same name. Excellent source for dyeing techniques as well as the history of Indian trade textiles. Includes pictorial supplement, glossary, and bibliography.

———, *Splendid Symbols*, Textiles and Tradition in Indonesia, New Haven, Conn.: Eastern Press, 1979.
Exploration of the role of textiles in the social customs and religion of Indonesia. Scholarly work with photographs from collectors worldwide.

Glaman, Kristof, *Dutch Asiatic Trade 1620–1740*, The Hague: Martinus Nijhoff, 1981.
First published in 1958 in Denmark, this thoroughly researched work shows the importance of raw silk and piece goods to the Dutch-Asiatic trade. Full appendices and index.

Graff, H. J. de, *De Mord op Kapitein Francois Tack*, Ph.D. thesis, Leiden, Holland: Rijksuniversiteit te Leiden, 1935.
Interprets the politics of central Java at the beginning of the eighteenth century from reports collected by an embassy sent to capture Balinese rebels.

———, "Tome Pires 'Suma Oriental' en het tijdperk van godsdienstovergang op Java," *Bijdragen tot de Taal-, Land-, en Volkenkunde*, Vol. 108, 1952, pp. 132–171.
Discusses importance of Pires manuscript, comparing it to other accounts of Majapahit rule.

Hall, D.G.E., *A History of South-East Asia*, London: Macmillan and Co., 1964.
Standard Southeast Asian reference work.

Hall, K. R., "The Coming of Islam to the Archipelago: A Reassessment." *Economic Exchange and Social Interaction in Southeast Asia: Perspectives from Prehistory, History, and Ethnography*, Karl L. Hutterer, ed., Ann Arbor: The University of Michigan, 1977, pp. 213–231.
Discusses evidence that supports a Coromandel source for Islam and examines internal conditions on Sumatra that supported conversion.

Hall, K. R., and John Whitmore, eds., "Southeast Asian Trade and the Isthmian Struggle, 1000–1200 A.D.," *Exploration in Early Southeast Asian Statecraft*, Ann Arbor: The University of Michigan, 1976, pp. 303–340.

Hamzuri, Drs., *Batik Klasik*, Jakarta: Djambatan, 1981.
Excellent description of the process of making batik and the tools used. This book also identifies patterns by their Indonesian names.

Hare, Denise, "A Filmmaker in Asia," *Craft Horizons*, Vol. XXXV, New York: American Craft Council, April 1975, pp. 18–68.
Pictorial essay.

Hawkins, Everett D., "The Batik Industry: The Role of the Javanese Entrepreneur," *Entrepreneurships and Labor Skills in Indonesian Economic Development: A Symposium*, Monograph Series, New Haven, Conn.: Yale University, 1961.
One of the few articles about modern batik. Original research and useful.

Holt, Claire, *Art in Indonesia: Continuities and Change*, New York: Cornell University Press, 1967.
Good overall reference.

Hordonin, E. H., and W. L. Riffer, *Java Tooneelen uit het Leven*, Leiden, Holland: A. W. Sythoff, 1855.
Excellent illustrations by Lemercier.

Hurwitz, J., *Batikkunst van Java*, Rotterdam: Museum voor Land-en Volkenkunde, 1962.
Discussion of history, technique, motifs, uses, and industrialization of Javanese batik.

Jacqué, Jacqueline T., *Chefs-D'oeuvre du Musée de l'Impression sur Etoffes Mulhouse*, Vol. 2, Tokyo: Editions Gakken, 1978.
Fantastic survey with great color plates plus bibliography and glossary. Unfortunately, batik is not well identified.

Jasper, J. E., and Mas Pirngadie, *De Inlandsche Kunstnijverheid in Nederlandsch Indië*, Vol. 3, The Hague: Mouton and Co., 1912.

The classic study of Indonesian handicrafts, now out of print. Excellent hand drawings. Volume 3 is especially relevant. (Vol. 1: Weaving Baskets, Vol. 2: Weaving Textiles, Vol. 3: Batik, Vol. 4: Gold and Silk, Vol. 5: Metalwork.)

Jonge, J.K.L. de, et al., eds., *De Opkomst van het Nederlandsch Gezag in Oost-Indie: Verzameling van Onuitgegevene Stukken uit het Oud-koloniaal Archief 1595–1814*, The Hague: 1862–1909.
Documents relating to the first Dutch voyages to Indonesia and the development of the VOC.

Kafka, Francis, *Batik, Tie Dyeing, Stenciling, Silk Screen, Block Printing, The Hand Decoration of Fabric*, New York: Dover Publications, 1973.
How-to-do-it for the craftsman.

Kahlenberg, Mary Hunt, *Textile Traditions of Indonesia*, Los Angeles: L.A. County Museum of Art, 1977.
Exhibition catalogue for exhibit at L.A. County Museum of Art. Description of Indonesian textiles with glossary and bibliography. Many color and black-and-white photographs. Several articles are written by scholars.

Kat Angelino, P. de, *Rapport betreffende eene gehouden enquête naar de arbeidstoestanden in de batikkerijen op Java en Madoera*, 3 Vols., Weltevreden: Kantoor van Arbeid, publicatie no. 6–8, 1930–1931.
Detailed study of conditions in the batik industry based on inspection of each major region. Draws on earlier official reports as well. Photographs.

Kennedy, R., *Bibliography of Indonesia Peoples and Cultures*, revised and edited by T. W. Maretzku and H. T. Fischer, New Haven, Conn.: 1962.
Useful although now outdated.

Kertanegara, "The Batik Industry in Central Java," *Ekonomi dan keuangan Indonesia*, Vol, 11, No. 7, 1958, pp. 345–401.
Economic analysis of the batik industry.

Kroese, Dr. W. T., *The Origin of the Wax Block Prints on the Coast of West Africa*, Hengelo, Holland: N. V. Uitgeverij Smit van 1876, 1976.
Scholarly and interesting, showing close relationship of Javanese and Ghanaian batik. Unfortunately, terribly written.

Langewis, Laurens, and Frits A. Wagner, *Decorative Art in Indonesian Textiles*, Amsterdam: van der Peet, 1964.
Major resource for the study of Indonesian textiles. Color plus black-and-white photographs.

Larsen, Jack Lenor, with Alfred Bühler, Bronwen Solyom, and Garrett Solyom, *The Dyer's Art: Ikat, Batik, Plangi*, New York: Van Nostrand Reinhold, 1976.
Excellent text, profusely illustrated. Section on batik somewhat uneven. However, as an overview, an important source.

Lasker, Bruno, "Bondage Through Worker Indebtedness in the Batik Industry of Java," *Human Bondage in Southeast Asia*, Appendix C, Chapel Hill: University of North Carolina Press, 1950.
A view of postwar labor relations in batik factories.

Lattimore, Owen and Eleanor, *Silks, Spices, and Empire*, New York: Delacorte Press, 1968.
Excellent original sources, both Asian and European.

Legge, John D., "Indonesia Since 1600," *Encyclopaedia Britannica*, Vol. IX, Chicago: H. H. Benton, 1974, pp. 483–491.

Lewis, Albert Buell, *Javanese Batik Designs from Metal Stamps*, Anthropology design series, No. 2, Chicago: Field Museum of Natural History, 1924.
Catalogue of *cap* exhibit; slightly outdated.

Linschoten, Huygen van, *His Discours of Voyages into East and West Indies*, London: John Wolfe, 1598.
Four books with separate titles written by Linschoten, a great traveler,

commentator, with wonderful maps. Marvelous reading.

————, *Itinerario*, Voyage of H. v. Linschoten, Ship Captain to the East Indies, Amsterdam: Cornelius Claesz, 1596.
World maps; see above.

Loeber, J. A., *Das Batiken, Eine Blüté Indonesischen Kunstlelebens*, Oldenburg, Germany: Gerhard Stelling Verlag, 1925.
One of the best books on batik: thorough, well illustrated, and even interesting.

Mackie, J.A.C., ed., *The Chinese in Indonesia*, Five Essays, Nelson in association with the Australian Institute of International Affairs, West Melbourne: Thomas Nelson, Ltd., 1976.
Excellent series of essays; an important book for the study of the Chinese in Java.

Mangkudilaga, Drs. D. Sufwandi, et al., *Batik*, Exhibition of selected pieces from the collections of the Jakarta Textile Museum and the Yogyakarta Batik Museum, Jakarta: PT Djaya Pirusa, 1980.
Exhibition catalogue of batik with brief history and description. Written in both Bahasa Indonesia and English.

Marzuki, Jazir, N. Tirtaamidjaja, and Benedict Anderson, *Batik: pola dan tjorak-pattern and motif*, Jakarta: Djambatan, 1966.
History and origin of Indonesian batik written in English and Bahasa Indonesia.

Maxwell, John and Robyn, *Textiles of Indonesia*, an introductory handbook, Melbourne: Gardner Printing and Publishing, 1976.
Brief synopsis of Indonesian textiles and photographs of cloth from the National Gallery of Victoria.

McEvedy, Colin, *The Penguin Atlas of Modern History (to 1815)*, Hong Kong: Penguin Books, 1972.
Brief but excellent general history, with maps of trade routes, especially to the Orient.

Meilink-Roelofsz, M.A.P., *Asian Trade and European Influence in the Indonesian Archipelago Between 1500 and 1630*, The Hague: Martinus Nijhoff, 1962.
Important history of trade in Indonesia.

Mills, J. V., "Chinese Navigators in Insulinde about A.D. 1500," *Archipel*, Vol. 18, Paris: 1979, pp. 69–93.
Examines fifteenth-century Chinese navigational theory and practice.

Mintz, Jeanne S., *Indonesia: A Profile*, Princeton, Toronto, London, New York: D. van Nostrand Co., 1981.
Published in cooperation with the Asia Society, this work is a valuable overview of Indonesian history and culture.

Monzie, A. de, *Les Batiks de Madame Pangon*, Paris: Editions D'Art Charles Moreau, 1925.
Color and black-and-white plates of Art Deco batik; interesting designs.

Moussinac, Leon, *Etoffes Imprimées et Papiers Peints*, Paris: Editions Albert Lévy, 1924.
French portfolio of wallpaper patterns in which plates 46 and 60 are batik patterns.

Mylius, Norbert, *Indonesische Textilkunst: Batik, Ikat und Plangi*, Vienna: Notring der wissenschaftlichen Verbände Osterreichs, 1964.
Early technique is described in individual chapters. Thorough bibliography and many photographs.

Naipaul, V. S., *Among the Believers*, New York: Random House, 1981.
Good reading on Islamic countries, including Indonesia.

Neill, Wilfred T., *Twentieth-Century Indonesia*, New York and London: Columbia University Press, 1973.
An excellent history and cultural geography of Indonesia.

Newman, Thelma R., *Contemporary Southeast Asian Arts and Crafts*, New York: Crown Publishers, 1977.
Ethnic craftsmen at work with how-to instructions for adapting their crafts.

Nieuhoff, Johan, *Voyages and Travels into Brazil and the East Indies*, London: 1704.
Fascinating travelogue of seventeenth-century Dutch voyager. Detailed description of cities, their people as well as customs, with extraordinary etched illustrations, especially of Batavia. Nieuhoff took three major voyages to the East Indies and Brazil and accounts of these trips were published in Dutch and French between 1665 and 1668.

Nieuwenhuys, Rob, *Baren en oudgasten*, Tempo doeloe-een verzonken wereld, Fotografische documenten uit het oude Indie 1870–1920, Amsterdam: Querido, 1981.
Excellent source for colonial Java; profusely illustrated.

Ogilby, John, and Arnold Montanus, *Embassy from the East-India Co. of the United Provinces to the Emperor of Japan*, Dedicated to Charles II, London: Tho. Johnson, 1670.
History of early exploration plus a long description of embassies from Batavia to Nagasaki. Excellent illustrations.

Ostmeier, S.S.B., *Kleeding en Sieraden van de Inlandsche Vrouw op Java en Madoera*, Batavia: Albrecht and Co., 1913.
Interesting, although out of date on batik techniques and motifs.

Osumi, Tamezo, *Printed Cottons of Asia*, The Romance of Trade Textiles, revised by George Saito, Tokyo and Rutland, Vermont: Bijutsu Shuppan-Sha and Charles E. Tuttle Co., 1963.
Excellent overall survey that includes a brief section about batik.

Palmer, Ingrid, *Textiles in Indonesia, Problems of Import Substitution*, New York: Praeger Special Studies, 1972.
Presents brief summary of the history of economic aspects of batik, then concentrates on contemporary economics.

Palmier, Leslie H., "Batik Manufacture in a Chinese Community in Java," *Entrepreneurships and Labor Skills in Indonesian Economic Devel-*

opment: *A Symposium,* Monograph Series, New Haven, Conn.: Yale University, 1961.
Unfortunately outdated, but nevertheless relevant.

Pfister, R., *Les toiles imprimés de Fostat et de l'Hindustan,* Paris: 1938.

Pigeaud, Th., *Java in the 14th Century, A Study in Cultural History,* Vol. IV, Commentaries and Recapitulation, The Hague: Martinus Nijhoff, 1962.
Translation and interpretation of the poem "Nagara Kertagama" written in honor of a Majapahit king. A most important source on fourteenth-century Java.

Pringgoadisurjo, Luwarsih, and Kosam Rimbarawa, *Informasi literatur untuk tekstil dan batik,* Jakarta: Pusat Dokumentasi Llmiah Nasional, 1974.
Comprehensive bibliography on Indonesian batik.

Purcell, Victor W.W.S., *The Chinese in Southeast Asia,* London: Oxford University Press, 1965.

Raadt-Apell, M. J. de, *De batikkerij van Zuylen te Pekalongan* (Midden-Java 1890–1946), Uitgeverij Terra-Zutphen, 1980.
Excellent small volume about van Zuylen's batik that includes full information about her life, her family, and her work. Color photographs.

———, "Van Zuylen Batik, Pekalongan, Central Java (1890–1946)," *Textile Museum Journal,* Vols. 19 and 20, Washington, D.C.: The Textile Museum, 1982, pp. 75–92.
Excerpted from her book. Well translated, good reference.

Raffles, Thomas Stamford, *The History of Java,* 2 Vols., reprint of 1817 edition, Kuala Lumpur, Malaysia: Oxford University Press, 1982.
Written more than one hundred fifty years ago, these two volumes are classics: the writing is succinct and elegant. The material is relevant and thought provoking. Fully illustrated with aquatints by Daniell. Both volumes essential reading for the history of Java and its batik.

Rawson, Phillip S., "The Visual Art of [the] Southeast Asian Peoples," *Encylopaedia Britannica,* Vol. 17, Chicago: H. H. Benton, 1974, pp. 250–273.
Excellent discussion of all Southeast Asian arts with an outstanding bibliography.

Réal, Daniel, *Les batiks de Java,* Paris: A. Calavas, n.d., Paris: Libraire des Arts Décoratifs.
Forty-six plates of batik from museum and private collections.

———, *Tissus des Indes Néerlandaises,* Paris: Libraire des Arts Décoratifs, 1927.
Forty-nine plates of textiles including both batik and ikat at the Exposition de l'art décoratif aux Indes Néerlandaises in France.

Robinson, Stuart, *A History of Dyed Textiles,* Cambridge, Mass.: The M.I.T. Press, 1969.
A complete history and discussion of dyed textiles. Includes appendices for further study on the topic.

Rouffaer, G. P., and H. H. Juynboll, "Batikken," *Encyclopaedia van Nederlandsche-Indie,* Vol. 1, Gravenhage: Martinus Nijhoff, 1917, pp. 192–203.
Useful, albeit rather dry, material about batik.

———, *De Batik-kunst in Nederlandsch-Indë en haar Geschiedenis,* 2 Vols., Utrecht, Holland: A. Oosterhoek, 1914.
Important and first major study of Javanese batik. Written between 1900 and 1914 in six volumes and reissued in this edition of two volumes.

Rouffaer, G. P., and J. W. Ijzerman, eds., *Schipvaart der Nederlanders naar Oost-Indie onder Cornelius de Houtman 1595–1597,* Vols. I and II, Leiden, Holland: Linschoten Society, 1915–1925.
Dutch records of their first travel in the East. Important details regarding items traded in the archipelago.

Schouten, Joost, "Rapport na de overgave van Malaka," *Berigten van net Historisch Genootschap te Utrecht,* Vol. 7, No. 1, 1859, pp. 258–375.
Records of materials seized by Dutch when they captured Malacca.

Schrieke, B., *Indonesian Sociological Studies,* Part 1, The Hague: W. van Hoeve, Ltd., 1955.
Very important historical analysis of the rise of Java in trade.

Seydel, Agnes en Kate, *Het Batikken,* Leiden, Holland: A. W. Sijthoff's Uitgeversmaatschappij.
How to batik cloth and how to use this material; useful household hints of the 1920s.

Smith, Datus C., Jr., *The Land and People of Indonesia,* Philadelphia and New York: J. B. Lippincott Co., 1963.
Although this book is now twenty years old, its historical insights are interesting. Written for the young person, it is valuable for any age.

Soekmono, R., *Pengantar Sejarah Kebudajaan,* 2nd vol., 5th ed., Jakarta: Penerbit Yayasan Kanisius, 1973.

Solyom, Garrett, and Bronwen Solyom, *Textiles of the Indonesian Archipelago,* Asian Studies at Hawaii, No. 10, Honolulu: University Press of Hawaii, 1973.
Overall description of the different textiles made in Indonesia.

Spée, Miep, *Traditionele en moderne batik,* Cantecleer bv. de Bilt, 1977.
Batik techniques, especially those of Java.

Steinmann, Dr. Alfred, *Batik, A Survey of Batik Design,* Leigh-on-sea, England: F. Lewis Publishers, Ltd., 1958.
Only four hundred copies printed. Excellent, concise description in a clear style.

———, "Batiks," *Ciba Review,* No. 58, 1947, pp. 2,090–2,125.

Suryadinata, Leo, *Pribumi Indonesians, the Chinese Minority and China,* Kowloon, Hong Kong: Heinemann Educational Books (Asia), Ltd., 1978.
Indonesian Chinese economy, politics, and culture.

Sutton, Thomas, *The Daniells: Artists and Travellers,* London: The Bodley Head, 1954.
Very good overall description of the two Daniells, their extraordinary voyages and excellent art. William Daniell illustrated Raffles's book.

Tirta, Iwan, and Raymond Lau, *Batik, The Magic Cloth,* n.p., 1974.
Small handbook with glorious color plates of batik from all regions of Java.

——— (Tirtaamidjaja, N.) *Batik-pola dan tjorak* (English text by Benedict Anderson), Jakarta: Djambatan, 1966.
Plates of hand-made batik with brief introduction and description of history and batik technique and motifs, written in both Bahasa Indonesia and English. Brief bibliography included.

Valentijn, Francois, *Oud en Niew Oost-Indien,* Vol. 1, Dordrecht and Amsterdam: J. van Bramm, 1724–1726.
This work by an explorer is in five parts and of interest for early exploration: Java, the Philippines, and even Acapulco are discussed.

Veldhuisen, Harmen, *Blauw en Bont,* Delft: Volkenkundig Museum "Nusantara," 1980.
Important new material and analysis contributing to the history of batik, especially that of the north coast.

Veldhuisen-Djajasoebrata, Alit, *Batik op Java,* Rotterdam: Museum voor Land-en Volkenkunde, 1972.
Written by one of the experts on batik and a good reference.

Vreeland, Nena, et al., *Area Handbook for Indonesia,* Foreign Areas Studies of the American University, 3rd. ed., Washington, D.C.: Government Printing Office, 1975.
Excellent overview but nowhere near as thorough as articles from the *Encyclopaedia Britannica.*

Wagner, Frits A., *Indonesia: The Art of an Island Group,* New York: McGraw-Hill, 1959.
Survey of Indonesian art.

Warming, Wanda, and Michael Gaworski, *The World of Indonesian Textiles,* Kodansha International, 1981.
Recent book on batik, profusely illustrated. Although much detail, not well organized and not very interesting.

Warni, Puspite, *Pameran Kain koleski pribadi Gusti Kanjeng Putri Mankunegoro VIII (1923–1978),* Jakarta: Museum Textil Jakarta, January 1980.
Batik collection of the wife of a local prince.

Wassing-Visser, Rita, *Weefselsen Adatkostuums uit Indonesië,* Delft: Volkenkundig Museum "Nusantara," 1982.
Mrs. Wassing-Visser is curator of this excellent show and introduces the catalogue. Illustrations are particularly useful in showing how cloths are worn. Unfortunately only five batik are included in the show and only one is from the north coast. Color and black and white.

Wojowasito, Prof. Drs. S., and Drs. Tito Waito W., *Kamus Lengkap,* Inggeris-Indonesia Indonesia-Inggeris, Bandung: Angkasa Offset, 1980.
Useful English–Bahasa Indonesia dictionary.

Wolters, O. W., "Indonesia to the End of the 16th Century," *Encyclopaedia Britannica,* Vol. IX, Chicago: H. H. Benton, 1974, pp. 476–483.
Excellent reference.

———, *Early Indonesian Commerce,* Ithaca, N.Y.: Cornell University Press, 1967.
Chronicles the rise of Srivijaya in Sumatra.

Wright, Arnold, ed., *Twentieth Century Impressions of Netherlands India, Its History, People, Commerce, Industries, and Resources,* London: Lloyds Greater Publishing Co., Ltd., 1909.
Detailed account of East Indies with photographs.

Yoshimoto, Shinobu, *Indonesia Shenshoku Taikei* (Systematic Study of Indonesian Textiles), 2 Vols., Kyoto: Shiko-sha Publishing Co., 1978.
Exhaustive study of all Indonesian textiles with excellent color plates. Volume 2 deals mostly with batik. Notes are comprehensive. Most textiles are from Japanese collections.

Yoshioka, Tsuneo, *Sekai No Sarasa,* (Dye-Patterned Fabrics of the World), Kyoto: Kyoto Shoin Co., Ltd., 1980.
Excellent photographs with some inaccurate information.

Unpublished Works

Abdurachman, R. A. Siti Katidjah, *Kenang-Kenang,* Reminiscences of childhood, Private family papers, Jakarta: unpublished, 1965.

Segal, Shari, *The Fabric of Javanese Life: Cultural Meanings of Batik,* submitted in partial fulfillment for the Master of Arts (Anthropology), Hunter College, The City University of New York, 1974.
Excellent thesis, dealing with central Java. Bibliography and illustrations.

Independent Field Research

Abdurachman, Paramita, 1983
Basharahil, 1970–1983
Hajadi, Atmadjaja, 1972–1983
Hardjonagoro, K.R.T., 1972–1983
Hendromartono, Jane, 1982–1983
Masina, H., 1982–1983
Oey Soe Tjoen, 1982–1983
Said, Achmad, 1977–1983
Shiraishi, Takashi, 1983
Sutjahjo, Hadi, 1983
Tan It Long, 1982
Tirta, Iwan, 1970–1983
Yahya, Achmad, 1972–1983

ACKNOWLEDGMENTS

The rewards of this work have been enormous. I have been particularly gratified by the willingness of so many people and institutions to open their minds and their doors and to share their knowledge. My thanks to the following people is boundless. I wish I had the space to write in detail how helpful and kind everyone has been on this project.

In *Amsterdam*: Rita Bolland, curator of textiles at the Koninklijk Instituut voor de Tropen; K. Goulooze of Gré Nabrink; Andreas and Yook Landshoff; Rob Nieuwenhuys; and Benjamin J. Stein. In *Auckland*: Lau Wai Man. In *Brussels*: Mr. and Mrs. Fritz J. Schmidt. In *Cirebon*: Mr. and Mrs. H. Masina. In *Cologne*: Brigitte Majlis of the Cologne Museum; Rudolph Smend of Smend Gallery. In *Delft*: Suwondo Sudewo and Rita Wassing-Visser, curator of the Delft Volkenkundig Museum "Nusantara." In *Enschede*: Bernard van Heek. In *The Hague*: Meur. M. E. van Opstall of the Royal Archives. In *Honolulu*: Garrett and Bronwen Solyom. In *Ithaca*: Professor George Kahin.

In *Jakarta*: Asmara Arifin; Joop Avé; H. Munir Djody; H. Sa'adiah Djody; Wieneke de Groot; Atmadjaja Hayadi; Ambassador and Mrs. John Holdridge; Adrian Idris; Frank and Cheng Lammers; Soelaeman Pringgodigdo; Thomas Spooner; Drs. Suhardina of the Museum Nasional; Bambang Sumadio, director of the Museum Nasional; and Dra. Kartiwa Suwatia also of the Museum Nasional; Mohd. Amir Sutaarga, director of the Indonesia museums; Johnny and Gwat Widjaja; Toky Wan.

In *Kedungwuni*: Mrs. Oey Soe Tjoen; Mr. and Mrs. Muljadi Widjaya. In *Krefeld-Linn*: Marianne Frings; Dr. Carl-Wolfgang Schumann of the Textile Museum. In *Leiden*: Dr. Jan B. Avé, curator at the Rijksmuseum voor Volkenkunde; Dorothée Burr and L. Manputty-Tentua at the Koninklijk Instituut voor Taal-Land-en Volkenkunde; Winnifred de Groot; Rens Loedin. In *London*: Dr. Brian Durrans at the Museum of Mankind; Henry Ginsburg; John Hillelson; Lisbet Holmes. In *Longboat Key*: Julian and Goldie Kossow. In *Los Angeles*: Gordon and Judi Davidson; Mary Kahlenberg; Dr. Anne Summerfield. In *Melbourne*: Mary Drost; Joan Grant; John Guy, curator of Asian Art at the National Gallery in Victoria; Christopher and Veronica Hazzard.

In *Milan*: Sergio Feldbauer; Francesca Testa. In *Montreal*: Jacques Gadbois. In *New York*: David and Lova Abrahamsen; Richard Arkway; Morag Benepe; Barbara Butt; Millia Davenport; Katherine Duncan; Nancy Elliott; Cornelia Foss; Suzanne Goldstein; John Guare; Titi Halley; Helen Jessup; Mrs. Seti-Arti Kailola; Robert Katz; the Honorable C.J.M. Kramers, Consul General of the Netherlands; the Honorable Rudy Lengkong, Indonesian Consul General; Fanny Littell; Judith Lowry of Argosy; Robert Oxnam of the Asia Society; Alain Morvan; Shannon Mulligan; Elise Nelson; John Rathe and Daniel Tierney of the Rare Book Room and Tobin Sparling of the Print Room at the New York Public Library; Gail Perry; Dr. D. J. Reis; Frieda Rosenthal; Sandra Ruch and Herbert Schmertz of Mobil Corporation; Helen Schwartz; Anita Spertus; Lisa Taylor, director of the Cooper-Hewitt Museum; Alan Wardwell.

In *Pekalongan*: Fan Kei San; Fan Lie Ching; Jane Hendromartono; Tan It Long; Achmad Said; Mr. and Mrs. H. Achmad Yahya. In *Ronco*: Hans W. Siegel. In *Rotterdam*: Harmen C. Veldhuisen; Alit Veldhuisen-Djajasoebrata, curator Indonesian department, Museum voor Land-en Volkenkunde. In *Singapore*: B. Basharahil. In *Surakarta*: Danar Hadi; K.R.T. Hardjonagoro; Nora Yap. In *Stonington*: Judith Backman; Ann Fuller; Rosalie McKenna; Eleanor Perenyi; Jon Rosenthal; Grace Stone. In *Sydney*: Lisa Purser. In *Tokyo*: Akiko and Bernard Krisher; Hiro Oka; Takashi Shiraishi; Meredith Weatherby. In *Washington, D.C.*: Patricia Fiske, director of the Textile Museum; Cornelia Noland; Annette Valeo; Pandqi Surya; His Excellency A. Hasnan Habib, Ambassador from Indonesia.

In *Yogyakarta*: Mr. and Mrs. Ardiyanto Pranata; Dr. Djoko Soekiman, director of Sonobudoyo Museum; Johnny Sunu; Achmad Yusuf, head of collections, Sonobudoyo Museum.

Very special thanks go to Carol Southern of Clarkson Potter, who believed in *Batik* when no one else did, and to Gael Dillon, the art director, for her sensitive work with Kiyoshi Kanai, a brilliant graphic designer. Kathy Powell ably assisted on all aspects of the manuscript.

It was at the home of Brian Brake that I saw the first antique batik and it is thanks to him that much of this visual opulence is possible.

Robert J. Holmgren generously shared his enthusiasm for textiles and without him I would never have looked as far afield; his criticism of my manuscript was invaluable.

The manuscript was also read by Jagat S. Mehta, former permanent foreign secretary of India, who provided scholarly insight into the roots of Hinduism, the Javanese language, and Asian nationalism.

Paramita Abdurachman and Iwan Tirta helped in the research and writing. Their points of view were always important and lively.

Mattiebelle Gittinger, curator of Textiles at the Textile Museum in Washington, D.C., first suggested the idea of an exhibit of batik from the north coast and then urged me to organize and write this book. Her scholarship, research, and friendship were essential.

My colleague Susan Schwartz Blum has shared with me some of the best and worst moments in this endeavor. Her tireless research, enormous enthusiasm and energy, as well as modesty recommend her to enthronement. To my other colleagues at China Seas, especially Christina Diekman, go my thanks for keeping things going smoothly throughout.

My family has suffered with unsilent good humor, and despite the din and too many cold suppers, they were always a source of encouragement and kindness.

I did not know when I met Osborn Elliott in Hong Kong, nearly two decades ago, that my life would change and become inexorably linked with his. In retrospect it seems fitting that we have been together from the time we remet on a hot tarmac at Jakarta airport, he waving the *Newsweek* flag and I that of north-coast batik. This book is dedicated to Oz, the finest editor, friend, and lover.

I.M.E.

INDEX

CREDITS

All pictures © Brian Brake except for the following:

© Abdurachman, Paramita, private collection, pp. 89, 97 (top).

Bettman Archives, p. 38.

© Blum, Susan, pp. 68–69.

Bry, John Theodore de, *Petit Voyage*, Latin ed. 1601, Part V, plate 17, p. 29.

Burrows, Larry, *Life* magazine © 1968, Time, Inc., p. 187 (left).

Cassagne, Armand, after A. van Pers, "Eene Inlandsche School in De Kampong," tinted lithograph, originally published in The Hague 1855, pp. 40–41.

Cause, H., Decker, G., vander Gouwen G., engravers of Johan Nieuhoff's *1618–1672 Voyages and Travels into Brazil and the East Indies*, pp. 27, 30–31.

Daniell, W., original appeared in Raffles' *History of Java* 1817; this is a Parisian lithograph ca. 1850, p. 32.

© Firmenich, Jo, pp. 102 (right), 156, 221 (bottom and third from bottom), 223 (second from bottom).

Florea, Johnny, *Life* magazine © 1968, Time, Inc., pp. 179, 183.

© Hendromartono, Jane, private collection, pp. 122, 124 (bottom).

© 1983 Kahlenberg, Mary Hunt, and Summerfield, Dr. Anne, pp. 86, 161 (center right and lower left), 164–165, 205 (top, second and fifth from top), 213 (bottom).

© Koeth, Alice, p. 23.

© Lau Wai Man, pp. 25, 58–59, 132 (left).

Lemercier after E. Hardouin and W. L. Ritter from *Java Tooneelen uit het Leven, Karakterschetsen en Kleederdragten van Java's Bewoners* (Sythoff, ed.), Leiden, 1855, colored lithographs, pp. 35, 37, 41.

© McCabe, Inger, pp. 26–27, 52, 85, 97 (bottom), 174–175, 178, 190–191, 193 (top left), 195, 198.

Mieling, C. W., after A. van Pers, "Een Chinees in Een Tandoe," colored lithograph from *Nederlandsch Oost-Indishce Typen*, The Hague, 1853–1862, p. 42.

© Nardiello, Carl, pp. 8–9, 136, 171 (lower right), 176–177; 205 (bottom).

Nieuwenhuys, Rob, private collection, p. 103.

Photographic Archives of the Royal Tropical Institute, pp. 33, 64–65.

© Stegemeyer, Werner, pp. 119, 146 and 147 (top), 161 (center left), 163, 168 (top), 221 (bottom), 204 (bottom), 205 (fourth and sixth from top), 211 (second from top).

© Varon, Malcolm, jacket.

Woodbury and Page, from an original album entitled *Vues de Java*. Woodbury and Page established themselves in Batavia in 1856. For the next several decades they made thousands of photographs throughout Java. Sometimes their photographs appeared as chromolithographs, such as "De Landraad" by Armand, published between 1865 and 1876. Pp. 43 (top and bottom), 44–45, 46–47, 48–49, 114.

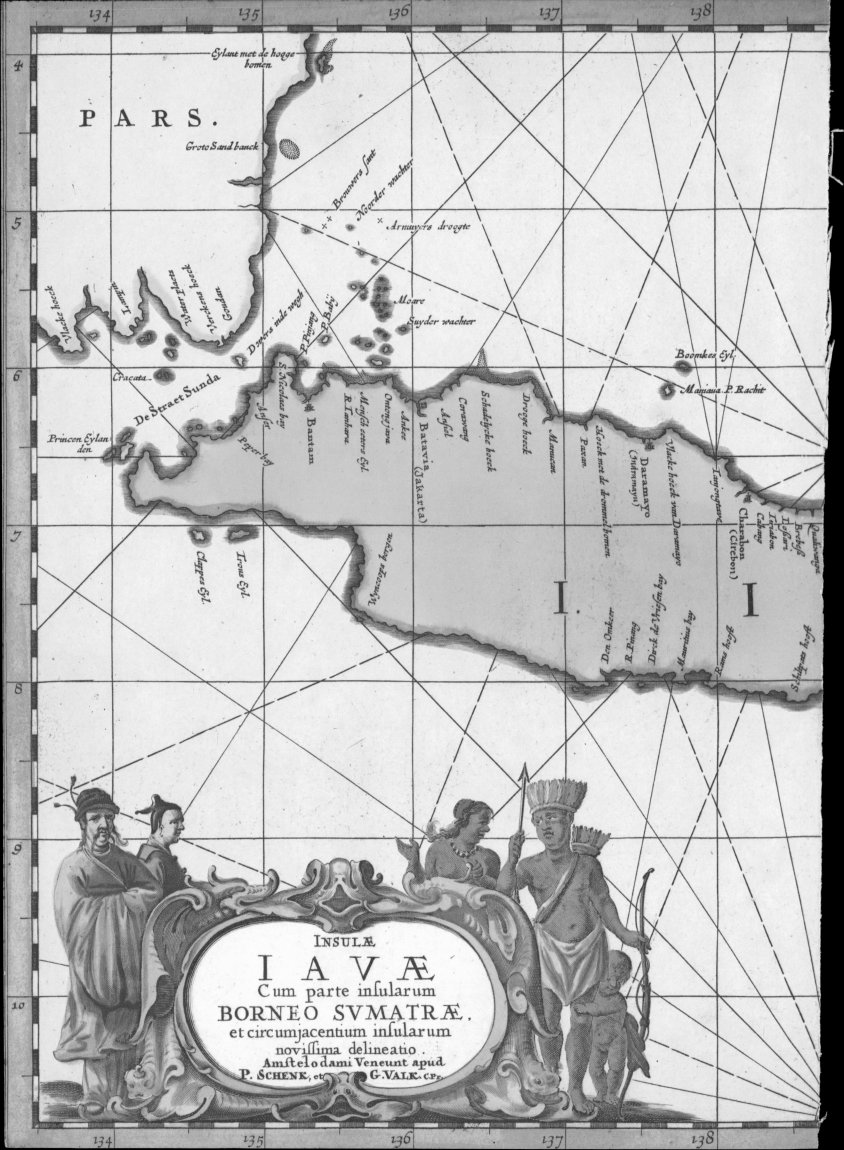

PARS.

Eylant met de hogge bomen.

Groto Sand banck

Brouwers sant

Noorder wachter

+ + +   × Arnuyers droogte

Eylant met de hogge bomen.

Moare

Suyder wachter

Vlacke hoeck

Langit

Water plaets

Verckens hoeck

Goudan

Boomkes Eyl.

Maniaua P. Rachit

Cracata

De Straet Sunda

Dogers inde wegh

P. Pipang

P. P. Baby

S. Nicolaes bay

Anser

Bantam

Peper bay

Ontong java

Menijch ceters Eyl.

R. Tanhara

Ankee

Batavia
(Jakarta)

Coravang Anjol

Schadelycke hoeck

Droge hoeck

Mamican

Paian

Hoeck met de drommel bomen.

Daramayo
(Indramayu)

Vlacke hoeck van Daramayo

Langongtange

Charabon
(Cirebon)

Cabary

Tayadon

Dobari

Brebcy

Qualiauara

Princen Eyland
den

Clappes Eyl.

Irons Eyl.

Vermuysen wegh

I.

I

Den Omleer

R. Pinang

Dirck Vries bay

Maurits bay

Rams hoeft

Schulpen hoeft

INSULÆ
IAVÆ
Cum parte insularum
BORNEO SVMATRÆ,
et circumjacentium insularum
noviſsima delineatio.
Amſtelodami Veneunt apud
P. SCHENK, et   G. VALK. C.P.E.

134   135   136   137   138